The Family in Crisis in Late Nineteenth-Century French Fiction focusses on a key moment in the construction of the modern view of the family in France. Nicholas White's analysis of novels by Zola, Maupassant, Huysmans, Hennique, Bourget and Armand Charpentier is fashioned by perspectives on a wide cultural field, including legal, popular and academic discourses on the family and its discontents. His account encourages a close rereading of canonical as well as hitherto overlooked texts from *fin-de-siècle* France. What emerges between the death of Flaubert in 1880 and the publication of Bourget's *Un divorce* in 1904 is a series of Naturalist and post-Naturalist representations of transgressive behaviour in which tales of adultery, illegitimacy, consanguinity, incest and divorce serve to exemplify and to offer a range of nuances on the Third Republic's crisis in what might now be termed 'family values'.

Nicholas White is Lecturer in French at Royal Holloway, University of London. He is editor (with Naomi Segal) of *Scarlet Letters: Fictions of Adultery from Antiquity to the 1990s,* and he has also edited Zola's *L'Assommoir* and Huysmans's *Against Nature*.

CAMBRIDGE STUDIES IN FRENCH 57

THE FAMILY
IN CRISIS IN LATE
NINETEENTH-CENTURY
FRENCH FICTION

Recent titles in this series include

A complete list of books in the series is given at the end of the volume.

THE FAMILY
IN CRISIS IN LATE
NINETEENTH-CENTURY
FRENCH FICTION

NICHOLAS WHITE

CAMBRIDGE
UNIVERSITY PRESS

PUBLISHED BY THE PRESS SYNDICATE OF THE UNIVERSITY OF CAMBRIDGE
The Pitt Building, Trumpington Street, Cambridge CB2 1RP, United Kingdom

CAMBRIDGE UNIVERSITY PRESS
The Edinburgh Building, Cambridge CB2 2RU, United Kingdom   http://www.cup.cam.ac.uk
40 West 20th Street, New York, NY 10011–4211, USA   http://www.cup.org
10 Stamford Road, Oakleigh, Melbourne 3166, Australia

© Nicholas White 1999

First published 1999

Printed in the United Kingdom at the University Press, Cambridge

Typeset in Baskerville MT 11/12½ [SE]

A catalogue record for this book is available from the British Library

ISBN 0 521 56274 0 hardback

In memory of Jack Morris
teacher, scholar, raconteur

Contents

Acknowledgements

Chapters 4, 5 and the second half of chapter 6 have their origins in a Ph.D. thesis completed in the University of Cambridge in September 1993. I am grateful to the British Academy for a Major Award between 1990 and 1993, and to Fitzwilliam College and the Faculty of Modern and Medieval Languages in Cambridge for assistance of many kinds dating back to 1986. I would also like to thank Royal Holloway, University of London, for providing the sabbatical leave during which the bulk of the completed draft was written, and colleagues for fostering an atmosphere conducive to research. Versions of two chapters have appeared elsewhere in somewhat different forms. I thank the editors for permission to use this material. Portions of chapter 4 appeared in *French Studies Bulletin*, 47 (1993), pp. 12–14, and in French translation as '*Le Docteur Pascal*: entre l'inceste et l'"innéité"' in *Cahiers naturalistes*, 68 (1994), 77–88. Versions of both parts of chapter 6 have appeared elsewhere, in the case of Hennique in *Essays in French Literature*, 32–3 (1995–6), pp. 41–63, and in the case of Zola in *Neophilologus*, 81 (1997), 201–14. Much help has been gratefully received from librarians in London (the British Library and the libraries at Royal Holloway), Cambridge (the University Library and the Radzinowicz Criminology Library), Paris (the Bibliothèque Nationale), and Oxford (the Taylor Institution Library). Linda Bree, Kate Brett and Alison Gilderdale of Cambridge University Press have provided invaluable support. It is also with great pleasure that I take this opportunity to express my gratitude towards friends, teachers and colleagues, some of whom have read this material in different versions, all of whom have offered through conversation and correspondence many instances of comment, encouragement and advice germane to this project. They include Jennifer Birkett, Malcolm Bowie, Peter Collier, Stephen Gundle, Robert Hampson, Ruth Harvey, Stephen Heath, Edward Hughes, John Leigh, Karl Leydecker, Robert Lethbridge, Jann Matlock, Timothy Mathews, Michael Moriarty,

Patrick O'Donovan, Christopher Prendergast, Naomi Segal, Michael Sheringham, Jonathan Thacker, Andrew Walsh, Tony Williams and Robert Ziegler. The debt to members of my family – Nikola, my parents and my brothers – is ongoing.

Introduction: fin de siècle, fin de famille?

> Vous croyez entendre un soupir, c'est une citation, – serrer une
> femme sur votre cœur, c'est un volume.[1]

> En ce moment, tous les littérateurs, et les plus dissemblables comme
> talent, affirment descendre de Flaubert . . . Ah! s'il était vivant,
> comme ils tairaient cette prétendue descendance![2]

8 May 1880 . . . Amidst the numerous *faux débuts* which might be said to
have inaugurated the *fin de siècle*, perhaps none has the capacity to engage
scholars of French literary and cultural studies alike more productively
than the death of Gustave Flaubert. Indeed, few names resonate more
profoundly in the echo chamber of nineteenth-century family life (and
the fictional representation of its discontents). A point of rupture which
was at the time far more conspicuous in its public splendour, and towards
which present-day cultural analysts and readers of poetry might turn
more immediately, is the burial of Victor Hugo on 1 June 1885, not least
because this facilitated the self-liberation of Mallarmé's *Crise de vers*. In
Roger Shattuck's words, 'By this orgiastic ceremony France unburdened
itself of a man, a literary movement, and a century'.[3]

However, critics of the novel, not least those whose reading responds
in varying ways to the paradigm of bourgeois fiction enunciated in Tony
Tanner's classic account of *Adultery in the Novel*, will need little persuasion
about the importance of Flaubert for the generation of Naturalist novelists who published in Paris in the final decades of the century.[4] In very
different ways *Madame Bovary* and *L'Education sentimentale* examined the
issues of marital ennui and extra-marital seduction, and the *fin-de-siècle*
imperative of retrospection compelled Zola *et al.* to respond to these
accounts of unhappiness. Ever since Denis de Rougemont's famous
study of the representation in the West of unhappy desires, it has been
a critical commonplace to assert the permanence of the theme of adultery.[5] As Catherine Belsey notes, 'people like reading about desire';

indeed, 'in this field everyone is an expert'.[6] In the terms of Léon Jaybert's study, *De l'adultère dans les différents âges et chez les différentes nations*, 'L'adultère est de tous les temps et de toutes les nations, parce que toujours et partout il y a eu des passions aveugles et des unions mal assorties'.[7] More specifically, though, Tanner's account of such transgression in the 'bourgeois novels' of Rousseau, Goethe and Flaubert is only the most famous of a number of analyses which highlight the theme's particular urgency, seen as coincident with the rise of the middle classes in much of Europe and as prior to the birth of Modernism. This urgency is merely set into relief by the self-conscious literary perversity of Gustave Droz's bestseller *Monsieur, madame et bébé* (1866) which, in Zeldin's words, 'proposed to do what no one else had done: write about love in marriage'.[8] What needs to be defined is the relationship between claims about the apparent ubiquity of the theme of adultery and the historical specificity identified within the bourgeois novel.[9]

Tanner suggests that a shifting of social norms around the turn of the century is reflected in a 'move from the more realistic novel of contract and transgression . . . to what might be called the novel of metaphor'.[10] In Tanner's terms, 'as bourgeois marriage loses its absoluteness, its unquestioned finality, its "essentiality", so does the bourgeois novel'. This notion of a shift is echoed in Adam Phillips's book, *Monogamy*: 'Since the second half of the nineteenth century a lot of people have become agnostic about monogamy.'[11] The disaffection with the 'novel of contract and transgression' which inspires the development of Modernist prose is sketched by Tanner in terms of a triple impulse, embodied by Lawrence, Proust and Joyce. This image of literary practice in mutation needs to be clarified by a more exact historical and geographical focus on the precise manner in which bourgeois realism reached its culmination with the advent of naturalism towards the end of the nineteenth century, and then waned. As Maupassant observes in a piece which anticipates the publication of Zola's *Pot-Bouille*:

Le sujet n'est pas neuf; il n'en apparaît que plus intéressant, l'adultère ayant toujours été la grande préoccupation des sociétés, le grand thème des écrivains, le grand *joujou* de l'esprit des hommes. Et on ferait une bien curieuse étude en recherchant de quelle façon, tantôt plaisante et tantôt tragique, les générations successives ont jugé les manquements à cet accouplement légal qu'on nomme le mariage.[12]

The subject is today far from moribund as a source of literary inspiration, and quite naturally those so-inclined will also be able to cite examples of subsequent texts which still manipulate the motif of adultery in more banal ways (most visibly in the form of television soap operas). However, this may articulate merely the residual influence of family structures fashioned largely during the bourgeois century, or in other words the extent to which we still find classic family narratives so readable and habitable.

Beyond (or rather behind) the canonical nineteenth-century versions of Balzac, Stendhal and Flaubert, researchers will also find an array of commonplace examples by figures such as Kock, Feuillet, Champfleury, Cherbuliez, and Ponson du Terrail.[13] It may not be simply because of its multiple manifestations that adultery in nineteenth-century fiction holds such fascination. This motif also acquires a symptomatic quality when we analyze a culture established by the disestablishment of 1789, and engaged in an obsessive quest for political legitimation through property and propriety. As Lynn Hunt explains, the revolutionary value of *fraternité* is merely the most conspicuous sign of the way in which 'the French had a kind of collective political unconscious that was structured by narratives of family relations'.[14] Implicit in the conceptualization of the home as 'référence ultime, unique bastion des convenances et des hiérarchies',[15] the metonymical relationship of family to state clearly raises the stakes in the fictional analysis of the transgression which most directly threatens the *foyer*. Jules Cauvière, for example, a professor at the Institut Catholique de Paris, defined the home as the 'molécule initiale de la société civile'.[16] Moreover, male paranoia about wifely adultery implicitly acknowledges the limits of what might be termed the bourgeois culture of possession. Krafft-Ebing, for instance, says that female infidelity 'is morally of much wider bearing, and should always meet with severer punishment at the hands of the law. The unfaithful wife not only dishonours herself, but also her husband and her family, not to speak of the possible uncertainty of paternity.'[17] As Flaubert writes to Louise Colet on 13 March 1854:

Où y a-t-il . . . une virginité quelconque? Quelle est la femme, l'idée, le pays, l'océan que l'on puisse posséder à soi, pour soi, tout seul? Il y a toujours quelqu'un qui a passé avant vous . . . Si ce n'a été le corps, ça a été l'ombre, l'image. Mille adultères rêvés s'entrecroisent sous le baiser qui vous fait jouir . . . Et dans la vraie acception du mot tout le monde est cocu – et archi-cocu.[18]

The inventory of objects of desire in Flaubert's opening question suggests the metaphorical association between forms of possession which operates in and on nineteenth-century French culture: firstly, sexual–domestic control over women; then, decadent cynicism about 'intellectual property'; finally, mastery on land and sea upon which depends the colonial adventure (the reference to 'le pays' perhaps also implying land-ownership to which the bourgeoisie aspires in avaricious imitation of the aristocracy it wishes to depose).

As Maupassant realizes, the fabled anxiety of influence habitually imposed upon authors is experienced by *fin-de-siècle* writers as a pervasive state in such a self-consciously degenerative culture. Like Flaubert he wonders whether an idea can ever be truly original:

Il faut être, en effet, bien fou, bien audacieux, bien outrecuidant ou bien sot, pour écrire encore aujourd'hui! Après tant de maîtres aux natures si variées, au génie si multiple, que reste-t-il à dire qui n'ait été dit? Qui peut se vanter, parmi nous, d'avoir écrit une page, une phrase qui ne se trouve déjà, à peu près pareille, quelque part. Quand nous lisons, nous, si saturés d'écriture française que notre corps entier nous donne l'impression d'être une pâte faite avec des mots, trouvons-nous jamais une ligne, une pensée qui ne nous soit familière, dont nous n'ayons eu, au moins, le confus pressentiment?[19]

Such a corrective from this latter-day La Bruyère articulates the fears of those who wrote (and those who write) about late nineteenth-century fiction. Though Mallarmé might have been able to target Hugo, Flaubert appears to have been more resistant to parody, not least because of his own parodic strategies. Earlier critics are clear-sighted in this regard. André Maurois quotes Thibaudet's description of Flaubert as 'le Cervantès du roman français' and develops this comparison in the context of the Spaniard's parodic verve:

Vers 1850, le public français, déçu par la monarchie et par la république, par le drame lyrique et par le roman historique, par les excès de la passion comme par ceux de la révolution était tout prêt à goûter un livre qui brûlerait ce qu'il avait adoré, tout comme le public espagnol avait été prêt au temps de *Don Quichotte* à accueillir une parodie des romans de chevalerie.[20]

It is in the ambivalence of parody that we may measure the ambivalence of Flaubert's treatment of adultery, a motif much cited, exciting readers and inciting litigation, which nevertheless revels in its own vainness and vanity.

Beyond the realm of literature, the debates of politicans and intellectuals in the early years of the Third Republic inflect as much as they reflect a crisis of family values, in which our own *fin de siècle* – and indeed *fin de millénaire* – cannot help but find its embarrassed reflection. To the extent that legislation can be viewed in hindsight as a precipitation of such debates, readers of family fictions cannot ignore the *Loi Naquet* of 1884. This is important not only because in practical terms it might have freed unhappy couples in numbers and ways which the previous laws on separation did not permit, and redefined the liberational quality some-times ascribed to adultery, but also because it signalled the fragility of state-sponsored idealism about the indestructibility of the married couple. However unrecognizable as an adequate divorce law it might appear to a late twentieth-century audience, the *Loi Naquet* did articulate an admission on the part of the French state that the family unit was not indissoluble. Roddey Reid suggests that the notion of 'crisis' is really just a general effect of modern discourse: 'The so-called modern domestic family . . . has been always already dysfunctional, in crisis, *en miettes*, porous, and open to the outside . . . [It] has existed only insofar as it has been lamented in discourse as loss or absence and thus desired'.[21] Even if one acknowledges Reid's argument that the term 'crisis' should not conceal a counterfactual (or should one say 'counterfictional'?) idealism in narratives of familial discontents, it would be hard to deny the his-torically specific role of legal issues such as divorce, cohabitation and paternity suits in the reconstruction of the material social fabric of the Third Republic (which is of course fought out through opposed dis-courses). Indeed, here one might recall Tanner's admission of 'the absence of historical and sociological material' in his own landmark study.[22]

It is at the intersection of these twin parameters of cultural retrospec-tion and historical crisis that the narratives of domestic disorder explored in this book unfold. Central in the tradition of the novel of adultery to which Zola, Maupassant, Huysmans, Hennique, Bourget and Charpentier respond is, of course, the tale of the seduced wife on which critics have understandably focussed. Yet such a narrative pattern also implies the importance of the role of the seducer. A *nouvelle* typical in this regard is André Theuriet's 'Paternité', published in two parts in the *Revue des deux mondes*.[23] It tells of the return of the bachelor, Francisque Delaberge, from Paris to the provinces. As government inspector sent back to his home region he develops a rivalry with Simon Princetot which is exacerbated by their pursuit of the widow, Camille Liénard. In fact Simon was born shortly after Delaberge's affair with Mme Micheline Princetot of the *Soleil d'Or* at Val-Clavin twenty-six years earlier. The physical resemblance between these men only adds to Delaberge's suspicions, as does Micheline's keenness for him to return to Paris before he can discover the truth of his paternity. But the truth comes out and Francisque understands the *enjeux* of paternity which oth-erwise may so easily have remained latent: 'Il comprenait de quel poids les anciennes fautes que nous croyons vénielles pèsent plus tard sur nos

destinées. Ces amourettes que nous traitons si légèrement au temps de
notre jeunesse, laissent des semences éparses qui peuvent, dans l'âge
mûr, devenir autant de plantes envahissantes et meurtrières'. For Simon
embodies the *lex talionis*, the nemesis of the father's guilty desire, which
inverts the classical tale of sexual transgression so that Delaberge feels
'comme un nouvel Œdipe' (though he is in fact the father in this tale of
generational jealousy). Even when the old laundry woman from the *Soleil
d'Or*, Zélie Fleuriot, confirms his suspicions in chapter 7 and Marceline
finally admits this illegitimate paternity in response to his plea, 'vous
seule pouvez m'en donner la certitude', doubt is never quite erased, for
his ex-lover teases him with the implication of her own married status:
'est-ce qu'on est jamais sûr?' Perhaps Simon is the product of a legitimate sexual encounter. In one of those philosophical moments where
authorial and protagonistic positions collude, Delaberge asks, 'Dès
qu'on pénètre dans ces mystères de la filiation, peut-on jamais posséder
une certitude? L'adultère a cela de fatal qu'il laisse toujours planer une
ombre sur la véritable origine de l'enfant'. Subsequently Delaberge realizes that he must return to Paris without disturbing the amorous designs
of the next generation. Whereas Camille Liénard initially saw herself as
the 'trait d'union entre ses deux convives', by the end of the tale the
sexual syntax has been refashioned so that Delaberge realizes that 'je
puis servir de trait d'union entre ces deux cœurs qui se désirent et n'osent
se l'avouer'. In fact it is the love of the paternal seducer for his biological son which dare not speak its name, and when Simon drives him to
the train station in the final chapter he simply gives his son his watch and
hence the future it will measure. He can only momentarily return to biological paternity, whether it is real or fictional, and it is certainly not a
place which he could call home.

It is quite clear from Champfleury's *Histoire de l'imagerie populaire* that
literary tales of the adulterous wife often both reflect and dictate popular
narratives of misogyny. This is evident in the appendix which
Champfleury devotes to the mythical Lustucru (or as it is recomposed:
L'Eusses-tu-cru): 'Lustucru, au dix-septième siècle, avait entrepris
d'adoucir le caractère des mauvaises femmes.'[24] His means, though, are
far from gentle: 'Lustucru proposait d'envoyer cette tête [de femme]
chez le forgeron et de la reforger à coups de marteau, jusqu'à ce que l'ouvrier en fît sortir les principes pernicieux.' The reaction invited by this
figure fuels a war of the sexes to which the novel of adultery does in a
strong sense belong. Champfleury cites a number of rejoinders to the
myth such as *Lustucru massacré par les femmes, L'invention des femmes qui fera*

ôter la méchanceté de la tête de leurs maris, and Saumaize's play of 1660, *Véritables précieuses*. He even wonders whether the misogynist tradition can be tracked in *Bibliothèque bleue* titles such as *Méchanceté des filles* and *Misères des maris*. Lustucru might well be seen as the patron saint of patriarchal fictions which take it upon themselves to diagnose and cure the female malady of immorality. In this vein of violent misogyny, the infamous pamphlet by Dumas fils, *L'Homme-Femme* (1872), advises deceived husbands to kill their wives. The attendant double standard is demystified by that *fin de siècle* version of Stendhal's *De l'amour*, Paul Bourget's *Physiologie de l'amour moderne*: 'Un des plus étonnants cynismes de l'homme consiste à prétendre que la faute de la femme est pire que la sienne – parce qu'il peut en résulter des enfants – comme si, entre une maîtresse qui devient enceinte et l'amant qui l'engrosse, il y avait la plus légère différence de responsabilité.'[25]

Léon Jaybert's history of adultery until the Second Empire also provides the classic answer to the question 'Pourquoi cette différence?': 'Un mari est-il adultère, il manque à ses serments; mais sa faute ne fait à sa femme qu'un tort très passager et bien faible, surtout quand elle l'ignore. La femme est-elle adultère, et le mari l'ignorerait-il momentanément, l'ignorerait-il toujours, les résultats peuvent être bien différents.'[26] The *Grande Encyclopédie* is unambiguous in its article on 'Famille' about the relationship between the certainty of lineage and the cohesion of society:

Quand le mariage s'est consolidé, régularisant l'union de l'homme et de la femme, s'effectue une véritable révolution par *la reconnaissance de la paternité* et la substitution de la parenté masculine à la parenté féminine . . . La solidarité entre parents et enfants étant une force, une cause de résistance dans la lutte pour l'existence, les lignées où elle est le plus intense prospèrent et survivent aux autres; le sentiment de la paternité progresse d'une génération à l'autre.[27]

In his 'réflexions en faveur des femmes' however, Jaybert goes on to blame the Donjuanism allegedly characteristic of French society:

C'est là la principale excuse de la faillibilité des femmes . . ., partout on cherche à les séduire . . ., partout on emploie mille moyens pour y arriver . . ., on tire parti contre elles de la faiblesse que l'on a fait naître, excitée, encouragée . . ., on applique son amour-propre à surprendre leur vanité . . ., on met son bonheur, sa gloire à les faire succomber . . ., et ensuite on se plaint d'avoir trop bien réussi . . . et, le dirons-nous à la haute de la société . . ., celui qui compte le plus de victimes est souvent le plus recherché.

Indeed, our analysis of the Don Giovanni fictions of Emile Zola's *Pot-Bouille* (1882) in chapters 1 and 2 and Guy de Maupassant's *Bel-Ami*

(1885) in chapter 3 of this book suggests ways in which this tradition of adultery in fiction might be reconsidered not merely as a defensive misogyny typical of patriarchy but also as an indulgence of male fantasies of promiscuity. As Rachel Fuchs reminds us, 'Throughout the nineteenth century at least one-quarter of all births in the department of the Seine were to single mothers, and Paris had one of the highest illegitimacy rates in the western world'.[28] Our revision questions the tendency of previous critical practice to analyse such fiction simply from within the family unit. Though of course men's seduction of women to whom they were not married might produce children who could be seen in biological terms as illegitimate, in the legal terms of nineteenth-century France only the seduction of unmarried women would show up in these statistics, for the status of paternity was attributed automatically to husbands, thereby erasing visible demographic markers of female adultery. By attending to male fantasies of seduction, we might then take account not only of manifest general forms of patriarchal domination within that culture but also of particular issues, not least the debate over paternity suits (*recherche de paternité*) which resurfaces as a key feminist issue during the early years of the Third Republic.

In order to develop a comprehensive account of the pattern of sexual relations in the late nineteenth century, this study moves beyond adultery in fiction to suggest how tales of infidelity can be read in the wider context of sexuality's material (in this case socioeconomic and legal) as well as psychoanalytic determinations. The latter have been amply elucidated by Naomi Segal and Alison Sinclair's analyses of adultery in fiction.[29] Naturally there are accounts of the novel of adultery informed by relevant historical data but, unfortunately, such illuminations of social, family and legal history have usually been absorbed in a theoretically unambitious design.[30] But the vast project of recent social history and theory allows us to reconstruct this network of sexual relations in ways which unpick the moral alignments of bourgeois culture.[31] Such alignments are both articulated and contested by those novelists whose very intensification of realist ways of seeing takes 'the order of mimesis' to breaking point.[32]

In particular, the spatial model which distinguishes so powerfully between the private and the public domains (typically gendered female and male respectively) reflects not only the approachs of much modern social theory but also from another perspective the prejudicial dispositions of many nineteenth-century social commentators. As Reid notes: 'The distinction between public and private (and male and female) became part and parcel of a new process of social mapping whereby the middle groups now constituted themselves through discourses and the practices of the new social sciences and philanthropy as middle class over and against the urban labouring classes.'[33] According to the socio-medical account of the causes of wifely adultery offered by J.-P. Dartigues, '[La femme] règne dans l'intérieur du gynécée, tandis que l'homme est formé pour vivre au dehors',[34] and as Peter Gay asserts, 'There were literally thousands of such pronouncements, in several languages, scattered across publications in every civilized country'.[35]

This closeting of female existences was not only a means of imposing social order; it also represented a danger for the well-oiled machine of intersubjective relations, and Alain Corbin offers pertinent examples of the contemporary pathologisation of female *pudeur*. 'Physicians described the clinical symptoms of "ereuthophobia", modesty of the second degree: a morbid fear of being unable to refrain from blushing. . . . The same type of anxiety was at the root of the "white ailment" in women, that is, the refusal to go out of the house for fear of being seen by strangers'.[36] The 'white ailment' was not an anomalous idiosyncracy (rationalised by doctors as the 'irrationality' of women), but in fact a symptom of the spatialisation of power in terms of private and public domains. Public space, and thus also the world of prostitution, belonged in this way to husbands. In the most extreme instances, it becomes the playground of the wayward husband, as it does for Baron Hulot in *La Cousine Bette*. Moreover, for women to escape the home for affective, sexual reasons was, in the paranoid patriarchal imagination, but a step from the professional liberation of housewives. In Colette Yver's *Princesses de science* (1907) Thérèse's husband is wracked with jealousy when his wife, a doctor, returns after visiting a patient one night:

A six heures, le bruit d'une porte qu'on ouvrait le fit sursauter. Thérèse était devant lui toute fraîche sous sa voilette, fleurant l'humidité matinale, frissonnant un peu dans sa jaquette de drap; et ce retour de l'épouse, au petit matin, le soin qu'elle prenait d'assourdir le bruit de ses bottines, tout avait un air clandestin, malséant, qui rappelait les romans d'adultère.[37]

This spatial model will allow us to contrast on the one hand the paradoxical conservatism latent in the inward disposition of incestuous fiction and, on the other, adultery's rupture of the symbolic divide which attempts to house female desire within the safe space of the *foyer*. To find such a blithely comforting reaction afforded by the very archetype of sexual transgression, incest, we need only recall the euphoric tonality of the narrative of uncle–niece incest in Zola's *Le Docteur Pascal* (1893) which is treated in chapter 4. In symbolic terms, it may be said that whereas incest imprisons desire within the domestic space, as if the walls around the home were impenetrable, adultery has little regard for this rigid division of private and public, inverting as it does the institutionalised binarism inside/outside. Adulterous desires are, so to speak, transmural.

This distinction between inside and outside is reflected in much family history and family theory.[38] David Cheal identifies specifically 'the nineteenth-century separation of public and private spheres', 'the ideological exaggeration of the contrast between "the home" and "the world" that developed during the nineteenth century'. This distinction is said to be characteristic of 'modernization'. Cheal recounts how theorists and historians have linked it 'to other kinds of dualism, such as those of the political and the personal, the instrumental and the expressive, and male and female'. An influential example of the critique of the private/public binarism is to be found in Lynda M. Glennon's *Women and Dualism*:

The technocratic society splits selfhood into the instrumental and expressive self; it divides social life into public and private spheres. It presupposes polar opposites. An increase in one's instrumentality *must* mean a decrease in one's expressivity, and vice versa. The assumption that this choice must be made is the crucial logical link to conventional views about male and female roles.[39]

In reality, 'the division . . . dissolves into a multitude of overlapping and interdependent contexts for social interaction'. Jürgen Habermas has stressed the tendency for market transactions to invade the private sphere.[40] More specifically, Cheal cites the networks of female friendships and the way in which a wife's performance in a traditional domestic role could help to further her husband's career. Another form of 'enjambement' between private and public that undermines this conjugal relation, however, is, of course, adultery.

The politics of public space in the Third Republic has been well mapped, not least by Kristin Ross in her study of Rimbaud. She argues that, 'the Commune raises its fist against conventional spatial hierarchies – between distinct Parisian *quartiers*, country and city, and, by implication, that global carve-up of terrain between France, the imperial metropolis and its client colonies'.[41] Gaston Bachelard's model of interiors and exteriors, however, allows us to interrogate the relationship between public space and the domestic realm. In practical terms, the sites of this drama of inside and outside are the doors and windows which facilitate the passage between public and domestic space. Bachelard notes:

La porte, c'est tout un cosmos de l'entr'ouvert. C'en est du moins une image princeps, l'origine même d'une rêverie où s'accumulent désirs et tentations, la tentation d'ouvrir l'être en son tréfonds, le désir de conquérir tous les êtres réticents. La porte schématise deux possibilités fortes, qui classent nettement deux types de rêveries. Parfois, la voici bien fermée, verrouillée, cadenassée. Parfois, la voici ouverte, c'est-à-dire grande ouverte.[42]

The family novel offers a peculiarly privileged opportunity to track the rhythms and patterns of these liminal moments within the architecture of everyday life. The door allows illicit passage both into and out of the domestic space (in the novel of adultery) and between various rooms within that domestic space (in the novel of incest). Windows allow the desirous gaze to stray outwards as a psychological, narratological and architectural *projection* of transgression (a prime example would be Emma Bovary waiting for Rodolphe). The door facilitates the passage that the window promises. Bachelard's notion of *entrouverture* also suggests an analogy between the eroticised nature of the half-opened domestic spaces of the novel of adultery and the narrative unclothing of the body described by Roland Barthes in *Le Plaisir du texte*:

L'endroit le plus érotique d'un corps n'est-il pas *là où le vêtement bâile?* . . . c'est l'intermittence, comme l'a bien dit la psychanalyse, qui est érotique: celle de la peau qui scintille entre deux pièces (le pantalon et le tricot), entre deux bords (la chemise entrouverte, le gant et la manche); c'est ce scintillement même qui séduit, ou encore: la mise en scène d'une apparition-disparition.[43]

　　Michelle Perrot stresses the symbolic force of the *seuil*: 'The threshold was sacrosanct, and no one crossed it without invitation unless unusual noises were heard or suspicious effluvia or noxious odours were detected. Parents could beat their children, and husbands could beat their wives; that was their affair, and no one would call the police for such a thing.'[44] Perrot goes on to cite Viollet-le-Duc's *Histoires d'une maison* of 1873 which 'was intended to be a model [and] lavished a great deal of attention on vestibules, corridors, and stairways, which were supposed to act as avenues of circulation and communication as well as escape'.[45] The development of the bourgeois concept of privacy was intimately related to the reorganisation of domestic space such that the individual or the couple might have a room of their own. The marriage bedroom in nineteenth-century France became, as Perrot puts it, 'the approved altar for the celebration of sexual rites . . . protected by thick bedroom walls and by a locked door through which the children were rarely allowed to pass, whereas parents could enter the children's bedroom at any time'.[46] What really mattered was not merely having a room of one's own but also having a key of one's own. As much as compartmentalised individual space guaranteed privacy and sanctuary, the multiplication of rooms also allowed their private dramas to go unobserved. Any collective policing, which traditional rural and proletarian domestic spaces had provided, was now largely halted.

The cultural perception of such material arrangements of domestic space was informed by a romanticization of love relationships which cherished the uniqueness of the amorous bond. In this modern version of the platonic myth two halves of a whole meet in a lovers' embrace and become the one they originally were and always needed to be. Cynical narratives of adultery, however, remind readers of the mythical nature of this romanticization of bourgeois marriage. Adultery is always a second relationship, an afterthought, the overspill borne of the failure of our narratives of desire to close in an idealistic fashion. Counter to cynical versions, though, there is an idealistic strain which sees in the melodrama of adulterous fulfilment the tragedy of the *trop tard*. Adultery could be seen from this perspective as a 'perversion' which typifies the spirit of the Decadence. Such idealistic narratives therefore want to defend themselves on all counts; they try to resist the accusation of naivety by bemoaning the failings of married life whilst fuelling the fantasy that life and love are to be found elsewhere, at the end of that journey of desire between actuality and aspiration. It is this idealistic narrative which Emma Bovary wants to believe in, only to find that Rodolphe is living out the cynical version of the love plot.

Cynical plots put into question the uniqueness of the ideal relationship. This questioning of uniqueness can be done either by an addition or a subtraction of passionate relationships. Cynicism is measured in classical plots of addition in the distance from the ennobling depiction of a lone bond of love. The cynical addition to the unique bond is seen in the exaggeration of a text such as *Pot-Bouille* where Octave pursues a series of women (and yet which is absent from Bernard Gallina's account of *fin-de-siècle* fictions of adultery).[47] The cynical subtraction from the unique bond is to be found in certain novels of adultery *manqué* whose nineteenth-century model is *L'Education sentimentale* (though such an interpretation of the novel as a whole is to be distinguished from the hero's own sublimation of the initially unobtainable object of desire). In novels such as this the narrative resists the banality of the enactment of adultery. Edith Wharton's *The Age of Innocence* provides a slightly later example of this pattern. Such novels of adultery *manqué* can be usefully read as complements to *Pot-Bouille*.

In fact these plots, which we might term the *Brief Encounter* plot, also echo a model borne of the pre-bourgeois age, Madame de La Fayette's *La Princesse de Clèves* (1678), traditionally identified as the mother of the French *roman psychologique* and cherished by feminist criticism. This fiction shows that the plot of subtraction can carry the mood of idealism as well as that of cynicism. The major crime of the noble heroine is not the consummation of adultery but her notorious *aveu*. She confesses to her husband that she has an admirer whom she is unwilling to name. This confession effectively leads to the death of her husband who cannot believe in his wife's claim of self-restraint. He dies because he cannot believe that in this context of multiple courtly intrigues his own wife's personal plot is actually one of adultery *manqué*. Even after the death of her husband she continues to resist the pleasures offered by M. de Nemours. So La Fayette does offer the reader a version of the plot of subtraction in which the uniqueness of passion is denied, but this plot is lost at the heart of the cynical plot of addition, exemplified by the satellite narratives of courtly intrigue which function as ambiguously cautionary tales. Ironically, this death makes the consummation of a once adulterous passion perfectly feasible. But the very accessibility of romantic fulfilment renders the self-denying heroine all the more admirable or, in the final words of the novel, all the more inimitable, as the princess denies her passion for Nemours and retreats from the court. What distinguishes this seventeenth-century novel from the nineteenth-century tales about Mme Duhamain and Frédéric Moreau are the motives for restraint we find in these fictions. In these cynical bourgeois plots of subtraction restraint looks like a mixture of boredom and indecisiveness; in the pre-bourgeois plot of subtraction cynicism is countered by the heroism of moral choice (for all the unhappiness this brings). In the wake of May 1880 the most explicit homage to Flaubert was Henry Céard's *Une belle journée* (1881), centred on (or rather decentred by) the non-event of Trudon's tryst with Mme Duhamain at the restaurant des Marronniers. The heroine, Mme Duhamain, agrees to the meeting only to find that her admirer is simply a further example of the banality she regularly encounters, rather than an exception to the rule of tedium; in a self-conscious echo of Flaubert, 'rien n'arrive'.[48] So adultery seems to have lost its subversive vitality as the characteristic threat to the ideology of the bourgeois family values.

This sectarian cult of Flaubert (validated, as we shall see, by Huysmans's preface to the 1903 edition of *A Rebours*) can be identified in the response to the second edition of the new version of *L'Education sentimentale*, published in November 1879, half a year before Flaubert's death. Céard writes to Zola on 10 December 1879 after reading the latter's article on *L'Education* printed in *Le Voltaire* the previous day:

Vous avez fait un bien bel article sur *L'Education sentimentale*, bien vibrant et bien juste. Imaginez que le malheureux livre n'est nulle part: pas un exemplaire aux étalages. Personne de nous n'a vu qu'on en ait parlé dans les journaux. Du reste, figurez-vous bien ceci: c'est que nous sommes, en tout, une quinzaine seulement à Paris qui pratiquons ce chef-d'œuvre-là. Je me rappelle le grand coup qu'il m'a porté alors que je le découvris en 1874: je l'ai depuis enseigné à bien du monde, faisant de bien rares conversions. Certaines de mes amitiés sont venues uniquement de là: les plus littéraires et les plus solides.[49]

Much later in a letter to René Dumesnil (dated 13 July 1916) Céard charts the development of this allegiance to around 1878, 'une époque où, définitivement renseigné par Flaubert et *Les Trois Contes*, je me suis détaché des procédés de Goncourt et de Zola. *Une belle journée* fut le symptôme de ma transformation'.[50] As will become particularly clear in our analysis of Hennique's *Un accident de Monsieur Hébert*, the dynamics of envy and provocation are never far from the literary friendships evidenced by the mutual support between Naturalist writers. Supporting Flaubert is for Céard, as for Huysmans, also a way of resisting the shadow of Zola, and this operates at a somewhat base psychodynamic level as well in the nobler reaches of æsthetic choice traditionally charted by critics such as Colin Burns who argues, 'it is to Flaubert rather than Zola that one must turn in order to determine the true nature of Céard's development'.[51] Indeed, this is not to say that Zola and Flaubert should be seen as cultural enemies. Zola's praise at least for the realism of Flaubert's fiction is well-documented. Nevertheless, within the mind games practised by the *petits naturalistes* Flaubert represents an alternative form of cultural paternity. Certainly Zola's novel of adultery which is analysed in part 1 offers a contrast to the Flaubert / Céard model of adultery in fiction, identified in *L'Education sentimentale* and *Une belle journée*, as well as to the notorious focus on the adulteress which is recast by *Madame Bovary*.

Both types of novel (and in particular the plot of addition) have parodic possibilities. In the Flaubert/Céard model, adultery never quite happens; in Zola's novel, it seems to happen virtually all the time, which is in keeping with the critical distinction between, on the one hand, a Flaubertian world from which materiality and experience are in some sense erased and, on the other, the world of Zola in which copia is the order of the day. Here copia should be understood in the dual sense identified in another context by Terence Cave.[52] As Cave shows, the history of the development of the term from Latin generates two conflicting notions: firstly that of copia as abundance, and secondly that of copia as copy. In addition to its 'connection with . . . general notions – abundance, plenty, variety, satiety, resources' from the parent forms *ops*, in medieval Latin 'owing to a productive accident of usage, *copia* comes to mean a "copy" accompanied by its cognates *copiare* and *copista*'. The complementary relationship between parodic models is implicitly affirmed in *Au bonheur des dames* which transposes Octave's private *éducation sentimentale* to the public realm of capitalist adventure. His dictum that 'tout arrive et rien n'arrive' suggests that the multiple scenarios of Octave's *Bildung* do in some sense cancel each other out, only to conclude in the *bonheur* of 'cette belle journée'.[53] A vital form of irony in novels of adultery lies in the fact that adultery is itself reduced to the same form of sameness identified in marriage itself. Indeed adultery, it might be argued, is a parody of the marriage it undoes, often playing through a similar repertoire of binary emotional permutations, but within the ensnaring geometry of the triangle.

It is a critical commonplace to define nineteenth-century public space as an exhilarating and perturbing locus of defamiliarization (typically in a version of the capital of modernity, Paris, as the city of pleasure or as the city of revolutions), and yet the quest for privacy is not confined to the family home. On the contrary, the quest of the adulterous spouse is often a search for another place where, to borrow Michael Wood's phrase, 'secondariness is home'.[54] This is then a quest for refamiliarization, as Corbin suggests in his description of the rise of the *maison de rendez-vous* during the *fin de siècle* as a location for prostitution which imitates the cosiness of home life.[55] The desire for privacy outside the family is motivated by the need for secrecy which turns the denouements of traditional narratives of adultery into moments of exposure and revelation. What this suggests is an active link between questions of space and questions of knowledge. Treatment of what might be termed the imperative of triangularity in fictions of adultery has a long and distinguished lineage.[56] Exceptions to the pattern of narrative instability borne of triangular structures of desire are limited to anomalous cases such as the anonymous *Confessions d'une jeune femme* (1906), whose heroine ends up living happily between her husband and her lover.

It is perhaps most useful for critics attuned to the potential of social theory to consider the classic triangular pattern of cuckolded husband and fallen wife – whose *common ground* is the home itself – and the seducer from the extra-familial space in terms of a structure of cognition. What the wife and seducer share is knowledge, not only the carnal knowledge of sexual pleasure apparently forgotten by the married couple, but also at a second degree the knowledge of the secret fact of their passion (in other words, the knowledge of such erotic *connaissance*). As Sedgwick stresses, knowledge and sex had become 'conceptually inseparable from one another'.[57] In rhetorical terms, therefore, the classic tale of adultery is characterized by the figure of dramatic irony. By a spatial paradox this figure lends to the fallen wife a knowledge of the extra-domestic situation superior to that of her husband, who at least in theory participates in the male dominion of this extra-domestic space. As in Molière's ironic interrogations of the authority of fathers, the imbalance which undermines the patriarchal family structure and facilitates the plots of family fiction comes from the mismatch whereby the theoretical power of husband and father no longer coincides with actual knowledge (in the case of comedy not until the denouement, and in the case of tragic fictions not until it is simply too late). This problem with the deficit in husbands' knowledge is only exacerbated by men's fears of being duped under the legal principle which presumes a husband's paternity. In the unambiguous terms attributed to Barbey d'Aurevilly by Paul Bourget, 'Et puis, vous qui parlez toujours d'hérédité, il n'y a qu[e les femmes], entendez-vous bien, qui en connaissent les secrets, parce qu'il n'y a qu'elles qui connaissent vraiment de qui est leur enfant, quand elles en ont.'[58]

Just as adultery can be understood as an enigma to be resolved or concealed by the individual – depending on his or her position within the cognitive triangle of dramatic irony – so as a phenomenon of social history its secret nature poses an enigma of referentiality which resists factual analysis. Nevertheless it does invite fictional analysis as the love which cannot help but speak its name. One answer to why the fictional motif seems so prevalent is simply that the representation of adultery in the form of an encounter between consenting heterosexual adults has been the most palatable form of cultural curiosity about perversion. Due to the great difficulty in proving the *constat d'adultère* by finding lovers *in flagrante delicto*, the police were compelled to act on the far from satisfactory assumption that 'deux êtres, de sexe différent, enfermés dans une chambre à un seul lit suffit pour constituer le délit d'adultère'.[59] For adultery resisted the normal judicial procedures, and the forces of order were allowed to indulge in circumstantial evidence, such as exposing characters for being in the wrong place at the wrong time. This procedure provided an addled response to the forensic crisis of a legal process forced to deal with adultery. But even if we feel that, because in sociological terms it enjoys the privacy of the perverted, adultery can ultimately hide its face as necessarily one of the most private moments in any history of privacy, the argument that there is an intense *fin de siècle* reflection on the matter of adultery is hardly diminished by the conclusion of a social historian such as Anne-Marie Sohn that

it was during the Third Republic that a decisive new approach to adultery developed. Public opinion on the subject changed quite rapidly, while at the same time the participants themselves subverted its meaning. Rates of adultery almost surely increased, given changes in social habits as well as a more tolerant outlook.[60]

Michel Foucault's account of modernity's discursive foregrounding of sexuality needs no introduction. In his much cited words, 'le sexe n'a pas cessé de provoquer une sorte d'éréthisme généralisé'.[61] But as with Roddey Reid's generalizing argument, this nevertheless leaves room for a spotlighting of the *fin de siècle*'s particularly vocal concern for matters sexual. As Marc Angenot puts it: 'La fin du XIXe siècle, c'est le grand moment du sexe-en-discours, celui où il est le plus tabou, le plus obsédant, le plus récurrent et protéiforme dans ses dissimulations, la méconnaissance de ses symbolismes et les ruses de sa représentation.'[62] The pertinence and irony of writing a book on the family in crisis at the end of the nineteenth century as the twentieth century comes to its own close is made clear by Jeffrey Weeks's comment that 'this present is, perhaps, more preoccupied with sexual issues and controversies than ever before'.[63] All this being said, of course, it would be a mistake to conflate discourses on sex and those on the family, as if sex and family were coterminous. What adultery surely proves is that they are not. The traditional family may well be viewed as a way of socializing sexual desires. Adultery, however, seems to exert a destructive, anti-social force, by threatening to reassert the sexy nature of sex in a way that is apparently lost in that process of socialization.

Fin de siècle France's process of reflection on the family was fuelled by the translation of Engels's *Der Ursprung der Familie, des Privateigenthums und des Staats*. In it Engels states, 'l'histoire de la famille date de 1861, de l'apparition de *Droit maternel* de Bachofen'.[64] Family history, it seemed, was now a self-conscious element in academic discourse. It was seen as something amenable to systematisation and to theory. Engels goes on to develop L. H. Morgan's division of family history into four periods, translated as *la famille consanguine, la famille punaluenne, la famille syndiasmique*, and *la famille monogamique*. The shift from barbarism to modern society, between the third and fourth stages, is described in terms of a rigidification of the rules of fidelity. Under this system, Engels sees wifely adultery as a residual memory of ancient sexual practice. Suspicious as he is of 'un ennui mortel que l'on désigne sous le nom de bonheur domestique', Engels realises that the ideal of the monogamous family now acts as 'la forme cellulaire de la société civilisée'. Of modern France he notes:

L'adultère, défendu sous des peines sévères, rigoureusement puni, mais inde-structible, devint une institution sociale inéluctable. La certitude de la paternité des enfants reposa surtout, après comme avant, sur la conviction morale, et pour résoudre l'insoluble contradiction, le Code Napoléon décréta: 'Art.312: l'enfant conçu pendant le mariage a pour le père le mari'.

The prioritisation of legal over natural paternity is seen as an admission of the cognitive limits in patriarchy's attempts to ensure the validity of its own lineage: 'la monogamie est née de la concentration de grandes richesses dans les mêmes mains – celles d'un homme – et du désir de transmettre ces richesses par héritage aux enfants de cet homme, à l'ex-clusion de ceux de tout autre'.

Adulterous patterns of sexual, spatial and cognitive transgression contravene the homosocial bonds upon which patriarchal structures depend. This term 'homosocial' is usefully defined by Eve Kosofsky Sedgwick as 'a word occasionally used in history and the social sciences, where it describes social bonds between persons of the same sex; it is a neologism, obviously formed by analogy with "homosexual", and just as obviously meant to be distinguished from "homosexual"'.[65] The irony of adultery breaking male homosocial bonds is reflected in a cultural com-monplace in which the cuckold is betrayed not only by his wife but, just as significantly, by one of his friends (or at least fellow men). The numer-ous popular responses to the irony of this situation can be exemplified by the success of the Charlton Horn Fair in London, which thrived during the eighteenth and nineteenth centuries. Notorious for its inde-cencies and frequent riots, it was suppressed by Order in Council in 1872. Tradition had it that King John granted the right to hold the fair to a miller whose wife he had seduced after a hunting expedition in the area. The miller was given the land visible from Charlton to the bend of the river at Rotherhithe, and amused neighbours christened the river boundary of his land 'Cuckold's Point'. In its heyday thousands of people would attend the fair by boat dressed as kings, queens and millers with horns on their heads.

Rather than taking the psychoanalytical track back to the homosexual analogy so persuasively elucidated by Sedgwick, this book analyzes the social mechanisms of male friendship which are threatened by fictions of homosocial betrayal but persist outside marriage in the figure of the *célibataire*, most notably in the recoupling of Frédéric and Deslauriers at the end of *L'Education sentimentale*, which asserts the apparent naivety of heterosexual romance.[66] The associated questions of rivalry and jealousy as well as the matter of affiliation are played out not merely within the novels in our corpus but moreover within the field of literary relations which surround the *maître de Médan*. Whereas Paul Bourget stands at some distance from Zola and, along with Maupassant, offers an alternative psychological approach to character and narrative, Huysmans, Hennique and Céard appear to be initially bound by the twin affiliations of Flaubert and Zola. This bubbles over into internecine strife with the publication of Huysmans's *A Rebours* in 1884.

The issue of illegitimacy so often cited in the context of fictions of adultery not only underpins fears of wifely misbehaviour; it also underscores the potential delusion of such male concerns, for of course even the non-adulterous mother of 'legitimate' children may herself be the product of a defective bloodline associated with illegitimacy by the bourgeois culture of which *Les Rougon-Macquart* is typical. It will be suggested, then, that rather than being simply avatars of ailment, *fin-de-siècle* narratives of consanguinity (such as *A Rebours*) and of incest (such as *Le Docteur Pascal*) fulfil a conservative function by appearing to resist the uncertainties of sexual interaction with the world outside one's own family. They seem to allow characters to 'keep it in the family'. Huysmans's novel is presented in chapter 5 as the extreme moment in this resistance to otherness of all kinds. As the last in a long line of consanguineously degenerating aristocrats, the sterile des Esseintes embodies the *fin de famille* against which the ever burgeoning family tree of Zola's fictions unfolds. For des Esseintes the world external to his domestic realm exists only as a projection of imagined or recollected communities. The ending which deports the antihero back to the capital city diagnoses the decadence of family fiction as such, for more typical realist and naturalist fictions also collude with bourgeois readers' self-inflation to the exclusion of counterdiscursive possibilities outside their own social space. Indeed, the problematic use of uncommon languages from across the social spectrum in *L'Assommoir* may be read as an expression of the difficulties in actually escaping the contractual demands of legibility imposed on bourgeois fiction.

These counterdiscursive possibilities are explored in chapter 6 which concludes part 3 of our study by examining a pair of texts where the question of radical politics threatens to detonate at the heart of the family romance. In the case of Léon Hennique's *Un accident de Monsieur Hébert* (1883) the presentation of a fragment from a radical newspaper, which rewrites the tale of a middle-class *partie de campagne* interrupted by *paysans* from the locality, enlists the ironies of gender and social differences inherent in the history of pictorial *déjeuners sur l'herbe*. Zola's *Paris* (1898) offers an altogether more literal detonation of the well-worn tale of sibling rivalry by allowing an anarchist bomb to hold to ransom the very readability of a Naturalist narrative which looks as if it might collapse under the weight of its own multiple plot structures.

The model for these imbrications of the sexual and the political as understood by contemporaries (and thus without the awareness of sexual politics as now understood) is *L'Education sentimentale*, invoked in Huysmans's preface of 1903 ahead of the oft cited *L'Assommoir* as the paradigm for a form of Naturalist fiction which seems to write itself dry in *A Rebours*. The indispensable equivocation of Flaubert's text lies in the possibility of seeing not only an allegorical relationship between the missed political opportunities of 1848 and the missed romantic opportunities of Frédéric, but also of identifying the figurative force of that very act of missing. For it is perhaps to the extent that the sexual and the political in *L'Education sentimentale* are skewed, and thus miss each other, that the much glossed possibility of the 'livre sur rien' operates most effectively as a self-evacuating focus of thematic dislocation. This contrast between the interiority of des Esseintes's universe and the gesture towards the political by Hennique and Zola projects the inner / outer model onto extreme scenarios where family narratives appear, in the case of Huysmans, to be excessive, and in the case of Hennique and Zola, to be insufficient. Manifestations of a discontent with the cultural limitations of this obsession with adultery were widespread. We may note as an example Emile Verhæren's privileging of Huysmans's writing at the expense of the 'et'-school of Ohnet, Theuriet, Bourget and Daudet, as he labels them: 'Le mal de mer vous prend à être tangué et roulé dans la chaloupe de l'éternel adultère, ce lieu commun inextirpable du roman français. On hurle au changement. On l'attend, on l'espère, et alors qu'une première colombe de l'arche tournoie au-dessus de nous (telle cette *Bièvre*), on soupire: Enfin!'.[67] In a letter-card encouraging Arnold Goffin to spread the name of Ruysbroeck, Huysmans explains, 'ce serait plus intéressant que l'histoire de l'adultère de Mme la

Duchesse une telle avec le Comte un tel, suivant la formule de Bourget ou Prévost – quelle vieille galanterie on nous sert tout de même!'[68]

This inadequation between the novel as a genre and its key topic, the family, anticipates the formal ruptures which prose fiction is to undergo as the century turns. In France in particular, though, a paradigmatic shift in the conceptualization of family matters is registered in the *fin de siècle*, as we have suggested above, in the debate on divorce which leads to the *Loi Naquet*. (As so often, it is in family law where the sexual and the political meet.) At the same time the discourse of the New Woman and the possibilities of alternative sexual, familial and emotional arrangements (not least in the form of *union libre*) provide in an altogether more radical way a capacity to deconstruct narratives of lives plotted around a unique conjugal bond.[69] It is indicative that Zola's presence is gradually effaced in the course of this book and is largely absent from the concluding chapter which considers the narratological implications for mainstream fictional forms of these shifts in the conceptualization of family life. This Coda draws together the major strategies of reading used in the preceding chapters by examining Paul Bourget's *Un divorce* (1904) and providing a brief taste of Armand Charpentier's now forgotten fiction which at its best liberates bourgeois female characters from the narrative of the unique conjugal bond. The historical span of the present account stretches from Flaubert's death in 1880 to the appearance of Bourget's novel. Bourget's rather more conservative account of what he perceives as the socially and morally pernicious effects of twenty years of divorce law nevertheless shares with Charpentier the desire to write from within the standpoint of the male-authored *lisible* bourgeois fiction to which this book is devoted.[70] What such fiction can no longer presume is that lives will unfold along a single narrative line towards those key transactional moments famously defined by E. M. Forster as the *telos* of the classic tale:

> If it was not for death and marriage I do not know how the average novelist would conclude. Death and marriage are almost his only connection between his characters and his plot, and the reader is more ready to meet him here, and take a bookish view of them, provided they occur later on in the book: the writer, poor fellow, must be allowed to finish up somehow, he has his living to get like anyone else.[71]

The recasting of fictional conclusions of death and marriage at the end of the nineteenth century (and such moments of historical termination themselves) share the desire to re-examine, under the influence of what Hegel calls 'the bitter wine of a sense of finitude',[72] the multiple meanings of that pregnant expression *faire une fin*.

PART I

The promiscuous narrative of Pot-Bouille

CHAPTER I

Demon lover or erotic atheist?

> What do men who can command, who are born of rulers, who evince power in act and deportment, have to do with contracts? Such beings are unaccountable, they come like destiny, without rhyme or reason, ruthlessly, bare of pretext.[1]

> At least religious atheists could believe that God was dead, but what can the erotic atheist believe?[2]

Though its origins precede the death of Flaubert, *Pot-Bouille* is at the heart of the rewriting of the Flaubertian novel which we observe after May 1880. Of course, it enjoys a literally and symbolically central location as the tenth novel in Zola's twenty-novel cycle. (As we shall see, there is a particular way in which the final novel, *Le Docteur Pascal*, responds to the patriarchal concerns voiced and ironised in Zola's own novel of adultery.) Indeed, the opinion of Lionel Trilling and George Steiner that *Pot-Bouille* is actually *the* archetypal bourgeois novel can be clarified in the cultural context of the novel of adultery, as well as in the social context of hypocritical bourgeois values. So whereas readings of this novel have traditionally stressed the satire of social norms, an awareness of hitherto uninvestigated intertextual links will highlight its parody of cultural forms, which might be described as 'authorized transgression'.[3] Zola's novel displaces the focus of the great nineteenth-century tradition of adultery in fiction by returning in a tragicomic (and thus Mozartian) vein to the Don Giovanni theme. Both novels and operas do form the major cultural fields of intertextual reference in *Pot-Bouille*, but these references (or at least the explicit ones) are not to Mozart and Flaubert, but to Meyerbeer and Grétry on the one hand, and Balzac and Sand on the other. The narrative describes the adulterous machinations of the inhabitants of an apartment block in the rue de Choiseul in Paris by following the adventures of Octave Mouret who arrives from Plassans (and, we might say, from *La Conquête de Plassans*). The novel of adultery is parodied by Zola's use of the Don Juan figure who enjoys a double-edged relationship to the patriarchy that the novel of adultery subtends. As a sexual peripatetic, the Don Juan figure, Octave, threatens husbands with the notorious uncertainty of paternity, and yet at the same time embodies a certain principle of virility, which is itself grounded in a crisis of masculinity and paternity.

What Zola does in this novel is to make the male seducer into the central figure (and not, as is so often the case in bourgeois fiction, a seduced wife such as Emma Bovary). This resolutely does not mean that he is the recipient of the reader's sympathy. Indeed, one of the characteristics of this archly cynical novel is the lack of sympathy elicited by the various characters, for within the scheme of dramatic irony which we have identified in general terms above, those characters in the know appear quite malevolent and those in the dark appear fairly dim. It is for this reason that the exceptional scene of the 'fausse couche' of Adèle is so painfully memorable. It would certainly be an exaggeration to read Zola's critique as an attack on the family *per se*. In the discussion about *union libre* over a decade later Zola still sees the family as the 'least worst' unit of social organisation: 'Toute notre organisation sociale repose sur la famille . . . [I]l faudra que l'union entre un père et une mère représente des garanties pour les petits. Ces garanties, le mariage seul les donne à présent.'[4] Although we are not invited to sympathise with Octave Mouret in any great measure, we are nevertheless constrained as readers by the focalizing mechanism of the novel.

Even the title *Madame Bovary* – in spite of its initial constructive indeterminacy as to which Madame Bovary we might be about to pursue – identifies a female focus of interest. The problematics of such a focus are made infamously clear in Flaubert's transgender identification with his heroine ('Mme Bovary, c'est moi'), and this effect is sharpened by Flaubert's use of *style indirect libre*. What critics have noted, though, is the mobility of such narrative identification, such that the seducer's perspective is not wholly marginalised by Flaubert's narrator. It is this view which is tracked assiduously in *Pot-Bouille*, which might therefore be thought of as the seducer's tale.

Though *La Conquête de Plassans* and the comparisons it invites with other novels by Zola create one context which helps to define *Pot-Bouille*'s cultural location, there is a yet more specific context which surrounds the publication of the novel. The prelude to this was the appearance of three newspaper articles written by Zola. On 14 February 1881, *Le Figaro* published a satirical piece entitled 'Le divorce et la littérature' in which

Zola describes the crisis in subject matter that writers would undergo if those reformers promulgating a fresh divorce law were successful:

[les romans et surtout les drames] . . . sont toujours plus ou moins bâtis sur l'adultère, et ils ont tous des dénouements inacceptables, coups de couteau, coups de fusil, violences inutiles et odieuses. Du moment qu'on pourra lâcher sa femme, je compte qu'il ne sera plus permis de la tuer. . . Voilà donc notre répertoire détruit.[5]

Notably, the focus of this critique of contemporary writers is, once again, their sense of an ending. As examples, Zola cites *La Femme de Claude*, the plays of Dumas fils, Augier and Sardou. Once more the self-conscious nature of the obsession with adultery in nineteenth-century literature emerges: 'Faut-il tuer la femme? Faut-il tuer l'amant? Faut-il tuer le mari? On a retourné la question de cent manières, on a sauté sur place dans cette «toquade» de notre temps, que le dix-huitième siècle a ignorée et qui fera hausser les épaules du vingtième.'

Two weeks later *Le Figaro* published 'L'Adultère dans la bourgeoisie' which compares middle-class infidelity with proletarian prostitution.[6] In both instances, the apparently fallen nature of women can be explained, Zola tells us, by reference to 'milieu' and 'éducation'. In a mode which echoes Balzac's warning that 'ce n'est pas le mari qui forme la femme',[7] he proceeds to analyze three forms of upbringing, which can be mapped onto specific characters in *Pot-Bouille*. Firstly, he considers the neurotic effect of spatial enclosures on 'une race atrophiée par les plafonds bas' which generates 'l'adultère physiologique par le déséquilibre des névroses héréditaires', witnessed in Valérie Vabre. By a rhetorical sleight of hand it is such a woman, and not just the progeny of such an adulterous relationship, who is described as illegitimate, 'une créature abâtardie'. Zola concludes this description by suggesting that at least four out of ten adulteresses fall into this category. (To perceive self-irony in this taxonomical zeal would be a generous interpretation.) So what we might have expected to be merely a psychological case turns out to be a socially identifiable type, and it is in this displacement from case to type (to which Naturalism as a literary movement is so sensitive) that the decadence of contemporary mores becomes quite visible.

In the second instance, the link between prostitution and adultery is manifest. What Zola dislikes is the homosocial bonding of mother and daughter which excludes the father, who is criticized by his wife. This is represented in the novel by the Josserand family where the mother chaperons her daughters on the social circuit in search of husbands. Such a mother's 'véritable cours de prostitution décente' teaches her daughter 'des révérences et des clins d'œils, des pâmoisons de gorge, tout l'art du libertinage reconnu nécessaire et autorisé par les familles'. We see this in action in the 'scandale de la fenêtre' which seals the union of Berthe and Auguste Vabre.[8] The aim is a socially and economically advantageous marriage. Once the bait is taken and the daughter is married off, the game of seduction starts all over again: 'Et la chasse recommence, non plus au mari, mais à l'amant. Même tactique, d'ailleurs. Sa mère lui a appris le métier'.[9] So adultery mimes marriage. This is 'l'adultère de la femme sortie de sa classe, gâtée par les appétits de son milieu, élevée par une mère respectable et prude dans cette idée que les hommes sont mis au monde pour fournir des robes de femme'. Like Octave's, this is a desire that seems to know no end, caught up on the wheel of bourgeois possibilities in this post-revolutionary world.

If this second category equates adultery with greed, then the final section considers the other extreme in which the perpetuation of innocence produces 'l'adultère le plus commun, dans la bourgeoisie'. So if four out of ten adulteresses are hysterics, then by Zola's reckoning perhaps five out of ten are simpleminded, with the odd materialistic woman thrown in for good measure! In the novel Marie Pichon is guilty of 'l'adultère par bêtise... l'adultère sentimental, où la chair n'est encore pour rien, et qui n'est jamais que la faute de la sottise du milieu et de l'étrange conception de l'honnêteté chez les parents.' As will be suggested in chapter 2, if the first scenario depicts domesticity as asphyxiation, in like fashion, this final category depicts domesticity as incarceration, 'on calfeutre les portes et les fenêtres, pour que le dehors n'entre pas'. This resistance to the realm of external desires cannot be repeated in married life.

Zola's cynicism generated a deal of public reaction which led him to nuance these views in an article on 'Femmes honnêtes' in *Le Figaro* on 18 April 1881.[10] In place of this misogynistic image of female foibles, Zola offers three alternative scenarios which suggest how Valérie, Berthe and Marie might have been other than they are: firstly, the assiduous, frugal and moral housewife; then, an instance of 'l'intelligence française', 'cette souplesse à tout comprendre'; and finally native intelligence which resists the naïvety otherwise fuelled by a convent education. In the first case, the fusing of capital and desire acts as a positive moral force. So busy is the wife of the watch repairer, 'brûlée du seul besoin d'aider son mari, afin d'arriver tous deux à quelque chose', that 'il n'y a pas de place pour un vice, l'adultère est supprimé par les faits'. Unlike Berthe who expects to be served by the income of a man, this wife 'devient une volonté et une force, au même titre que l'homme'. Whereas Berthe's adulterous desire is fuelled by her indolence and triggered by her material aspirations, material improvement in their quality of life becomes a form of desire for this valiant wife: 'une passion, où elle met toutes les forces nerveuses de son être'. For she represents labour, whereas Berthe embodies consumption.

Zola's second case of the laudable bourgeoise is also defined by her active engagement with her husband's business activities. Whereas the watch repairer's wife walks the streets of Paris returning completed work and collecting payments whilst her husband works inside the boutique that is also their home, this second figure runs the family business whilst her husband is away on business at Le Havre or Marseille. Theirs is really a marriage of 'associés' and she is 'un autre lui-même' who manages sales and accounts. Once more Zola suggests a contrary vision to the diagnosis of idle hands which readers will see in *Pot-Bouille*: 'Ceux-là s'entendent et se resteront fidèles; ils sont trop occupés, ils ont trop d'intérêts communs'. Of particular interest is the vision of sexual equality which Zola perceives amongst the industrious bourgeoisie (as he brushes over questions of birth, childcare and the value of domestic work): 'Lui, la traite en égale, avec une nuance de respect pour son activité. Elle, cesse d'être une femme, lorsqu'elle est en bas; et, si un homme se montre galant, elle demeure surprise, oublieuse de la beauté pleine, de la santé superbe de ses trente ans.' The *femme de trente ans* made notorious by Balzac is rendered a paragon of virtue by the desexualizing qualities of robust labour.

The final type of faithful bourgeoise represents the triumph of 'une hérédité lointaine et compliquée' over 'son milieu', over a convent education which usually produces 'une poupée aimable' like Marie. What such a wife inherits is a kind of native good sense which makes her an invariably accurate source of business acumen on which her husband can draw behind closed doors; she is the power behind the man. Though she loves to go out dancing in Paris, she has 'rien d'une héroïne de roman, pas même l'allure un peu garçonnière de la femme de commerçant', as though her happiness lies in her capacity to escape contemporary narrative possibilities, to live a life untracked by literary culture. Even though she is depicted as 'une vraie femme', once more it is the virtual desexualization of women which guarantees happiness: 'Après les adorations de la lune de miel, les deux amoureux deviennent deux amis; et, dès lors, le bonheur du ménage est indestructible'. Zola's ideal consists of a heterosexual marriage tie which discovers the virtues of homosocial friendship. Such friendship between men and women might thus be termed *heterosocial*. As the article concludes, 'Dans tous les ménages honnêtes que j'ai connus, la femme vivait étroitement la vie du mari. La moralité du mariage est uniquement là'. Ironically, this heterosocial partnership is what Octave appears to find by the end of the novel in both his commercial-conjugal relationship with Mme Hédouin and, even more ironically, in his largely unexplored (because unspoken) friendship with Valérie.

What all of these these positive scenarios imply, however, is the potential link between socioeconomic decline and moral decadence. Although this article is largely a tactical response to virulent criticism, it nevertheless becomes clear from this pair of articles that Zola was both immersed in the misogynistic motifs of the literature of adultery and yet also suspicious of the pernicious effect such social stereotypes might exercise upon the literary imagination. It is in this ambivalent context that *Pot-Bouille* was written, apparently intended as a novel of adultery to end all novels of adultery.

These female types can, as has been suggested, be mapped onto characters in the novel. As such Zola's moral and social typology of women is culturally sanctioned in the press before publication of the novel. As the lender of books Octave comes to dominate the circulation of cultural capital before his sexual circulation can come into its own. As we have already noted, both of these forms of capital are but preludes to his triumph in the true capitalist exchange of financial capital. Marie Pichon receives a kind of literary titillation from her reading of romantic and post-romantic fiction such as George Sand and Honoré de Balzac which Octave procures for his mistress-to-be, borrowing so as to be able to lend. As such Octave operates as a sort of literary pimp. Indeed, it is in the realm of literature rather than that of sex where Octave seems to provide Marie with the greatest pleasure.

The fact that critiques of reading such as Léon's and Duveyrier's prove so pointless suggests a similarly ambivalent attitude towards that Flaubertian critique of the romantic education of Emma's sensibility. Octave seduces Marie Pichon in chapter 4 of the novel, when an implicit parallel is drawn between the 'désordre' in the household of the *hystérique*, Valérie Vabre, and the 'désordre' – the same word is used – in the Pichon household as Madame is overcome by a rereading of George Sand's *André*. What is interesting is that it is Mme Pichon, and not Mme Vabre, who yields to Octave's seductive manœuvers (although Valérie indulges her desires elsewhere). The moral disorientation triggered by reading romanticism is diagnosed in the foreground of the novel whereas the effects of a much-pathologized hysteria are marginalized in the text as rumour and connotation. Zola's letter to Baille (dated 4 July 1860) situates Sand's writing at the heart of the tradition of adultery in fiction, when he qualifies his criticism of *Jacques* with an assertion of the general validity of the situation it recounts: 'rien de plus strictement vrai que cette situation d'une femme n'aimant plus son mari et ne pouvant s'empêcher d'aimer un autre homme'.[11]

Rather than copying *Madame Bovary*'s critique of such reading, however, one is left wondering whether even this *lieu sûr* of Flaubertian irony is not also subject to Zola's parody. The moral lesson becomes a comically heavy-handed set scene. Marie complains of the effects of reading, 'Quand ça vous prend, on ne sait plus où l'on est . . .' (p. 75), and it is made quite clear that she is playing *not* so hard to get . . . She faints, Octave diagnoses, 'C'est d'avoir trop lu', and subsequently – in a scene that is both ridiculous and brutal – we learn how 'il la posséda, entre l'assiette oubliée et le roman, qu'une secousse fit tomber par terre' (p. 77). This sense of a parodic overplaying of the topos of dangerous reading is particularly important given that even in Culler's destabilising reading of *Madame Bovary*, he maintains this critique of romanticism as a Flaubertian certainty.[12] This parody of the proscription of reading makes mincemeat of the final line in chapter 4 where M. Campardon tells Octave: 'L'éducation dans la famille, mon cher, il n'y a que ça!' (p. 78).

One of the benefits of married life is that Marie escapes from the cultural censorship of her father, M. Vuillaume, whose educational theory runs thus: 'pas de romans avant le mariage, tous les romans après le mariage' (p. 67). The sense that Marie's upbringing has been isolated and uninspiring is brought out early in chapter 4 when Octave enjoys afternoon tea with the Pichons and Marie's parents. The piano is a far more acceptable bourgeois pastime for a young lady, hence the 'gêne' when Octave expresses shock at the fact that Marie cannot play. This immediately puts into question their bourgeois status, to which Zola's inane characters aspire. She can, however, sing and her mother recalls 'cette chanson sur l'Espagne, l'histoire d'une captive regrettant son bien-aimé'. What Zola suggests is that the culture of romance is pervasive, and will prove especially attractive only to a woman who has known such a cloistered upbringing. The ultimate irony is that it is her father who originally allowed her to read *André* a few months before her marriage, thinking it to be 'une œuvre sans danger, toute d'imagination et qui élève l'âme'.

The choice of *André* as the accessory to adultery is itself revealing, for this is a novel which already invokes the subject of reading. The eponymous hero, the son of the marquis de Morand, is a Walter Scott fan, and when his friend, Joseph, tries in vain to denigrate the character of Sand's heroine Geneviève, he pretends that she is a major consumer of novels: 'elle fera pis que les autres; je me méfie de l'eau dormante et des filles qui lisent tant de romans'.[13] So both the indulgence and the proscription of romantic reading seem equally pathetic. André's own fantasies about novelistic heroines are already subject to irony in Sand's account, and this is only exacerbated in Zola's novel. André hides books in his jacket and goes out into the wilds of nature with 'Jean-Jacques ou Grandisson'. Unlike that other secret reader, Julien Sorel, André does not consume Napoleonic texts (for unlike Julien, he is not a social aspirant; his family has already 'arrived'). The fantasies of André (unlike the Lovelace figure, Joseph) are of 'les chastes créations de Walter Scott, Alice, Rebecca, Diana, Catherine', of 'les soupirs éloignés des vierges hébraïques de Byron', and of course 'la grande et pâle Clarisse'. There is, however, a musical counterpart to these 'chœurs délicieux', as 'quelquefois un chœur de bacchantes traversait l'air et emportait *ironiquement* les douces mélodies'.[14] Zola's novel represents a displacement from romantic fantasy to this ironic Bacchanalian mode to which even André is attracted in spite of himself. In the terms which Sand borrows from Richardson, Zola takes us back from Grandisson to Lovelace. Indeed as we shall see, the very name Clarissa is desublimated by Zola in the form of Clarisse Bocquet.

In her chapter on 'Educating Women: *André* and *Mauprat*' which raises these very questions of milieu, upbringing and their romantic transcendance, Kathryn J. Crecchius stresses the cautionary element in Sand's account of 'society's lack of place for unusual women'.[15] *André* can thus be read in a manner which Zola would have appreciated as 'an epistemological enquiry, one that seeks to define the use and meaning of knowledge to a woman'. The *grisette*, Geneviève, is elevated in this Pygmalion tale by her acculturation which seems at first to make her eminently suitable for André, but Geneviève dies during a stillborn birth, disappointed by her timid husband and hurt by her father-in-law's unkindness. As Crecchius observes: 'Geneviève's passage from a calm, semi-educated maker of flowers who does not have an inkling of the meaning of passion to a loving, knowledgeable artist parallels, and then surpasses Galatea's transformation from inert marble to warm flesh.' Ovid's tale is reformulated in the reading imagination of the bourgeoise,

Marie Pichon, as a fantasy of social aspiration which is particularly intriguing because its *grisette*–aristocrat relationship actually brackets out the middle classes. This tale of a 'love between two spheres' reminds the bourgeoisie of their origins but also of their goals.[16] In her 1851 preface Sand explains how she wrote the novel in Venice and delights in quoting the Italian proverb, '*Tutto il mondo è fatto come la nostra famiglia*'.[17] The ironic twist for bourgeois readers in this quotation is that the Pygmalion plot forces them to consider the links between their own families and not only those socially superior but also those socially inferior. This makes such readers recall their class's origins amongst the *peuple*, as does Zola's uncomfortable analogy between the homes in *Pot-Bouille* and the image of the cess-pit at the back of the house.

André is in both senses of the term an accessory to adultery. At one level it seems to be an accessory to the crime of adultery, aiding and abetting the seduction; but at another it is also presented as but one more aspect of domestic furnishing, a further banal instance of bourgeois *bricabracomanie*. Indeed Sand's novel is specifically invoked in that moment of 'seduction' in chapter 4 of *Pot-Bouille* which shares the brutality of Ventujol's 'seduction' of Gabrielle Hébert in the Hennique novel discussed below in chapter 6: 'il la renversa brutalement au bord de la table; et elle se soumit, il la posséda, entre l'assiette oubliée et le roman, qu'une secousse fit tomber par terre' (p. 76). So these icons of two forms of consumption (culinary and literary) frame the tragicomically brief moment of sexual consummation. The heavily symbolic determination of the book falling (like wifely virtue) is a sign of the collapse of the romantic culture to which the naive Marie has subscribed, as we have learnt only pages earlier:

Quand elle était jeune, elle aurait voulu habiter au fond des bois. Elle rêvait toujours qu'elle rencontrait un chasseur, qui sonnait du cor. Il s'approchait, se mettait à genoux. Ça se passait dans un taillis, très loin, où des roses fleurissaient comme dans un parc. Puis, tout d'un coup, ils étaient mariés, et alors ils vivaient là, à se promener éternellement. Elle, très heureuse, ne souhaitait plus rien. Lui, d'une tendresse et d'une soumission d'esclave, restait à ses pieds. (pp. 72–3)

This fantasy of *fin'amor* appears to locate idealized love in the natural realm of the woods, and in particular in the type of clearing set up as the focus of satire and parody in the *déjeuner sur l'herbe* scene in *Un accident de Monsieur Hébert* discussed below in chapter 6. The state of decadence to which this hackneyed rhetoric has been reduced is indexed by the simile 'comme dans un parc' which offers a contextualization for the image of the flowering roses. Rather than asserting its originary status within the stock of 'natural' commonplaces, this metaphorical figure suggests a quasi-Wildean inversion whereby the natural wood (like life) seems to be imitating the urban artifice of the park (like art). Besides, in *Madame Bovary* (as in Béroul's *Tristan et Yseut*) the woods are the site of adulterous consummation. The defloration of Marie as a new bride within this fantasy is brushed over in the flourish of a single line which leaves the newly weds walking off (into the sunset one presumes). Conjugal satisfaction is reflected in the calming of desire ('Elle, heureuse, ne souhaitait plus rien') which novels of adultery bring into question.

When Octave does seduce Marie, such illusions are shattered, as Marie tries in vain to defend herself with the words: 'Vous allez gâter le bonheur que j'ai de vous avoir rencontré . . . Ça ne nous avancera à rien, je vous assure, et j'avais rêvé des choses . . .' (p. 76). Octave's misogyny comes to the fore when he replies by whispering to himself what he truly feels about Marie: '«Toi, tu vas y passer!»' The disrespect which anticipates his brutal act of possession is registered in the shift from her use of 'vous' to his use of 'tu', and the fact that intersubjective dialogue is replaced by his internalization of discourse reflects the narcissism of the Don Juan as a cultural type and thus of this 'desire that desires *itself*'.[18] He has already made it clear that he is not interested in protracted conversation. When Marie explains her passion for fictional 'déclarations', he retorts, 'Moi, . . . je déteste les phrases . . . Quand on s'adore, le mieux est de se le prouver tout de suite' (p. 72).

This puts a particular gloss on Shoshana Felman's observation that 'the myth of Don Juan's irresistible seduction . . . dramatizes nothing other than the success of language, the felicity of the speech act'. Her use of Mozart and Molière suggests the particularity of the seducer's position within the social system of language which is echoed not only in *Pot-Bouille* but also in *Bel-Ami*. As in these novels the seducer in Molière's play enjoys the power of a kind of linguistic minimalism which allows him to seduce with very few words. As he tells Charlotte and Mathurine in Act 2 Scene IV, 'Tous les discours n'avancent point les choses. Il faut faire et non pas dire; et les effets décident mieux que les paroles.'[19] In Felman's words, 'To seduce is to produce language that enjoys, language that takes pleasure in having "no more to say".' As such Don Juan embodies the performative power of language ('performance' to be understood in its theatrical, linguistic and erotic senses), which confronts a constative faith in the truth-potential of language. The latter view is represented by the enemies who pursue Don Juan (usually angry fathers or fiancés). As such the Don Juan figure represents a threat to the referential system which reaches its summum in naturalism for 'the trap . . . of seduction consists in producing a *referential illusion* through an utterance that is by its very nature *self-referential*: the illusion of a real or extralinguistic act of commitment created by an utterance that refers only to itself.' This is the challenge which Octave and Georges Duroy present to the realist-naturalist literary system which houses them.

Indeed, Octave and Marie have nothing to say to each other after the seduction, until Octave notices that they have failed to close the door leading onto the stairs, which is itself a metaphor of the adulterous transgression of spatial proprieties. The 'malaise' that he feels relates to the homosocial betrayal of which he is guilty: 'il se rappelait que, fraternellement, il avait projeté de pendre la jeune femme au cou de son mari.' 'Animé d'intentions fraternelles' (p. 71), Octave has encouraged her husband to take her to the theatre and he plans to take them out for dinner in order to 'les pendre au cou l'un de l'autre' (p. 72). But this 'amitié singulière' and his 'accès de bonté' have given way to his misogynistic cocktail of disdain and desire. The emotional vacuity of the seduction scene is impressed upon the reader by continual reference to banal materiality when we might expect the language of idealized passion. This shift from the ideal to the material is witnessed most clearly in the concern they show for the damage done to the binding of 'ce beau volume de George Sand' (p. 77). Marie had even wrapped the book in paper so as not to dirty it, and her assertion of innocence resonates in the intertextual echo chamber of sexual morality: 'Ce n'est pas ma faute' (p. 76). The wider implicit question of moral fault runs through representations of adultery, normally at the expense of a guilty wife like Marie. In Zola's tale wives tend to be pathetic or indifferent rather than particularly malevolent. The role of judge may fall to the aggrieved husband, though often it falls to society at large, and the most ambiguous assertion of ambivalence in such matters is surely the famous conversation between Rodolphe and Charles towards the end of *Madame Bovary*. For there is a radical undecidability in Charles's observation that 'C'est la faute de la fatalité!'[20] Is this a supreme act of interpretative generosity and moral relativism on Charles's part, as the narrator would have it, 'un grand mot, le seul qu'il ait jamais dit'? Or is Charles's pronouncement just one more candidate for the *Dictionnaire des idées reçues* (as Rodolphe thinks, 'comique même, et un peu vil')? More precisely, Marie's claim echoes the words of the Don Juan figure, Valmont, in Laclos's *Liaisons dangereuses* who, at the Marquise de Merteuil's behest, repeats the very same words as he tries to abandon Madame de Tourvel.[21]

In chapter 5 Berthe Josserand traps Auguste Vabre into marriage when they are exposed behind a curtain at the Duveyriers' party. This victory represents a triumph for the androphobic triumvirate of Berthe, Hortense and their mother: 'et, dans leur triomphe, reparaissaient les leçons de la mère, le mépris affiché de l'homme' (p. 93). In the battle of the sexes such behaviour is represented as a grotesque complement to Octave's own misogyny. The textual complicity of marriage and adultery, which might be thought of as two moments in the same system of sexual organisation, is symbolized most acutely in chapter 8 at the wedding of Berthe and Auguste where Théophile wrongly accuses Octave of seducing his wife, Valérie. This accusation actually takes place in the church and the ironic counterpoint of marital and pre-marital scenes is resolved by the triumph of the narrative of adultery, as virtually everyone is fascinated by the sideshow which becomes the main event. As such we return in another key to Flaubert's parodic reading of a romantic sentimentality which privileges individual desire as an assertion of splendid subjectivity. Indeed, this vital scene is perhaps best read as a reply to Flaubert's famous 'Comices agricoles' scene in *Madame Bovary*. What this reveals is a contrapuntal relationship between these two counterpoints. The irony of Zola's counterpoint is of course particularly acute because he interrupts a public celebration of marital life – what Stephen Kern calls 'one of the most comforting and yet frightening moments in family life',[22] with a stock scene of marital discord as the reader is taken back and forth between the discourses of consent and accusation with comic effects. Auguste's accusatory line, 'vous avouez . . .', is greeted with the piercing '*Amen*' of a young chorister. At the start of chapter 8 we learn that Théophile Vabre has discovered an unsigned love letter which he falsely believes to have come from Octave who has been seen in public with Valérie – ironically in this very same church the day before the marriage takes place. With overbearing symbolism, marriage therefore competes on home territory against adultery . . . and loses: 'personne ne faisait plus la moindre attention à la cérémonie'.

The conclusion of this countrapuntal movement between the public avowal of fidelity and the indiscreet accusation of adulterous infidelity is hinted at in the sentence which follows the moment when Octave opens the letter he is supposed to have written: 'L'émotion avait grandi dans l'assistance' (p. 146). For at this instant in the text it is not clear which scenario the 'émotion' refers to. In the next sentence, though, it becomes clear that the spectacle of the wedding ceremony has been displaced by the counter spectacle of accusation: 'Des chuchotements couraient, on se poussait du coude, on regardait par-dessus les livres de messe'. So in more than one way the servicebook functions as what might be termed an alibi text, allowing the congregation to spy on the rival event rather than the main attraction, and the carnivalesque humour of the scene comes in large part from this inversion of the public spectacle of marriage and the secrecy of adultery. (The servicebook as alibi text echoes ironically the function of *André* as a textual accessory to adultery.) The conflict between the public discourse of marital consent and the private-cum-public discourse of accusation is played out not only by conflicting speech contexts but also through the interpretation of conflicting texts: the biblical text and the mysterious love letter. The one sanctions marriage; the other betokens its failure. The one defies attempts at ambiguous interpretation; the other refuses to give its reader any firm interpretative base (the true answer to Théophile's quest for authorial attribution is not just Valérie's lover; in terms of Barthes's famous question 'Qui parle?' the mysterious text also seems to be an encoded projection of husbandly paranoia). The religious text offers solace; the love letter is profoundly disturbing for all but its author and intended reader. The one interests nobody except the 'homme sérieux', Auguste, who says yes to the priest only after careful consideration; the other provides the audience with a collective *jouissance* (the initially ambiguous 'émotion' discussed above). So Auguste's cuckoldry is already prescribed in the dynamics of this ceremony.

Texts are not the only props in this tragicomic farce. Similarly, Berthe uses her veil to manipulate the visual logic of the event. Rather than merely fulfilling its symbolic function of obstructing any external gaze directed towards the blushing bride, the veil is used as a way of concealing her own transgressive gaze: 'Mais Berthe, ayant lu la lettre, se passionnant à l'idée des gifles qu'elle espérait, n'écoutait plus, guettait par un coin de son voile' (p. 147). As such the relationship of audience and actors is transformed by this refocussing of the narrative gaze. What this scene manipulates is the distinction between the public and private faces of desire with the secrecy of adultery undermining the publicly sanctioned marriage.

The paradox of this particular form of privacy (or secrecy) which undoes the privacy of family life is articulated most famously in Flaubert's 'Comices agricoles' scene, which draws a contrast between, on the one hand, the public world of the rural community and of economic exchange and, on the other, the secret prelude to Rodolphe's seduction of Emma Bovary. In the famous counterpointing of public and private (or official and transgressive) the reader is taken back and forth between scenes of natural fertility (with crops and animals on show) and the superior gaze of the would-be lovers looking down from the first floor of the townhall (where, ironically enough, the state registers marriages). In typical Flaubertian fashion the reader is invited by the demon of analogy to see a static comparison between private and public, instead of a progressive contrast leading to a resolution. It is as if the reader finds in seduction all the platitudes of the country market, with the effect that the dynamics of the counterpoint are haunted by the spectre of sameness. The official speech of the *conseiller* delivered before the prize-giving is as rhetorically inflated as Rodolphe's speech of seduction, both of whose *lieux* are indeed *communs*.

Overarching this is the implicit analogy with the 'meat market' of bourgeois marriage. In the context of this spatial arrangement of narrative discourse, flitting cinematically between two locations, only to find that they are reduced to the stultifying figure of sameness, it is particularly fitting that the *conseiller* should be called M. Lieuvain. It is at the level of the metaphorical that the reader draws connections between these public and private scenes, for example in Lieuvain's use of the image of the nation as a body to map out the growing freedom of travel:

Si . . . je reporte mes yeux sur la situation actuelle de notre belle patrie: qu'y vois-je? . . . partout des voies nouvelles de communication, comme autant d'artères nouvelles dans le corps de l'Etat, y établissent des rapports nouveaux; . . . enfin la France respire! . . .[23]

Emma can only compete with this liberation of the public (and by implication male) citizen, by looking for a particular type of 'rapport nouveau' to free her from the stultifying constriction which means that she will not actually be able to travel to the Paris of her dreams. This is one reason for her disappointment at not having a son. Emma imagines that a son would enable her to break the mimetic cycle in which the mother is reproduced in the daughter, a cycle which entraps her in the tyranny of metaphor, keeping closed the desirous realm of male adventure in a public sphere. Flaubert's way of reinvesting the sameness of comparison with the dynamics of counterpoint is to accelerate the pace of exchange so that ultimately we change focus from sentence to sentence, with no narratorial intervention, until Rodolphe seizes Emma by the hand. Emma's tragedy stems in part from the different ways in which she and Rodolphe conceptualize the space of desire. What for her is liberation is, in his mind, imprisonment: 'Rodolphe lui serrait la main, et il la sentait toute chaude comme une tourterelle captive qui veut reprendre sa volée'. This itself is merely a prelude to the appearance of the reluctant prizewinner, the simple Catherine Leroux.

This relationship between desire and the market (in its straightforward and conceptual forms) is echoed in *Pot-Bouille* in the syntagmatic unfolding of Octave's shift from private to public realms, from the house on the rue de Choiseul to Mme Hédouin's department store. The irony of Zola's scene of counterpoint is that it is Berthe, the bride, who will fall into the arms of Octave. It is thus fitting that when the priest asks her whether she promises Auguste 'fidélité en toutes choses, comme une fidèle épouse le doit à son époux, selon le commandement de Dieu' (p. 147), Berthe is already looking over her shoulder, not at her past, but at her future, as she watches Octave being accused. Like a naughty schoolgirl, she senses that life is elsewhere. Female economic dependency is reconstituted via Zola's misogynistic vision in the form of Berthe's materialistic aspirations. Inspired by her mother's desire to push her daughters up the socio-economic ladder, Berthe is seduced by Octave's little gifts. It is perhaps here that the thematics of prostitution in *Nana* meet *Pot-Bouille* most explicitly. The wife who is never satisfied rehearses a melodramatic stereotype, but what Zola's narrative offers is a bridge from a stereotype of materialistic, socioeconomic desire to another stereotype of the unquenchable sexual desire of women reformulated in Freud's notorious question 'Was will das Weib?' In other words, what constitutes the *bonheur des dames*? Part of the fascination exerted by the Don Juan figure is that he at least appears to know the answer to that question. The goal of *bonheur* is ironically invoked in the wedding scene. Théophile reads out to Octave the confirmation of adulterous *jouissance*, received by Valérie in an anonymous letter: '«Mon chat, que de bonheur hier!»' (p. 147), and the term is picked up in the reference to Berthe's distraction by this counter spectacle as she answers the priest's question about fidelity: 'Oui, oui, répondit-elle précipitamment, au petit bonheur.' The intensity of the eudemonic quest so central to the tradition of *Bildung* in fiction is undermined by the nonchalance and randomness of uninterested (and in a sense profoundly uninteresting) lives.

However, there are women who do resist Zola's Don Juan, not least the *hystérique*, Valérie Vabre, who, like the reader, laughs at the accusation made by her husband (which we may contrast with the tragic overtones of the Princesse de Clèves's rejection of the duc de Nemours and her anguished confession). The other characters take events rather more seriously, but Valérie keeps her distance from the 'incestuous' machinations of the apartment block into which she refuses to be drawn, although she too has a lover who is held in the shadows of textual allusion, outside the house. It is for this reason that her husband is the victim of a double humiliation in his accusation of Octave, for M. Vabre is both right (that he is being deceived) and wrong (about the lover's identity). Her lover (and her unmappable hysteric's desire which becomes a fantasy of the male homosocial clique) are in all senses ob-scene, displaced off stage in this theatricalized farce of bourgeois adventure. Paradoxically, all of this allows Valérie the privilege of sharing the reader's sense that what could be tragic is merely derisory. By resisting Octave she comes to share his omniscience, and when they say goodbye as the Duveyriers' party draws to a close at the end of the novel and she looks at him 'de son air d'amie désintéressée', it is clear to the reader at least that theirs is a special relationship: 'Lui et elle auraient pu tout se dire' (p. 383). As much as Octave once fought against it, they are, it seems, the true heterosocial couple of the piece, for she does not allow the ruses of desire to intervene. Catherine Belsey argues that 'what the stories of demon lovers suggest is that the desire defined in the fiction cannot be met by a mortal lover, because in the end desire is not of the other, but of the Other, and its gratification is both forbidden and impossible'.[24] In particular, the implicit heterosexual utopia in which the minds and bodies of men and women might fit together is deferred here due to Zola's cynicism about the ethical values of this historical moment. In this skewing of the desires of mortal lovers Zola comes closest to that literary fantasy of writing his own version of *L'Education sentimentale*.

CHAPTER 2

The rhythms of performance

Quand une femme se donne à un homme, ce dernier, s'il était poli, enverrait ses cartes au père et à la mère de sa nouvelle maîtresse, en écrivant au-dessous de son nom, comme il sied: «avec mille remerciements.» Quatre-vingt-dix-neuf fois sur cent, il la leur doit.[1]

The array of intertexts displayed by *Pot-Bouille* is not merely a source of *éducation* for characters such as Marie Pichon. Intertexts can illuminate the theme of *éducation* highlighted (perhaps unwittingly) in one of the English translations of the novel, *Lesson in Love*. Nor are the novel's intertexts simply other novels. As we have already seen, music played a vital role in the cultural competence of the bourgeoisie. In particular, piano arrangements of operatic arias were especially popular as forms of collective self-entertainment in middle-class homes. These transpositions were social and spatial as well as musical, for they allowed the bourgeoisie to absorb within the comfort and self-regard of their own domestic space high cultural forms reviewed in the newspapers they read. The narrator paraphrases the response of the audience to the performance in chapter 5 in this vein: 'Vraiment, on ne réussissait pas mieux au théâtre'.[2] The public forum of operatic performance is thus scaled down to size within the semi-private, semi-public domain of the Duveyriers' parties and the yet more intimate domain of the private rehearsal.

Rather than simply offering examples of the culture in which the bourgeoisie chooses to indulge, the two major operatic references in *Pot-Bouille* provide ironic perspectives from which readers can view the theme of *éducation* set out in chapter 4 in the conversation between Octave and Marie's parents when they come round for tea. At the Duveyriers' party described in chapter 5, Octave listens to the singing of the 'Bénédiction des poignards' scene from Giacomo Meyerbeer's opera, *Les Huguenots* (text by Scribe and Deschamps; first performed at the Opéra de Paris on 29 February 1836). This performance is orches-

41

trated by Clotilde Duveyrier who has just noted for future reference
Octave's possibilities as a tenor. When the performance is repeated as an
ironic coda in the final pages of the novel at another Duveyrier party,
Octave now participates as a happily married man. Meyerbeer's tragedy
of misunderstanding and the dramatic irony of tardy recognition (where
Saint-Bris discovers too late that he has been the murderer of his own
daughter) stands in contrast to Zola's comedy of deception. Likewise,
Pot-Bouille implicitly ironizes Grétry's *Zémire et Azor* (text by Marmontel;
first performed at the Comédie Italienne on 16 December 1771) in which
Octave participates in chapter 10. The happy ending of this comic opera
(the marriage of Zémire and Azor) is undermined by the cynicism of
Zola's black comedy. In this opera Sandor comes to realize that his
daughter actually enjoys her enforced partnership with Azor. Thus
necessity is aligned with desire and the potential tragedy is averted. *Pot-
Bouille* sits between the tearful gravity of Meyerbeer and the blithe
comedy of Grétry, both of which play out dramas of misunderstanding
between father and daughter (echoed in the family narratives of the
Pichons and the Josserands).

Critics have suggested the link between the grand scale of Zola's
writing and Wagner's music, but in the France of Zola's youth it was the
German Giacomo Meyerbeer who dominated grand opera.[3]
Mitterand's Pléiade notes rightly stress that Zola saw in Meyerbeer along
with Boïeldieu and Weber 'un répertoire usé' whereas he was 'acquis à
Wagner' (p. 1652). Heinz Becker's entry on Meyerbeer in *Grove* nevertheless suggests points of contact which may have embarrassed Zola: his
'expressive monumentalism', his 'deliberately "unbeautiful" sound' and
the way in which he was 'drawn to massive choral crowd scenes and
refused librettos offering little opportunity for such "tableaux", as he
called them'.[4] At a practical level too Zola, the public intellectual, may
well have admired this man of culture who was also one of the richest
men in Europe and who manipulated the press with aplomb. It is said
that Meyerbeer was the inventor of the modern press conference, providing refreshments for journalists! The notes to Zola's *Œuvres complètes*
merely note that '*Les Huguenots* transposait sur les scènes lyriques le
bric-à-brac romantique du mélodrame historique, qui avait connu le
succès au cours des années antérieures'.[5] The Pléiade edition is more
comprehensive in its refutation of any conscious intention in the use of
Meyerbeer (pp. 1652–3). It quotes Céard's letter of 22 September 1881
and Zola's reply of 1 October which suggest that the role of the
'Bénédiction des poignards' scene is as a mere accessory. In Céard's

words, 'Vous n'avez pas à vous occuper des détails', and in Zola's, 'ce n'est d'ailleurs qu'un fond de tableau forcément effacé'. Nevertheless, Céard sent a copy of the scene to Zola and took care to explain to him which voices he had at his disposal in order to render his version authentic. *Zémire et Azor* receives no such gloss in either edition, but this distant intertextual echo is not merely an operatic archetype of romantic fantasy; it also engages very precisely with Zola's concerns.

The particular relevance of both of these operas can only be measured, however, if readers are aware of some of the details in each libretto. *Les Huguenots* dramatizes events around the St. Bartholomew's massacre in Paris on 24 August 1572 in a tragedy where the private and the public interweave viciously.[6] The opera opens in a deceptively comic tone with young Catholic noblemen at play, as the hedonistic values so prevalent in *Pot-Bouille* are extolled, first by Nevers: 'Des beaux jours de la jeunesse dans la plus riante ivresse/ hâtons-nous/ le tem [*sic*] nous presse/ hâtons-nous de jouir', and then by the seigneurs and the choir: 'aux jeux à la folie consacrons notre vie et qu'ici tout s'oublie excepté le plaisir'. Even these opening scenes, however, are subject to a cynical irony. Raoul's idealized description of his unnamed beloved (actually Valentine) is undercut by the laughter of the chorus: 'Vraiment vraiment sa candeur est charmante'. Raoul's servant, Marcel, is also suspicious of the welcome his master has received. He senses trickery in all of this and prays to Luther to save Raoul from the diabolical temptations of Catholic indulgence.

In Act 2 Raoul is brought to Marguerite de Valois who plans to marry him to the Catholic Valentine in order to secure religious peace. This role as the female matchmaker bears comparison with Mme Josserand, but once again *Pot-Bouille* involves a lowering of the emotional register and a desublimation of roles; for Mme Josserand's motives for tricking Auguste into marrying Berthe are far from noble. The encounter scene involves another triangular structure of desire as Marguerite's loyalty towards Valentine is momentarily put into question by her desire for Raoul. As she tells herself in an internalized 'dialogue' between heterosexual desire and homosocial loyalty, 'si j'étais coquette, dieu, pareille conquête, moi, serait bientôt faite, mais, non, non, non, non, et je dois alors que sa belle compte sur mon zèle lui plaire par elle et non pas par moi.' So ironically it is not the famed seducer, Nevers, but the young romantic, Raoul, who is the object of the desires of both Marguerite and Valentine. The former heeds her duty to the principle of religious and political reconciliation and so sacrifices her desire, whilst the latter's desire is in principle reciprocated but actually repudiated because of Raoul's misinterpretation.

At the end of the act Marguerite's plans for Valentine falter because Raoul has seen his beloved alone with Nevers in Act 1 and mistakenly thought that she was deceiving him (in fact she was asking to be released from their engagement so that she might marry Raoul). This is echoed in the meeting between another lady-killer, Octave Mouret, and Valérie Vabre which is also misinterpreted as a tryst. (The further irony in Zola's novel is that Valérie is indeed an adulteress, but not with Octave.) Still in love with Raoul, in Act 3 Valentine warns his servant, Marcel, that the Catholic noblemen plan to ambush him and that he should not come alone to the duel. Her father, Saint-Bris, is appalled to learn that his own daughter has done this. The tragedy of misunderstanding is set up. In spite of her love she must marry Nevers.

The 'Bénédiction des poignards' scene occurs when in Act 4 Raoul hears of the Catholic plan for the Protestant massacre. The swords to be used in the massacre are consecrated by a monk (ironically played in chapter 5 of *Pot-Bouille* by the distinctly uncelibate Trublot, Octave's confidant). Again the military mode of the swordsmen is ironized by the unheroic Octave whose own duel with Auguste Vabre is replaced by dinner in the restaurant Foyot![7] The 'Bénédiction', inspired by Bellini's *Norma*, was rearranged by Meyerbeer as the censors had forbidden the representation on stage of Catherine de Medici. Ironically the Don Juan figure, Nevers, (played in chapter 5 by a junior official at the Conseil d'État) refuses to take part in the conspiracy saying that he is a soldier and not an assassin and is led away as a prisoner once he has yielded his sword. Only then does the consecration actually take place. It is centred around Valentine's father (sung by Campardon) whose role stretches from the solo, 'pour cette cause sainte, obéisses sans crainte' (the first moment to capture Clotilde's audience) to the end of the *stretta*, when the conspirators who are about to leave on their mission suddenly turn once more, swords uplifted, and swear their undying allegiance. This is homosociality run riot. As Céard warns Zola, 'Vous pouvez remarquer que, sauf Valentine, il n'y a pas de femmes dans cet épisode' (p. 1653). Clotilde Duveyrier, the pianist who organizes the performance, keeps this lone female role for herself, 'car elle ne voulait pas introduire de femme parmi ces messieurs' (p. 90). This bears ironic comparison with the behaviour of her husband's mistress, Clarisse Bocquet, who, as we shall see, insists that only men attend her salon. Music is not merely the social nicety coveted by Marie Pichon. It also offers access to a dynamic emotional life otherwise prohibited by the rules of decorum, hence Clotilde's 'cris de passion' (p. 90). Music is for her a realm of eroticized adventure and also a form of revenge against a husband. Their different attitudes towards its qualities are an index of their emotional incompatibility. As Trublot explains, 'le piano a gâté sa vie . . .' (p. 82). This is because 'il n'aime pas la musique', to which Octave replies, 'Moi non plus'.

Throughout the 'Bénédiction' Raoul (now in the role of seducer) has been hiding and the triumphalist consecration is thus subject to dramatic irony. After the departure of the Catholic noblemen at the end of the act Valentine tries to stop Raoul leaving to what she sees as an almost certain death by declaring her love for him once more. This starts with her exclamation, 'Oh, ciel! Où courez-vous?' and reaches its climax in the *cantilena*, 'Tu l'as dit, oui tu m'aimes'. This is adulterous passion rendered honourable in the eyes of the audience by the vicissitudes of tragedy (as we have seen, this desire only becomes adulterous in this fourth act of the opera). She even blocks Raoul's path as he attempts to enter the fray, but he simply flings open a window and leaps out into the street, from the private domain of intimacy into the public realm of politics (a reversal of that most famous of balcony scenes in Shakespeare's not dissimilar story of the tragic conflict between love and quasi-tribal strife where Romeo climbs *up* to his beloved Juliet). Ironically enough, it is a rather different type of threshold love scene which follows Zola's version of the *stretta*, when Berthe's imprisonment of Auguste behind the curtain is exposed, so that their engagement can be fixed. The timid Auguste is no Raoul, of course, and never thinks of escaping via the window! Zola's version of the 'Bénédiction' moves back repeatedly to his own rather different scene of concealment until the finale of exposure.

Raoul rushes to call his fellow Protestants to arms at the start of the final act. In the ensuing massacre Nevers is killed and Valentine is free to marry Raoul. Her passion is no longer adulterous. Having retreated to the grimly symbolic location of the graveyard outside the church, she renounces her faith in terms which foreground the vocabulary of recognition and misrecognition so central to the denouement:

> Je subirai sans toi l'exil sur cette terre?
> où nous avons souffert, où nous avons aimé?
> Sans toi! tu crois cela! mon Dieu! nous autres hommes
> au véritable amour votre cœur est ferme
> Eh bien tu *connaîtras* tout l'amour d'une femme . . .
> je ne te quitte plus ni cette âme en tumulte

> cette âme *ne reconnaît plus rien*
> toi tu maudis mon culte
> moi . . . j'adopte le tien. [our italics]

This ultimate *connaissance* of reciprocal love will entail her father's failure to recognize his daughter, but Valentine is enveloped by a passion which is also experienced as a loss of (re)cognitive faculties. What she no longer recognises is the pull of her own faith. Just as the priests have blessed the Protestant swords, so Marcel blesses the young lovers in a scene which contrasts with the *cortège de noces* of Nevers and Valentine at the end of Act 3. At this moment a contrapuntal dynamic is set up between this unofficial wedding party and the slaughter of Protestants (as in the case of Berthe Vabre, née Josserand, the party is looking on at its own fate). They escape from a besieged churchyard to the street where Valentine's own father, Saint-Bris, orders his men to fire on them, fatally wounding his daughter whom he recognizes too late ('ah que vois-je ma fille?'). This is the tragic misunderstanding (even to the point of misrecognition) played out to its fullest extent. As in Act 1 Valentine is the victim of misrecognition by men who love her. At the start of the play Raoul misinterprets her secret meeting with Nevers; at the end her father cannot even recognize her. She is in a sense therefore the inverse complement of the archetypal adulteress in fiction for she is the victim of false accusation and mistaken identity. So her conspicuously romanticized name, and tragically her person, are effaced by the distorting perspective of religious violence. For although the killing of Valentine is an error, she has switched faiths to have her love for Raoul blessed, and Saint-Bris has sworn in the 'Bénédiction': 'des huguenots la race sacrilège aura dès aujourd'hui pour jamais disparu'.

This very same theme of generational misunderstanding between father and daughter is played out in rather less taxing fashion in Grétry's late-eighteenth century *comédie-ballet, Zémire et Azor*.[8] Played out in four acts, this fantasy narrative tells a Beauty and the Beast tale which results in the happy ending of their wedding.[9] Octave is invited by Clotilde to come and practise whilst she accompanies him on the piano. Their practice is, however, interrupted by news of her father's imminent demise, and Octave must fetch her husband from his mistress's so that Clotilde need not stand alone. The ironic gap between this idealist art form and the low-life camaraderie of Bachelard, Trublot *et al.*,which is then recapitulated by the narrative, provides a brutal exposé of the kind of naivety which Duveyrier exhibits in his idealisation of Clarisse before he realises that she has fleeced him.

The starving Sander and his servant Ali are shipwrecked at the start of the opera and are alone in a deserted palace when magically a table of food and wine appears. Subsequently, as Ali sleeps, Sander cuts a rose ('un témoin qui dépose') from the arbour to fulfil a promise made to his youngest daughter, Zémire. The Persian prince, Azor, suddenly appears in a rage and agrees to return Sander to his daughters only if he sacrifices one of them as payment for this act of impudence. The flower is to be paid for, it seems, by a defloration.

This dynamic of exchange raises the issue of an individual's value at numerous points in the opera. In Act 2 the horticultural metaphor associated with the blossoming Zémire is desublimated by the comic cowardice of the lowly Ali who is afraid of flying on magic clouds and so forth:

> Plus de voyage, je veux mourir vieux,
> si je puis je ne serai plus qu'une plante,
> et je prends racine où je suis.

But a rose like Zémire can of course be plucked, and it is this process of transplantation which underpins the rapid scene changes characteristic of this fantasy opera. Later, in Act 3 Scene 4, just before her encounter with Azor, Zémire wonders, 'Sur ce trône de fleurs voudrait-on m'élever?' Azor's answer would of course be yes. The conceit which compares culinary consumption and sexual consummation provides a further articulation of the tragic theme of exchange as penance. Just as Ali and Sander have feasted from the table magically produced by Azor, so it seems that the latter will consume Zémire. According to Ali's aside:

> L'aimable enfant! quel dommage,
> D'être mangée à son âge!
> Il [Azor] n'en ferait qu'un repas.

Earlier in the act Sander and Ali are returned home where the father tells his daughters of the financial ruin they now face. Only Zémire had requested a simple gift – the rose – which she delights in, and she proposes to the family a life of honest toil. (Like the Josserand daughters, Fatmé wants lace and Lisbé wants ribbons.) The dramatic irony which perpetuates Zémire's innocence is soon broken, however. When she spies her father writing a farewell letter as he plans to sacrifice himself, Zémire forces Ali to take her to the palace with the words: 'le tems [*sic*] nous presse'. This dramatic device of time's constraints is echoed in comic vein from the very beginning of *Les Huguenots* in Nevers's ode to youth which again warns 'le tem [*sic*] nous presse'. The irony is that

Nevers's comedy precedes a tragic twist, whereas Ali's fearful warning prefigures a comic ending in which the elasticity of magical time (we may recall that the start of Act 2 takes us to a moment before the end of Act 1) allows for a reversal of Azor's fortunes – and, as we shall see, of the spell which has turned the handsome prince into a fearsome monstrosity. *Pot-Bouille*, on the other hand, unfolds in the postlapsarian world of contrived emotions where love is rarely innocent in the first place.

When she encounters Azor in Act 3, Zémire faints at the sight of this monstrous figure, but before long she is struck by the devotion of his words and sentiments, not least his aria 'Du moment qu'on aime', which is also sung by Octave in *Pot-Bouille*. The setting at the start of chapter 10 could well be one of seduction. The aria Clotilde has chosen is really a declaration of love by Azor, but this is not the 'petit opéra impromptu' of Angélique and Cléante who take the roles of shepherd and shepherdess in Molière's *Le Malade imaginaire*; this is not the innocent spontaneity of youth but a culturally sanctioned script of flirtation and seduction. M. Duveyrier is elsewhere this evening, and Clotilde's beauty strikes Octave: 'Elle lui paraissait très belle, seule dans l'appartement vide' (p. 183). They also claim to share a love of music, supposedly unlike the philistine M. Duveyrier. Zola quotes the aria's opening lines:

> Du moment qu'on aime . . .
> L'on devient si doux . . . (p. 184)

Clotilde's 'visage froid' is replaced by 'langueur' as the 'volupté assoupie' of the drawing room envelops them. Then leaning over her, his chest touching her hair, he continues:

> Et je suis moi-même
> Plus tremblant que vous.

But this emotion shown by Clotilde is dropped 'comme un masque', as she repeats this final line twenty times in a manner which exposes the limits of her emotional investment in this pastime (in spite of her performance in chapter 5): 'la passion musicale était à fleur de peau, dans la mécanique' (p. 184). We already know that Octave has confessed his actual dislike of music. The reference to trembling in the final line quoted by Zola echoes Clotilde's cry of 'Je tremble' in her role as Valentine (p. 91) and anticipates her response to the thought of having to fulfil her conjugal duties now that Clarisse Bocquet has absconded with all the furnishings bought by her husband: 'elle tremblait de ne pouvoir se refuser à l'abominable corvée' (p. 199). This 'répulsion physique qu'il lui inspirait' (p. 183) lends a particular irony to the context of Azor's repulsive appearance, overcome in large part by this beautiful aria sung by Octave. For Clotilde her husband's adultery is not a betrayal but a saving grace: 'maintenant . . . plus rien au-dehors ne la protégerait'. So, as with the Campardon's *ménage à trois*, the spatial logic of inside and outside is inverted.

The original aria, 'Du moment qu'on aime', continues:

> He quoi! vous craignez l'esclave timide sur
> Qui vous régnez! N'ayez plus de peur:
> La haine homicide est loin de mon cœur.

Azor wants this plot to end in love, not death. He has been condemned to this repulsive appearance as punishment for his vanity by a cruel fairy until he can inspire love:

> Tu m'avais donné la beauté:
> De ce don je fus trop flatté;

As we know from the feast and the rose, though (and as the logic of exchange implies), what might appear to be a gift is never just a gift. So a hierarchy of authority is set up with the fairy dictating to Azor who dictates to Sander who tries unsuccessfully to dictate to Zémire. But at the end of the act Azor agrees to let her visit her family for an hour before sunset and even gives her a ring which could free her from his power (unusually a ring which liberates rather than constrains; 'cet anneau vous rend libre'). As Azor realises:

> . . . puis-je à mon tour
> Me faire aimer par la contrainte?
> La haine obéit à la crainte;
> L'amour n'obéit qu'à l'amour.

Much of the idealism of this opera, buttressed by the anti-realist æsthetic, is grounded in this privileging of love above any hierarchy of constraining powers.

In the final act Zémire explains to her disbelieving family that she is truly happy with Azor whom she pities a great deal:

> Avec lui je suis moins à plaindre,
> Oui, bien moins que vous ne croyez . . .
> Ne vous affligez plus, mon père, sur mon sort.
> Je suis heureuse. Adieu.

They believe her to be bewitched and her father does not want to let her return, but she throws away her ring and vanishes. This time the paternal misunderstanding is overcome. It is because Zémire could stay that she must go. Will she, though, return in time? The scene switches to the forlorn Azor who retreats to a grotto, until the approaching Zémire recognises that she is in love with this 'stigmatised outsider who will at last be rewarded for his intrinsic worth'.[10] The fairy's spell is broken from the bottom of the opera's hierarchy of power and the stage is transformed to another enchanted location where Azor returns 'dans tout l'éclat de sa beauté' and in the presence of her family Zémire joins him in matrimony. The death plot (at first Zémire demands Sander's life, then his daughter's) is supplanted by the marriage plot. Clearly we are a long way from Zola's naturalist æsthetic and it is no surprise that such fantasy is criticized by the *maître de Médan*, but once again the potential tragedy of misunderstanding between father and daughter is played out as Sander tries to keep Zémire from returning to Azor.

Sublime happiness is achieved not least because the virtuous Zémire breaks the fairy's spell by falling in love with Azor. As such she solves the wicked conundrum: how can the ugly inspire love? Hence the causal and temporal snag (which runs along the lines that 'beauty inspires passion and love') is resolved by Zémire's willingness to see beyond surfaces ('Quelle figure horrible! et quel charmant langage!' Act 3, Scene 5): her love guarantees the return of his beauty. Desire usually precedes love, but in this case Zémire's love for Azor precedes her desire for him. The generosity of Zémire's response allows the logic of the gift to be stripped of its cynical implications as the limits of the material realm are highlighted. As Azor tells her:

> C'est vous qui me rendez à mon peuple, à moi-même
> Le trône où je remonte est un de vos bienfaits.
> Venez-y prendre place, et que le diadême
> Soit pour vous le moins cher des dons que je vous fais.

Whereas desire and politics meet head on in *Les Huguenots*, Zémire's love allows Azor to return to his political duties.

In an ending befitting Molière, Sander is repositioned in full possession of paternal authority ('Je sais tout') and the once dominant Azor submits to his authority. Fortunately generosity proves infectious as Sander gives Zémire's hand to Azor and all join in the final lines:

> Amour amour quand ta rigueur met à l'épreuve un jeune cœur
> A quelles peines, à quelles peines tu l'exposes . . .
> Qui mieux que moi mieux que moi saura jamais
> Quels sont les maux que tu nous causes
> Quels sont les biens que tu nous fais.

So the demands of moral philosophy are met as obligation imposed by Azor's original demand is aligned with desire as Zémire falls in love with Azor who proves to be obliging in an altogether different sense. The nobility of such a moral goal is also registered in *Les Huguenots* as Marguerite yields her desire for Raoul in the service of her obligation to the politics of religious reconciliation. *Pot-Bouille* suggests the irrelevance of such moral systems within the new bourgeois universe of self-interested desires and compromised obligations, not least the obligation of fidelity.

As we saw in the introductory chapter, it is the public space of the nineteenth-century city which belongs virtually exclusively to men, whereas the roles of bourgeois women in particular are scripted on the domestic stage of family life (as it is in the upbringing of children and the management of the home that the bourgeoise works, rather than elsewhere). An example of this masculinisation of public space is found on the very first page of *Pot-Bouille*. The reader arrives in the novel as Octave arrives in a Paris which is, we learn, 'publiquement ouvert aux appétits des gaillards solides' (p. 3). So it is out into the public sphere of what we might call this capital of desire that the 'débordements des appétits' may flow, a 'débordement' promised in the preface to *Les Rougon-Macquart* (vol. 1, p. 3).

The irony is that it is not until the end of the novel that Octave really makes his way in the world, marrying Mme Hédouin, the owner of the department store *Au bonheur des dames*, in preparation for the novel which bears that name. We might say that, meanwhile, Octave explores desire rather than capital, in the inner realm of a block of bourgeois apartments on the rue Choiseul rather than conquering the city as a public arena. In *Pot-Bouille*, the space of the house is in large part equivalent to the space of the novel, and thus the proximity of urban living provides a means of localizing desire in the Don Juan plot (with the 'stranger in the house' *dès le début*). Thus Zola inverts the action in *Madame Bovary* which reveals a woman escaping from her domestic realm in search of adulterous gratification, with Emma consummating her passion for Rodolphe in the woods (or out in the field according to the terms of the city/field opposition which Tanner borrows from the Bible). What Zola shows us in his novel is not so much women breaking out but instead men invading the domestic scene. Indeed, when he wrote to Hugo Wittmann who had bought the translation rights for the Viennese *Neue Freie Presse*, Zola suggested that a version of *Maison bourgeoise* or *Histoire d'une maison bourgeoise* be used in place of that untranslatable title, *Pot-Bouille*. In the novel itself this reciprocal mapping of fictional and domestic spaces is reflected in the use of the word 'roman' in the reference to the tale told by the owner, M. Vabre: 'enfin arriva l'histoire de sa maison dont la construction restait le roman de son existence'.

The theme of bourgeois hypocrisy ably mapped by Brian Nelson can be measured in the rhetorical distance between the facade and the back of the house. The architecture of female busts and of cupids on the front (presented to Octave and reader alike at the front of the book, on the very first page) is to be read ironically:

Au premier, des têtes de femmes soutenaient un balcon à rampe de fonte très ouvragée. Les fenêtres avaient des encadrements compliqués, taillés à la grosse sur des poncifs; et, en bas, au-dessus de la porte cochère, plus chargée encore d'ornements, deux amours déroulaient un cartouche, où était le numéro, qu'un bec de gaz intérieur éclairait la nuit. (p. 3)

This overwrought Second Empire style is itself parodied in the proliferation of textual details and the dizzying multiplications of scenarios within Zola's plot. The house conceals at its back a virtual cess pit into which the servants pour each apartment's rubbish. This metaphor of the moral detritus of bourgeois living relocates the figurative force of 'ordures' invoked as theme and image in the working-class context of *L'Assommoir*, misappropriated as a focus of ethical critique by reviewers working for an essentially middle-class press, and reclaimed in Zola's preface of January 1877. The well-worn theme of bourgeois hypocrisy is reconfigured in this space between front and back, or in other terms between the irony of romanticized architecture and the metaphor of 'ordures'. Irony and metaphor are both figures of rhetorical displacement which take naturalist writing away from the objective reportage it seems to want to mimic. Lanham defines irony as 'implying a meaning opposite to the literal meaning' and metaphor as 'changing a word from its literal meaning to one not properly applicable but analogous to it'.[11] So both figures stand at some distance from the literal responses of the naive reader (or bourgeois cuckold), and hypocrisy is inscribed in the distance between irony and metaphor, or between the beauty of the facade and the ugliness of the rear. The spatial order of front and back is also projected onto the temporal order of beginning and ending. For not only does the novel begin at the entrance to the house, but it also ends, as we shall see, with a discussion amongst the servants as they pour dirty water out into the yard.

A novel such as Zola's highlights the naivety of patriarchy's absolute model of how bourgeois women operate, namely the theory of 'separate spheres', because there are, of course, numerous cases represented in fiction of public events taking place in the private domain. It is, for example, in its miming of aristocratic social organisation that the privacy of the bourgeois household is undone. Octave Mouret is introduced to the other inhabitants of the house at various parties held by the Josserand and the Duveyrier families. In these scenarios the bourgeois wife fancies herself as a salon hostess.

As well as using this retrospective glance to highlight the actual and metaphorical permeability of the public/private divide, Zola himself also explores a not dissimilar reconstruction of social space within the modern city. For the segmentation of the house on the rue Choiseul into separate apartment blocks is typical of the way in which this divide is nuanced within the metropolis. So as well as suggesting that there is an analogy between the *trottoir* and the *salon*, the novel (and its hero) also exploit the way in which the inside/outside divide is imported within the apartment block. In Zola's text, moreover, the subversion of the spatial order of family life by the trajectory of adulterous desire is itself adulterated as Octave manipulates Campardon's warning: 'Seulement, mon brave, pas de tapage ici, surtout pas de femme! . . . Parole d'honneur! Si vous ameniez une femme, ça ferait une révolution.' Within the bourgeois imagination articulated here by Campardon who is, of course, hypocritical in this regard, it is telling that this threat to domestic propriety is conceived in terms of a bourgeois fear of politics fought out in the public realm of the street: namely revolution. Octave's logic is as treacherous as his behaviour: 'Il s'égayait, à l'idée des recommandations morales de l'architecte, car ce n'était pas amener des femmes, que d'en prendre une dans une maison' (p. 60). One of Octave's major provocations to the moral and territorial integrity of family life lies in his usurpation of the male role *within* the space of the family. When M. Pichon takes his parents-in-law back to the omnibus, Octave sits Marie on his knee and he drinks coffee with her from the same cup: 'en mari heureux du départ de ses invités, se retrouvant enfin chez lui, excité par une petite fête de famille, et pouvant embrasser sa femme à l'aise, les portes closes'. At the same time, though, Marie finds in such an arrangement a peculiar sense of what we might call spatial propriety, since she gets angry when Octave suggests that they sleep in his room . . . as if simply swapping her husband for another man *within* her own domestic space were somehow less transgressive.

Another piece of journalism which prefaces the publication of Zola's novel is Maupassant's article on adultery which appeared in *Le Gaulois*. Here Maupassant identifies the *ménage à trois* as the primary issue now facing family fiction:

Dans la bourgeoisie moyenne . . . on rencontre le plus souvent ces étonnants ménages à trois qui ont toujours fait et feront toujours la joie des spectateurs. Et toujours l'éternel doute se produit. Le mari est-il complice, témoin timide et désolé, ou invraisemblablement aveugle? De tous les problèmes de la vie, celui des ménages à trois est le plus difficile à démêler.

Zola's novel does voice this issue, but in a way which Maupassant's assertions do not quite anticipate. For Zola represents the importation of the husband's lover, Gasparine, into the Campardon household, and Campardon's response is one of shameful unease, as if the conflation of the husband's domestic and exterior sexualities were somehow improper (it is heavily ironic that Campardon should be an architect who thus effectively sets up the dispositions of private and public space).

In the light of all of the above it is with particular mirth that we read of M. Pichon thanking Octave for 'looking after' his wife with the words: 'Je suis toujours dehors'. Octave's decadence lies in part in his turning away temporarily from such a public role in his quest for sexual gratification amongst the women of the apartment block. In this way, the would-be Don Juan is feminized by his concern for the private world of sexual intrigue within the family. As we shall see in the next chapter, this initially paradoxical feminine trait is intensified in Maupassant's representation of Georges Duroy in *Bel-Ami* who is subsidized by women and their affections. That there is a relationship between gender and space is also suggested by other inversions of the norm. In Rachilde's *Monsieur Vénus* the effeminacy of Jacques Silvert's desire for the dominant heiress, Raoule de Vénérande, is voiced with particular eloquence through her control of his domestic arrangements. For Jacques, who loves Raoule with 'un vrai cœur de femme', is a kept man, living in a flat paid for by his benefactor.

One effect of the internal segmentation of the apartment block in terms of both public and private arenas is that the staircase becomes a place of public interaction, and the adulterous interaction across thresholds takes place *within* the bourgeois house. This interior pathway is policed by the figure of the concierge who thereby acquires a particular structural significance within the urban reconstruction of family life inside the apartment block. It is his role to control the comings and goings of tenants and strangers, and so we might say that he controls the divide between private and public, and therefore embodies a rival form of omniscience within the text. It is fitting that when Octave first encounters M. Gourd, he is reading the aptly titled *Le Moniteur*. This rival omniscience is only ironized by the awareness on the part of Zola's own omniscient narrator that M. Gourd is as corruptible as the rest of the dramatis personae, as he is persuaded to allow a mysterious wealthy gentleman to use a room for secret rendez-vous with his lady friend, but refuses to allow a joiner who is forced to work away from home to visit his own wife from time to time. The concierge can, of course, facilitate the adulterous scenario: one thinks of the 'prudence' of the concierge in *Bel-Ami* who turns a blind eye as Clotilde de Marelles installs Georges Duroy in their little love nest. One of the implications of Robida's well-known cartoon caricature of the novel which shows a bulbous-headed Zola lifting the lid and peering – like the limping devil, Asmodeus – under the roof of the bourgeois household, is that Naturalist omniscience in general is necessarily engaged in a rendering public of the private, and one might say that one of the key fantasies of Naturalism's epistemophilia is a refusal to accept the very concept of privacy itself, for in a sense naturalism ruptures the autonomy of private space by the very intrusiveness of its gaze.[12]

Octave plans to encounter his unattainable object of desire, Valérie Vabre, on the stairs and the staircases (in the plural, for there is also an *escalier de service*) have a menacing quality, not unlike one of Xavier Mellery's pictures. For the middle-class parent, it is clearly the focus of much anxiety. Campardon proclaims that: 'Je donnerais congé, le jour où ma fille serait exposée à rencontrer des créatures dans l'escalier.' Marie Pichon's mother recalls her daughter's upbringing thus: 'Pas de jeux dans l'escalier, la petite toujours chez elle, et gardée de près, car les gamins ne pensent qu'au mal.' The irony, though, is that her upbringing affords little protection: she is *mal gardée*. Thus it is in the theme of the education of girls that we may locate a primary experience of the gendering of domestic and public space. In the words of Campardon's wife: 'Une jeune fille est une responsabilité si lourde, il fallait écarter d'elle jusqu'aux souffles de la rue.' This resistance to invasion from external forces reaches extreme proportions in the censoring of literary and musical activities. The fact that Marie's parents cannot afford to pay for her piano lessons is explained away by reference to the ideology of separate spheres, as the piano and reading of fiction is associated with the intertextual invasion of domestic space by the evocation of emotional extremes apparently otherwise unavailable within the home.

Indeed the music which Octave hears from the staircase is used as a metaphor of the permeability (symbolic as well as literal) of the walls through which sound (like desire) passes. In the opening scene of Zola's novel, which depicts Octave's arrival in the house of apartments, we are offered an emblematic insight into this kind of spatial symbolism. If eyes can only look through open doorways, ears, of course, can hear through walls. As Octave leaves the Campardon's apartment, he hears the sound of Angèle playing the piano; this mingles with the same sound from the apartments of the Vabres, the Duveyriers and Mme Juzeur (p. 14). It is amongst this polyphony that Octave seeks his prey (note the musical symbolism of his name). It is exactly the same effect which we encounter at the start of Paul Alexis's *Madame Meuriot*: 'Les vocalises d'une voix de contralto . . . montaient d'un étage inférieur. D'autres pianos, dont il n'arrivait que des notes étouffées, jouaient dans plusieurs des nombreux appartements de la maison, vaste, très peuplée'. What such music invariably suggests is the emotional and moral fluidity behind (but also beyond) the sturdy bourgeois facade.

Prior to this polyphony of pianos in *Pot-Bouille*, Octave waits on the stairs for Campardon to fetch the key to his room and listens for sounds from above, but there is only 'une paix morte de salon bourgeois, soigneusement clos, où n'entrait pas un souffle du dehors' (p. 6). As he reaches his floor, however, he notices through 'une porte entr'ouverte' a mother with her child. The father is notably absent from the quasi-pictorial frame. Octave is struck by the woman's blonde hair and clear, vivid eyes . . . but the spell is broken, she blushes and closes the door. Octave's trajectory through the novel is characterized by an attempt to replay and play out this initial fantasy.

The spatial logic of the inside and outside which relates to representations of the social organisation of family life also applies to the generic space which Naturalist fiction inhabits. For parody places the naturalist novel within the generic system of adulterous fiction whilst retaining a kind of inner exile or a desire to be somewhere else. In Linda Hutcheon's words, parody is 'repetition with critical distance',[13] and it is, of course, Naturalism's way of responding to the stereotypical representations of adultery by authors such as Feuillet, Cherbuliez and Ponson du Terrail, but the ambivalence of Zola's position is revealed in the way that he indulges in the adulterous motif as much as he parodies its cultural predominance. Extra-marital affairs are multiplied to farcical proportions as Octave runs up and down the stairs, from apartment to apartment, at certain times succeeding and at other times failing in his attempt to seduce a string of bored housewives. So *Pot-Bouille*'s comedy is facilitated by the use of a Don Juan type rather than an adulteress. In a manner rather less sophisticated than Flaubert's[14] each step Zola takes towards parody is at the same time one more step away from Naturalism. As he himself admits about the novel in a letter to Henry Fouquier dated 26 April 1882: 'l'accumulation des faits en un même cadre lui donne souvent une intensité que le train-train réel de la vie n'a pas'.[15] In this context we might adulterate the words of Walter Benjamin in order to describe Zola's conception of Sex in the Age of Mechanical Reproduction. The tone of this anti-naturalistic quality is captured in David Baguley's description of the fairytale qualities of the hero which might seem to recall Julien Sorel, if Octave's *énergie* was less predatory and more boyish: 'As well as being endowed with the convenient virtues of mobility and irresistible charm conducive to revealing situations, Octave is invested with a penetrating, indirect look, which constantly gives him access to secrets hidden behind half-closed doors and to any woman's "heart".'[16] Zola's novel is, however, a *roman d'apprentissage* written from an even more cynical perspective, so that Stendhalian equivocations about the validity of idealism are replaced by a wholly unambiguous scepticism.

Parody is one way of both inhabiting and escaping the novel of adultery, and *Pot-Bouille* is therefore a fitting culmination to a cultural tradition, rather than a sudden break with the past. For parody is a way for the novelist to possess the form by which he or she is possessed. It is a way of speaking the language of adultery and, in that very same gesture, ridiculing such talk. It is a way of cheating on the novel of adultery. *Pot-Bouille* is therefore both inside and outside the novel of adultery, just as its hero, Octave, moves in and out of various domestic spaces within the house of apartments on the rue de Choiseul. Much of the ambivalence of the novel is clarified if we ask to what extent Zola's writing is seduced into colluding with the very motif it parodies.

As is revealed by Zola's reference to Sand's *Jacques* and the newspaper articles which we have quoted, Zola was fully aware of the cultural centrality of narratives of adultery. Written in the wake of this tradition, *Pot-Bouille* indulges in the motifs and ironies of such narratives and yet parodies their obsessions. At the Duveyriers' party in chapter 5, a group of men discuss a novel serialized in the *Revue des deux mondes*. Léon complains that 'il est bien écrit; mais encore un adultère, ça finit vraiment par être fastidieux!' (p. 94). Duveyrier argues that novelists overestimate the extent of bourgeois adultery: 'ces auteurs exagèrent, l'adultère est très rare parmi les classes bien élevées . . . Une femme, lorsqu'elle est d'une bonne famille, a dans l'âme une fleur'. What this raises is the vexed issue of frequency which will always remain cloudy as long as a notion of private life pertains. As such adultery stands as an enigma at the heart of a society's moral self-concerns. The abbé Mauduit is cited via *style indirect libre* as the voice of conservative opinion: 'Jamais l'Église ne disparaîtrait, parce qu'elle était la base de la famille, comme elle était le soutien naturel des gouvernements'. Doctor Juillerat smiles and refuses to be drawn into this debate, and when he does make a comment it only irritates Duveyrier who cannot bear people discussing politics in his home (comparable to similar proscriptions in *La Conquête de Plassans* and at the salon de la Mole in *Le Rouge et le Noir*). At the same time, moreover, Octave and Trublot plan their own underhand sexual adventures. Similarly, as Duveyrier affirms that 'la religion moralise le mariage', he sees Berthe and Hortense stuffing the gullible young Auguste with sandwichs in a pincer movement intended to secure an engagement for one of them. So Zola is both within and outside the genre, distanced from its more banal manifestations by a satirical sense of its farcical potential.[17]

Just as adultery is paradoxically held within the bounds of the house, so the language of adulterous paternity returns to haunt the language of the family that it has subverted. Believing he is the father of the child Marie is carrying, Octave gives her forehead 'le baiser d'un père qui cède sa fille à un gendre' (p. 171). Octave can only respond to the possibility of paternity by borrowing a gesture that truly belongs to the repertoire of family life that he has subverted. Indeed here as elsewhere we see replayed the Flaubertian sense that adultery is but a parody of the marriage it undoes. In *Une Belle Journée* Mme Duhamain comes to observe the sameness of husband and would-be lover, 'préoccupés tous deux des mêmes niaiseries, débitant des pauvretés équivalentes, ils se confondirent à ses yeux en un même individu. Ensemble, ils lui parurent résumer la platitude'.[18]

Auguste Vabre is also harassed by Berthe's brother, Saturnin, whose eroticized jealousy becomes evident in a conversation with Octave. Saturnin describes how he cared for his sister when, as a girl, she fell ill, 'des fois, quand elle se plaignait trop, je lui mettais la tête sur moi. Nous étions gentils' (p. 237). In a perversion of this perverse scenario, he exhibits 'des délicatesses de mère' towards his sister. This 'tendresse étrange' is locked within an infantile past, 'ses désirs d'homme arrêtés, fixés à jamais par ce drame de la souffrance'. These incestuous urges actually invert the relation of conjugal and extra-marital roles in a manner reminiscent of Ernest Feydeau's *Fanny* (1858), 'aussi poursuivait-il le mari d'une haine furieuse d'amant contrarié'. For this time it is the husband who is the object of indignation.

So as we have just seen, the tension between the architectural edifice and the moral dissolution it houses is reflected in the structure of the novel which threatens to break the bounds of *vraisemblance* and degenerate into farcical self-parody. Within the biological narrative of blood, female adultery is registered in a literal and figurative decomposition of the paternal order which echoes the mythologized death of Nana: 'Vénus se décomposait'. Docteur Juillerat diagnoses 'une décomposition du sang: c'était une usure de l'être entier, où tous les organes se prenaient, les uns après les autres' (p. 344). It is ironically fitting that the effect of a daughter's adultery is discussed at the end of the penultimate chapter by the doctor and the priest, abbé Mauduit, as they walk out of the house for the final time. For both are institutionally accredited with the right to enter and investigate the domestic space. This homosocial couple represent old and new metaphysical orders, neither quite competent enough to cure the ills of the Second Empire, already pathologized as we shall see in the decomposition of Nana's rotting flesh. When, on the steps of the *Bonheur des dames*, they pass Octave and Mme Hédouin, who are all smiles after the announcement of their imminent wedding, the reader senses that the future lies with this heterosexual couple's entrepreneurial spirit. As Juillerat remarks to Mauduit when they walk on: 'Cette dame qui vend du calicot . . . Elle se fiche de vous et de moi. Pas besoin de bon Dieu ni de remèdes. N'importe, quand on se porte bien, ce n'est plus intéressant' (p. 364).

It is with the doctor that we might expect Zola's narrator to make a philosophical alliance, but the latter keeps his distance (and thus sets up another, male triangle with these 'readers' of bourgeois life) by revealing the *Bouvard et Pécuchet*-style excesses of this man of science. Within the dialogue of priest and doctor (which foreshadows the conflicts between Clotilde and Pascal, and between the Froment brothers, discussed below in chapters 4 and 6 respectively) the reader is shown how Juillerat's own discourse deviates between the insightful and the stereotypical (in another complex contrapuntal form). This is best revealed in diagrammatic fashion:

Juillerat's opinions approved of by Zola's narrator	*Juillerat's opinions censured by Zola's narrator*
A: Elles sont mal portantes ou mal élevées, voila tout.	
	B: Et, sans attendre, il gâta ce point de vue, il accusa violemment l'Empire: sous une république, certes, les choses iraient beaucoup mieux.
C: Mais, au milieu de ces observations d'homme médiocre, revenaient des observations justes de vieux practicien, qui connaissait à fond les dessous de son quartier. **D:** Il se lâchait sur les femmes, les unes qu'une éducation de poupée corrompait ou abêtissait, les autres dont une névrose héréditaire pervertissait les sentiments et les passions, toutes tombant salement, sottement, sans envie comme sans plaisir; **E:** d'ailleurs, il ne se montrait pas plus tendre pour les hommes, des gaillards qui achevaient de gâcher l'existence, derrière l'hypocrisie de leur belle tenue; **F:** et, dans son emportement de jacobin, sonnait le glas entêté d'une classe, la décomposition et l'écroulement de la bourgeoisie, dont les états pourris craquaient d'eux-mêmes.	
	G: Puis, il perdit pied de nouveau, il parla des barbares, il annonça le bonheur universel. (p. 363)

What is clear is that Zola's narrator nods approvingly in the direction of those explanations which enjoy some sociological substance but disapproves of those 'explanations' which refer to the arrival of the barbarian hordes and thus remythologize the historical process of the Decadence. In this he brings into question some of his own rhetoric in *La Curée*. It is perhaps because of such moments of weakness that, as we shall see below, Zola can suggest that doctor and priest are not so dissimilar. Section A reintroduces the theme of education which is amplified in sections C–E, where Juillerat repeats Zola's three female types: those corrupted (like Berthe) or dulled by their upbringing, (like Marie) and those who are victim to hereditary neurosis (Valérie).[19]

In section F the jacobins' politicized version of this process, which borrows the discourse of bourgeois demise, seems almost to invite its own deluded mythologization in section G where utopian notions of 'bonheur' are satirized. Indeed, the ease with which wisdom slips into banality is witnessed at the start of sections B and G by the use of the non-contradictory conjunctions 'Et' and 'Puis'. For, as Bourdieu reminds us, 'lucidity is always partial'.[20] In section B it is the invocation of politics (republican as opposed to imperial) which is derided across the rhetorical historical irony of 1870–1 and the (not so) new republic of which Zola's readers have knowledge, unlike his characters of course. What the former know is that Empire and Republic (old and new, not unlike Mauduit and Juillerat) are not so far apart as they might like to think. Only in his 'better' moments does the doctor realize, as the narrator does, that political fluctuations in this century of revolutions cannot change the moral and social substratum of Paris ('les dessous de son quartier'). So we have confirmed by the narrator Zola's own humanist sociology which is at odds with an ultimately more convincing radical materialist analysis.

At the Duveyriers' party in the final chapter of the novel, the abbé Mauduit's limp retreat back from social analysis to theology is made explicit: 'il jetait une fois encore le manteau de la religion sur cette bourgeoisie gâtée, en maître de cérémonie qui drapait le chancre, pour retarder la décomposition finale' (p. 382). It is also ironic that the language of this hypocritical 'cover up' under the *manteau* of religion should echo so closely the language of his despair in the church of Saint-Roch in the previous chapter. After Juillerat's departure the reader observes how the *maître de cérémonie*'s perception of degeneracy puts into question his own function:

Oh! Seigneur, l'heure sonnait-elle de ne plus couvrir du manteau de la religion les plaies de ce monde décomposé? Devait-il ne plus aider à l'hypocrisie de son troupeau, n'être plus toujours là, comme un maître de cérémonie, pour régler le bel ordre des sottises et des vices? . . . Oh! Seigneur, quelle était la route, que fallait-il faire au milieu de cette société finissante, qui pourrissait jusqu'à ses prêtres. (pp. 365–6)

Such despair is already inscribed in the implicit onomastic play on the notion of the *abbé maudit*. Yet his anguish is not spared by Zola's satirical method, for there is a paradoxical similarity between the apparent rectitude of the bourgeois house and the still in the house of God:

Pas un bruit, pas un mouvement ne troublait la nef déserte, où les revêtements de marbre, les lustres de cristal, la chaire dorée dormaient dans la clarté tranquille. C'était le recueillement, la douceur cossue d'un salon bourgeois, dont on a enlevé les housses, pour la grande réception du soir. (p. 364)

In the following sentence *douceur* becomes *douleur* as we see a woman alone before the chapelle de Notre-Dame des Sept-Douleurs.

The connotations of this topological analogy between church and salon are even more unsettling, for they recall the explicit analogy in chapter 7 between the bourgeois interior and the home of oncle Bachelard's low-life mistress Clarisse Bocquet on the rue de la Cerisaie:

Le salon, avec son tapis à grandes fleurs, son meuble et ses tentures de satin grenat, ressemblait beaucoup au salon de la rue de Choiseul; et comme pour compléter cette ressemblance, plusieurs des amis du conseiller, qu'il avait vu là-bas, le soir du concert, se retrouvaient ici, formant les mêmes groupes. (p. 133)

So the analogical chain extends: church = family home = mistress's salon. It is as if the bourgeois man can find his feet (under the table) everywhere, and almost as if he can be in (at least) two places at once. There are, however, clear differences between the salons kept by mistresses and wives, for Clarisse refuses to welcome any other women into her salon. This demi-monde simulacrum of an already confected bourgeois domain fulfils male fantasy; this is domestic comfort without wives and children: 'Mais on fumait, on parlait haut, toute une gaieté volait dans la clarté vive des bougies' (p. 133). As Duveyrier tells Josserand, who realizes in vain that he is being railroaded into making a dowry contract on behalf of Berthe: 'Nous sommes ici mieux que partout ailleurs . . .' (p. 134). Similarly, the rectitude of the bourgeois salon is not the only analogical force at work in the church at Saint-Roch, for the most striking vision there is the Calvary, 'une apparition tragique, un drame déchirant et simple: le Christ cloué sur la croix, entre Marie et Madeleine, qui sanglotaient' (p. 365). This is not the Christ of the Holy Trinity, but another figure of three: the psychosexually potent triangle of mother, son and fallen woman. We return to this vision of 'l'humanité saignante de cette mort' at the end of chapter 17 only to witness the embarrassment of Mauduit's illusions. Like Marie and Madeleine he cries for 'la vérité morte, le ciel vide' (p. 366); this is death without resurrection: 'le grand Christ de plâtre n'avait plus une goutte du sang'. In the image of tears without blood the actual and the symbolic are brutally divided in this shaming of delusion.

Mauduit is not really interested in Juillerat's political mythology, but, until this moment, he does share his teleological vision of history. The catastrophic nemesis at the end of his vision is that of 'un Dieu de colère résolu à exterminer enfin le peuple coupable' (p. 365). So it is as if doctor and priest are administering the last rites on a moribund moral and social order, as if the novel does end with a death after all (and not just Octave's marriage). As such this scene recalls that in *Madame Bovary* in which another man of science, the pharmacist Homais, and another man of the cloth, the abbé Bournisien, stand either side of Emma's corpse. Like Flaubert, Zola suggests that his homosocial couple are not so far apart as they might at first seem. Even when they argue, Juillerat concludes with the paradox: 'Je suis plus religieux que vous' (p. 363). But his religion is merely historical mysticism. In their final diagnosis, the doctor and the priest seem to be supporting each other, as if the magical powers of explanatory discourse are waning under the forces of pessimism:

> – Que de misères! murmura-t-il [Mauduit] avec tristesse.
> Le médecin hocha la tête, en répondant:
> – C'est la vie.
> Ils avaient de ces aveux, lorsqu'ils sortaient côte à côte d'une agonie ou d'une naissance. Malgré leurs croyances opposées, ils s'entendaient parfois sur l'infirmité humaine. Tous deux étaient dans les mêmes secrets: si le prêtre recevait leur confession de ces dames, le docteur, depuis trente ans, accouchait avec les mères et soignait les filles. (p. 362)

Privy to the private lives of women, these guardians of rites of passage are agents of those transactional moments, births and deaths, which contractual texts (marriages and wills) are intended to control. Hence the particular vacuity of the already vacuous 'C'est la vie'. What for Octave seems to be a renaissance is for the wider social order but the sign of demise. Beginnings and endings coincide on the contrary paths of personal and collective fates as we approach the point of narrative closure.

This language of decomposition culminates in the final scene where the servants discuss the moral failings of the bourgeoisie. When Hippolyte complains that dirty water has destroyed the dress of his master's wife, the maids reply with a torrent of abuse: 'La bonde était levée, un flot de mots abominables dégorgeait du cloaque. Dans les temps de dégel, les murs y ruisselaient d'humidité, une pestilence montait de la petite cour obscure, toutes les *décompositions* cachées des étages semblaient fondre et s'exhaler par cet égout de la maison' (p. 384, our italics). This systematic migration of the diction of decomposition between ethical, political and social realms suggests how wifely adultery comes to represent a wider sense of the Decadence, as the solidity of civilisation is threatened by the flooding sewer of modernity.

This decomposition is characterised by the demise of the fathers, Josserand and Duveyrier. When Auguste visits Berthe's parents to demand the dowry he has been promised, he tells them of her infidelity. The effect on M. Josserand is devasting, 'Mon Dieu! il mourrait donc de son enfant?. . . Et voilà, maintenant, qu'elle tombait à l'adultère, à ce dernier degré de vilenie pour une femme' (p. 329). The Josserands' party in chapter 3 is echoed by the Duveyriers' at the end of the novel. Josserand has died eight months earlier; Duveyrier, driven from his home, cannot even manage to commit suicide efficiently. As this *fête* celebrates the demise of the fathers, it is therefore particularly apposite that the reference to Meyerbeer's opera of paternal misunderstanding is repeated in this scene (p. 382). What is so ironic here is that Campardon's Saint-Bris is at his most dogmatic in the 'Bénédiction' scene. Naturally Octave performs brilliantly and Clotilde only wishes that she could have offered him a solo part, but Valentine's (and thus her) partner, Raoul – who is the major tenor in the opera – is of course hiding in this scene. Duveyrier, however, cannot hide, as his blood boils: 'Et, au fond de la pièce voisine, derrière un triple rang d'habits noirs, on voyait Duveyrier serrer les dents pour ne pas aboyer d'angoisse, avec sa mâchoire de travers, dont les boutons irrités saignaient' (p. 382).

This demise is crowned by the reference to Octave's marriage to Mme Hédouin. The composition of the novel, which, as we have seen, is threatened by the entropic forces which David Baguley views as symptomatic of the Naturalist novel in general, is saved from radical decomposition by a recuperative circularity which allows the lover to become a husband:

Octave eut une singulière sensation de recommencement. C'était comme si les deux années vécues par lui, rue de Choiseul, venaient de se couler. Sa femme se trouvait là, qui lui souriait, et pourtant rien ne semblait s'être passé dans son existence: aujourd'hui répétait hier, il n'y avait ni arrêt ni dénouement. (p. 381)

Marriage, found at the end of this novel as of so many others, actually registers a sense of iterative experience, with the differences between extra-marital and conjugal encounters cynically elided. The circularity that guarantees a formal recomposition of a novel threatened by hæmic and ethical decomposition is paradoxically related to the sameness of experience: 'Le thé, ensuite, déroula le même défilé, promena les mêmes tasses et les mêmes sandwichs' (p. 382).[21] Similarly, 'comme tous les samedis, lorsque minuit sonna, les invités s'en allèrent peu à peu', which echoes the *piano* effect of the swordsmen disappearing into the distance whispering the words, '«A minuit! point de bruit!»' (p. 92). Octave's marriage offers an ironic prefiguration of the somewhat happier ending of *Au bonheur des dames*, and he lives to fight another day.[22] The society on which he is a parasite seems, however, to be in a less healthy state.

The circularity of bourgeois myths, remapped ironically onto the structure of *Pot-Bouille* (as, in another mode, they had been rewritten by Flaubert in *L'Education sentimentale*) is threatened by the linearity of Juillerat's narrative of historical transformation.[23] Indeed, it is in Octave's escape from the common plot that his disdain for others seems most comprehensible. This question of narrative linearity is also raised implicitly by Robida's '*Pot-Bouille* ou tous détraqués mais vertueux' which appeared in *La Caricature* on 13 May 1882.[24] One of the questions which arises here is how such a caricature is to be 'read'. One could play the multiple permutations of a game of sexual snakes and ladders up and down the staircase in the central column, or as Aimé Cournet puts it in another context in 1866 *L'Amour en zigzag*. But there is a more ordered reading suggested not only by the convention of reading from the top left-hand corner but also by the fact that the top left-hand caption recounts the beginning of the novel with Octave's arrival in Paris. This ordering suggests that the spaces of domesticity and the novel have now been mapped onto the demarcated spaces of the cartoon strip. One need only look at the work of Bertall to see that Robida is by no means alone in this kind of cutaway presentation of domestic space.

This order of reading has interesting implications – not only because it takes us back to Zola in the bottom right-hand corner – but also because we begin not downstairs at the front door but in the *chambres de domestiques* at the top of the house. This, of course, reflects the inversion of social hierarchies in the vertical structure of the house and also at the level of knowledge in narrative. For the servants do enjoy a kind of shared omniscience as they return to their quarters every night to swap stories about their respective bourgeois bosses. Perhaps it is they who come closest to a kind of omniscience in the household, as a kind of quasi-Flaubertian muted presence, 'présent partout' and thus the busiest dealers in gossip. If the caricature begins in the servants' quarters, then the novel itself closes with the words of the maid Julie who is about to change jobs but realises that 'celle-ci ou celle-là, toutes les baraques se ressemblent. Au jour d'aujourd'hui, qui a fait l'une a fait l'autre' (p. 386). It is as if the famous opening line of Tolstoy's *Anna Karenina* has been rewritten and that now all *un*happy families appear to be the same too. This perception of an underlying sameness is also a way of making sense of the copia of adulterous scenarios in a novel which risks running away with itself. Although this perception of sameness is a particularly banal form of synthesis, it does provide a response of sorts to the risk of mindless additions and multiplications both promised and threatened in the novel. The doubling of the present ('Au jour d'/aujourd') mutes the voice of a transformed future that is to reverberate so conspicuously at the end of *Germinal*.

The effect of aesthetic circularity is validated further by an implicit satire of inconclusive activities. At one of the Duveyriers' *soirées*, M. Vabre tells M. Josserand how he collects statistics about paintings in the official salon catalogue. Insensitive to the qualities of beauty and emotion, Vabre's project knows no end, 'jamais mon travail ne sera complet, c'est ce qui me tue' (p. 85). Here we have the existential insecurity of the Don Juan type displaced to another character. Most ironically, Vabre never gets to see the paintings themselves. His mindless collection of statistics is, in every sense, blind. Like Bouvard and Pécuchet, Vabre's project knows of no intellectual principle which would facilitate a conclusion to his activities. This is pointless repetition without end. A further ironic inversion of the social order is, of course, that the owner of the house is the embodiment of endless repetition, whilst the demystifying perception of sameness behind apparent multiplicity is the gift of the maid. More interesting still is that Vabre's project is made even more difficult by female artists getting married: 'lorsqu'une femme artiste se mariait et qu'elle exposait ensuite sous le nom de son mari, comment pouvait-il s'y reconnaître?' Caught upon the interminable track of history, Vabre's project knows of no intellectual order which would allow for a summarizing conclusion to his activities. It is this interminable quality which, at a metaphorical level, brings on the termination of death ('ce qui me tue').

However, Octave lives on and gets married, in contrast to the actual death at the end of the preceding novel in the series, *Nana*. Maupassant's article, written for *Le Gaulois* as pre-publicity for their imminent serialization of Zola's novel and appearing on 14 January 1882, concludes by emphasising this contrast between on the one hand Zola's novel of prostitution and on the other his novel of adultery 'qui, dans le système qu'il semble avoir adopté des contrastes de livre à livre, doit être le roman calme, après cet éclatant roman *Nana*'.[25] The novel of prostitution, though, is in a sense but a novel (or rather many novels) of adultery seen from the other side, with the effect that the family itself does not act as the focus for the narrative, in spite of the homeliness of Clarisse Bocquet's salon. Indeed, this is where we find the novel of 'adultery of unmarried women' which Bill Overton finds so conspicuously absent from the European tradition of the novel of adultery.[26] For Nana is the woman visited by men when they leave the private domain of the family and choose, in Bourget's memorable phrase, to 'courir les diverses sous-préfectures du département de la Haute-Noce'.[27] Indeed, the adulterous triangle is inscribed in the opening scenarios of the novel at the Théâtre des Variétés where, ironically enough, Nana plays the role of Venus, wife of Vulcan who catches her with her lover, Mars, the god of war. The historical relationship between the practice of prostitution in Paris and male fantasies of adulterous seduction can be tracked in the rise of the *maison de rendez-vous* (from about 15 in number in 1888 to probably 200 in the early years of the twentieth century) which Corbin terms 'the shrine of venal adultery'.[28] There men would pay the agreed fee to the mistress of the establishment so that 'the meeting between the partners involved a simulated seduction, apparently without money being discussed'. In this version of the brothel as theatre 'what one hoped to find', Corbin tells us, 'was another man's wife'.

The relationship of complementarity between Bordenave's theatre and Zola's novel is also revealed by what might be termed the dynamics of beauty. For Nana uses the cultural forum of theatre as a vehicle for the display of her beauty; whereas Zola uses Nana's body in the service of his literary æsthetics. In other words, Nana's beauty generates the audience's desire, whilst Zola uses the issue of desire to underpin the æsthetics of his writing. To see these complementary dynamics as analogous, however, is to imitate the naivety of Hector de La Faloise who insists on referring to Bordenave's 'bordel' as 'votre théâtre'. In fact, Bordenave's theatre-cum-brothel offers a parody of mythologies of sex, as does *Pot-Bouille*, but the error of Nana's male audience is a generic misinterpretation borne of desire: 'Personne ne riait plus, les faces des hommes, sérieuses, se tendaient avec le nez aminci, la bouche irritée et sans salive'.[29] This is the face of male desire busy misreading its own culture.

One way to conceive of *Pot-Bouille* and *Nana* is as experiments in promiscuity, both asking via the narrative machines of plot what happens to those who refuse even the semblance of monogamy. Particularly revealing is the way in which questions of gender and genre inter-relate in these narratives of polygamy. The respective endings of these novels reflect the generic persuasion of each text. For Octave's fate appears to be a happy one at the end of a novel which is comic (though, as in other comedies, studded with tragic possibilities), and Nana's fatal end reflects the ultimately tragic quality of the novel and the serious faces of her male audience at odds with Nana's own carnivalesque exhuberance. Octave's marriage and Nana's death correspond to the two narrative possibilities identified with such irony by E. M. Forster. The end of *Nana* echoes that of *Les Liaisons dangereuses*, a model of female promiscuity in fiction whose notoriety in the nineteenth century is evidenced by Balzac's *La Cousine Bette* for instance. Like Nana, the promiscuous woman in Laclos's novel, Madame de Merteuil, contracts smallpox at the end of the narrative. But whereas this moralistic nemesis merely disfigures Merteuil, it kills off Nana on the very day the Franco-Prussian War begins. As such Nana is seen to embody the moral demise of the Second Empire. This is a kind of dramatic irony which privileges the historical knowledge of Zola's Third Republic audience at the expense of his characters. Only the former can know how foolish the cries of 'A Berlin! A Berlin!' truly are.[30] Here the military register displaces the erotic as one inaccessible name-fetish (the capital city which Frenchmen will never reach) replaces another, the name of Nana whispered by the audience in chapter 1 of the novel. This twinning of sexual and political decadence is one more echo of *Les Liaisons dangereuses* which diagnoses the ills of the aristocratic *ancien régime*. Thus the adulterous relationship between Mars and Venus (war and sexuality) theatricalized in the opening scenes of the novel is reinstated in its allegorical closure. In *Pot-Bouille*, though, it is Octave who is the invading force whose strategies for ambushing women reflect a received rhetoric of military manœuvers.

To find a comic novel in the *Rougon-Macquart* series is a little surprising (not least to student readers). As such this provides a vital test case in the relationship between gender and genre. The Naturalist ethos would seem to invite tragic rather than comic plots. At the same time, though,

Pot-Bouille reflects a cultural tradition of comic Don Juans which includes work by no lesser artists than Molière and Mozart. So, in the event, the genre of the Naturalist novel is overwhelmed by the imperatives of the representation of gender, and this is the ground on which the ideology of Zola's novel is fought out. Most striking is the way in which these culturally dominant narratives of male promiscuity operate in this comic mode, one superficial effect of which is to lessen the gravity with which the reader is asked to consider the moral problematic. Indeed, if it is true that we laugh at Octave, then it is also the case that we laugh with him; and when we laugh *at* him it tends to be at moments of inadequacy when he fails to live up fully to the role of the Don Juan (in the case of Valérie in particular, as we have seen). This contrasts with the punitive ending of the adulteress's tale so often written. Archetypally, *Madame Bovary* may explain at an early stage the circumstances of Emma's marriage but it concludes by showing the aftermath of Emma's death, and her form of death is itself seen as another type of sin: suicide.

As George Bernard Shaw perceived, there is in the sexuality of the Don Juan figure something of the Nietzschean *Übermensch*, highlighted above in one of the epigraphs to chapter 1. His is not so much a compulsory heterosexuality as a compulsive one. Driven by a monomania where will meets desire, such a figure happily overrides the contract theory of bourgeois society; be it the sexual, financial and social contract of marriage, or the wider set of socioeconomic contractual obligations which inform capitalist interaction. This is one reason why it appears so 'natural' for Octave to make the shift from *Pot-Bouille* to *Au bonheur des dames*, in other words from the private realm of sexuality to the public world of consumerism. For although contracts can be designed to define the flow of capital, there is also a tension between the economics of capital and the sociology of contracts. The former is at times intent on sacrificing the latter on the altar of the free market. The economic *Übermensch* who runs parallel with the Don Juan type is the figure of the entrepreneur, and it is in the lexical field around the French term *entreprendre* that this parallel is made most explicit. For if *entreprendre* means to undertake, then it also means to woo; if Octave is wooed by Mme Hédouin's *entreprise*, then he is himself the master of sexual *entreprises*; and if he is in general economic terms *entreprenant*, then he is also particularly *entreprenant avec les femmes*.

Indeed, the contrast between the fates of Octave and Nana makes particular sense in terms of an analysis of these protagonists' respective relationships with the prevailing systems of exchange and circulation:

sexual, cultural and financial. As we have seen above, Octave has to dominate the circulation of cultural capital before his sexual circulation can come into its own, and both of these forms of capital are but preludes to his triumph over the prime object of capitalist exchange, namely financial capital in *Au bonheur des dames*. Nana, however, cannot move beyond the sexual plot precisely because her body marks out the realm of her financial interaction. This is why she does not have a third novel in which to shine (we should recall that Octave's origins are sketched in *La Conquête de Plassans* and Nana's drawn out in *L'Assommoir*). For the male who is afforded public as well as private roles each form of exchange represents a further stage in a developing plot. It is via a set of animating differences between what Michel Serres depicts as analogical fluids (for sex, culture and finance, read: blood, ink and gold)[31] that Octave constructs a life and a narrative. Nana, though, is not allowed this differential narrative structure as financial and sexual imperatives are collapsed into the infinitely possessed (and yet also unpossessable) *non-lieu* of her female body. The prostitute as public woman represents an interesting test case as she attempts (or is forced) to escape her private status as woman, only to find that there is nowhere left for her to go but literally back to her own body as an object of exchange.[32] The difference between Octave and Nana is that he (unlike she) is allowed to exchange these systems of exchange. What is backgrounded in all of this (in spite of Nana's motherhood) is that charmed fluid, milk, which flows so proudly through the ideology of fertility in which Zola indulges. As we shall see in part 2, it flows back to the narrative surface ten novels later in *Le Docteur Pascal* at the end of the *Rougon-Macquart*, having passed *inter alia* through the novel of cultural capital, *L'Œuvre*, and the novel of financial capital, *L'Argent*.

Pleasures and fears of paternity: Maupassant and Zola

CHAPTER 3

'Bel-Ami': fantasies of seduction and colonization

By reading *Pot-Bouille* as Rodolphe's novel, it is possible to see how not only fallen wives but the figure of the arch seducer can be used to focus narratives of adultery. Both, of course, belong to the same adulterous scenario. They are partners in that narrative of seduction which is typically diagnosed as an articulation of bourgeois patriarchal fears about the uncertainty of paternity. Such uncertainty was particularly disturbing in a post-revolutionary order where the newly dominant group was keen to assert its political as well as sexual legitimacy. As Tony Tanner reminds us, *pater semper incertus est* (though no longer to the same degree in our own times, of course). Nevertheless, it is worth noting that the notion of the fear of uncertain paternity is merely one way of reading masculinity, and that the Don Juan model offers an alternative version of men's relationship to the uncertainty of paternity. In plain terms, for the seducer who fears the responsibilities of fatherhood it may be argued that the uncertainty of paternity is in fact a source of fantasy, or a way of escaping the biological fate of his actions. This may operate at conscious as well as unconscious levels. More particularly, it is a strategy of seduction amplified by the issue of paternity suits which sits high on the feminist agenda as the century draws to a close. Counter to the fear of uncertain paternity runs not only this fantasy but also a symbolic resistance to that fear in the form of tales of consanguinity and incest. These tales not only characterize the *fin de siècle*'s sense of its own decadence; they can also be found within the Naturalist tradition, as we shall see in chapter 4, in Zola's *Le Docteur Pascal*.

Pot-Bouille is, of course, by no means the only Don Juan narrative published during the *fin de siècle* which dramatizes fantasies of uncertain paternity. As we have seen, it can be read as a prelude to marriage (and thus to *Au bonheur des dames*), which seems to signal the taming of the *célibataire*. As Jean Borie has shown, the bachelor is a key figure within the literary as well as sexual culture of the nineteenth century.[1] Zola is of course an exception to the rule of artistic bachelordom symbolized by Flaubert and the Goncourt brothers, and as we shall see the narrative of Zola's own married life plays a conspicuous role in the paratextual dynamics of desire (adulterous as well as incestuous) which surround the publication of *Le Docteur Pascal*. *Pot-Bouille*, though, examines the role that the bachelor plays within a house of apartments which functions as a kind of sexual ecosystem in its own right. As he seems to be an infinitely mobile agent adjacent to the conjugal domain, Octave offers a contrast with the sedentary master of each household (who is emasculated by the deficit in knowledge he suffers in the game of dramatic irony), and to the wives Zola depicts this contrast as in itself an incitement to desire. As Borie shows, the bachelor is a louche figure because of his resistance to what might be termed the normative narrative of conjugal resolution. The ultimately conservative turn in a Don Juan narrative such as Zola's lies in its failure to perpetuate itself without the closure of marriage (in Octave's case) or nemesis (archetypally via the appearance of the stone statue). Rather than exhibit the homoerotic possibilities of the bachelor figure, Octave, the compulsive heterosexual, manipulates in different ways the homosocial ties he shares with men such as Campardon and Pichon.

Many of these issues are also explored by Guy de Maupassant in *Bel-Ami* which takes the tale of the bachelor's marriage a step further by introducing the narratologically as well as socially novel issue of divorce. The dangerous legal potential of sexual misadventure is broached in the conversation between guests at the Forestiers' dinner party about the Gauthier trial, a 'cas d'adultère compliqué de chantage' in part 1 chapter 2 of the novel.[2] Implicitly this parodies the discussion at the Duveyriers' party in chapter 5 of *Pot-Bouille* of the relationship between adultery in literature serialized by the press and adultery in real life. Members of the press clique invited to the Forestiers dissect the case with 'une curiosité professionnelle et une indifférence absolue' (p. 214) which Louis Forestier correctly characterizes as the work of 'bons lecteurs de Zola' (p. 1358). Thus Maupassant takes us back a stage from the reception of the press to the conditions of its cultural production, as guests weigh up stories 'comme on examine, comme on retourne et comme on pèse, chez les commerçants, les objets qu'on va livrer au public' (p. 215). Hence the analogy between journalists and retailers, and thus between Georges and Octave, is thus reinforced. It is Maupassant's Don Juan narrative which we shall investigate in this chapter. As we have already seen, *Pot-Bouille* fuels Maupassant's interest in questions of adultery, paternity and legitimacy, which is visible in much of his short as well as long fiction. Serialized in *Gil Blas* between 6 April and 30 May and published in book form by Havard in May 1885, *Bel-Ami* again recounts the taming by marriage of a Don Juan figure, here Georges Duroy, and in addition his manipulation of the new legal possibility of divorce to which we shall return in the context of Paul Bourget.

In his invaluable edition Louis Forestier nuances the notion that this is a sexual *Bildungsroman* à la Balzac: 'Duroy ne se forme pas vraiment. Dès le début, il possède la séduction, l'esprit de décision, l'aptitude à profiter des occasions qui pourraient le servir' (p. 1335). This of course may say more about the impoverished moral resources of the society on which Georges preys than it does about Georges himself. As the regal name suggests, Georges seems to be born to this life. In fact, a contrast may be made with the seriality of Octave Mouret's progression from *La Conquête de Plassans* via *Pot-Bouille* culminating in *Au bonheur des dames*. Zola's expansive novelistic project distinguishes between the origins, the sexual *éducation* and the commercial triumph of Octave, whereas Maupassant's contrary art of concision makes Georges's successes in the private domain of sexuality and the public domain of journalism coincide so as to stress their mutual causality. Georges's rise through the ranks of *La Vie française* (which refers in specific terms to the banal title of a newspaper and more generally to this pathologically decadent society) puts a new spin on the concept of *une carrière ouverte à tous les talents*.

The patriarchal role into which Georges is drawn by his cynical manœuvering does not confirm his *nom du père*. This patronym is consistently modified at each stage of this career progression which is also marked out by a spatial drama of verticality: Georges Duroy to Georges Du Roy to Georges Du Roy de Cantel to the baron Du Roy de Cantel.[3] The potentially feminizing force of this onomastic malleability is witnessed once Georges is to marry Madeleine Forestier, who like Mme Hédouin exerts the domination of an older widow in the business world. The difference is that the latter immediately becomes Mme Mouret, whereas Madeleine plays wordgames with her new husband's name, conspicuously just after asking him to take her to meet his parents in Canteleu near Rouen. In a feint which attempts to conceal class behind gender, she presents her social aspiration for 'un nom noble' as a feminine caprice (p. 345). Her blushing is unnecessary as Georges admits to having had similar thoughts; in a pattern which we shall chart below, male and female roles are shown to be not so distant as the reader may expect to find in a Don Juan novel. What she desires is (if the pun might be excused) particularity, but she tries in vain to convince Georges that 'Du Roy' will not make him look ridiculous (and thus the victim of irony) precisely because 'tout le monde le fait'. For Georges, however, this is 'un procédé trop simple, trop commun, trop connu', so Georges becomes the co-author of his own name when he mentions his inclination to use his home territory as a name and Madeleine confirms their new title: 'Duroy de Cantel'.

We may note that it is Madeleine who writes down the name in order to ratify its suitability and when she offers it to him Georges sees not his name but his wife's: 'Madame Duroy de Cantel'. This he accepts because of the social *vraisemblance* of the manœuver; as Madeleine argues, 'Ça se fait tous les jours dans la presse et personne ne s'étonnera de vous voir prendre un nom de guerre'. This weapon of social warfare serves as a veritable *nom de plume* for the journalism which is also co-authored by this couple (again, though the articles bear his name, she is the dominant authorial force behind his textual productions). So in more than one sense she gives birth to her new husband, for in Balzacian terms it is she who enjoys the virile energy of creativity and speaks the language of *arrivisme*: 'Avec un rien de méthode, on arrive à réussir tout ce qu'on veut' (p. 346). Similarly, Georges must passively accept the croix de la Légion d'honneur which is procured by his wife and thus implies a stain on his honour. The scandal of her influence is that she outstrips the legendary desires of the Don Juan figure. As he complains, 'Rien ne te satisfait maintenant' (p. 446). What pleases him most is not the announcement of the award in the *Officiel* of the New Year, but the spelling of his name in two words: Du Roy. So the name of the patriarch is disturbed by the displacements and subterfuges of both the seducer and his matriarchal accomplice.

Hence the reader is not surprised when she determines the terms of their marriage contract (p. 352) and colleagues on the newspaper tease him by calling him Forestier. So by a process of adoption Georges is passed between *noms de famille* (p. 368). This jealous teasing in turn ignites 'ce travail lent de jalousie posthume' which ties Georges into a counter-genealogy of surrogacy (p. 370). When this teasing concerns the similarity of Georges's articles and Forestier's, Georges's inner fury takes the form of a quasi-Bloomian anxiety of influence, but the point of textual origin who ensures this similarity is, of course, the ghost-writing wife, Madeleine. It is as if Madeleine and not Georges is the paradox-ical centre of this novel, in spite of the way in which the text focuses on the Don Juan figure. As is ritually noted, in the first scene of the novel

Georges is on his way towards the aptly named Eglise de la Madeleine when he bumps into Forestier, and this church is where his marriage to Suzanne is celebrated at the end of the text. This patronymic mobility creates a word-phobia (experienced by Maupassant's reader as a textual fetish) which means that even the common noun *le forestier* makes Georges jealous (p. 372). In the hotel room in Rouen on the way to visit his parents Georges feels a certain disgust at the thought that Madeleine's dressing gown may have retained some residue of Forestier's touch. As Georges realises, the trousseau, like innocence, cannot be reconstructed, and it is in this asymmetry between his own sexual licence and the purity by which he reifies the objects of his desire that the reader sees most clearly his hypocrisy over the double standard. And it is, of course, the sign of a literary genealogy ironically super-imposed over Maupassant's satire of family genealogy that this deceived husband who returns as a phantom-like presence is called Charles. Until the divorce plot is triggered, this Don Juan character, even though unre-formed, seems in a sense to be tamed as he is now in the position of the other man, for now he is the potential *cocu*.

The traditional link between marriage and naming is made clear by Catherine Belsey: 'Marriage yokes the transmission of worldly goods to the reproductive process, and cements the alliance between them in the perpetuation of the family name.'[4] But in *Bel-Ami* names become a way of concealing rather than confirming identities. A moment of confusion ensues when père Walter, standing in the public location of the newspa-per's offices amidst a political crisis, makes the mistake of calling Georges by the nickname used by his wife and daughter. This transgres-sion of the linguistic form of the public/private divide leaves Walter confused and apologetic but it is too late to retract the transgression, 'Très bien, alors je vous baptise Bel-Ami comme tout le monde' (p. 401). Within a few paragraphs, though, Georges has responded to Walter's call for 'une actualité, une chronique à effet, à sensation' by slyly offering a piece on the North African situation which he knows he can rework from his first article, 'Les Mémoires d'un chasseur d'Afrique', and then present anew, '*débaptisé*, retapé et modifié' (p. 402, our italics). What genealogies (textual as well as sexual) preclude is genuine originality, even from that arch individualist, Don Juan.

The fact that Georges is preceded and followed by Madeleine's other lovers, Vaudrec and Laroche-Mathieu, only confirms his unwilling incorporation into a counter-genealogy governed by the desires of the matriarch. Already the sight at the Forestiers' dinner party in part I chapter 2 of that 'vieux beau', Norbert de Varenne, still gracious as he kisses Mme Forestier's wrist, offers our Don Juan a vision of his own fate. Likewise when his own father meets Madeleine, he admires this 'belle femme' with the admiration of one who has 'passé pour connaisseur dans le temps' (p. 358). *Tel père, tel fils.* When Vaudrec dies, the confusion of authority in the Du Roy–Forestier household is emphasized by his bequeathal of all his estate to Mme Claire-Madeleine Forestier (updated to Mme Claire-Madeleine Du Roy in a subsequent version). By law this needs the consent of her embarrassed husband who is caught between honour and wealth (of course, the times demand the triumph of the latter, but this needs to be carefully arranged). So the process of patrilinear inheritance is rudely interrupted by the play of adulterous desire. Indeed, Madeleine's recollection of her own illegitimate origins suggests that she is an avenging angel sent to upstage the strategems of Don Juan. For her mother was a teacher, seduced and impoverished, who died when Madeleine was twelve, and the latter was brought up with money provided by a stranger: 'Son père, sans doute? Qui était-il? Elle ne le sut point au juste, bien qu'elle eût de vagues soupçons' (p. 360).

The socially encoded fictionalisation of honour reflects the bourgeoisie's historically regressive imitation of an aristocratic code, and the main site of male honour is the wife whose integrity underpins her husband's value, hence the difficulty of Vaudrec's will. As Georges tells his wife, 'C'est drôle que ce soit toi qu'il appelle, et non moi qui suis légalement le chef de famille' (p. 424). The archetypal scenario for such resolutions of triangularity is the duel already degraded in *Le Rouge et le Noir* whose status as a model text is, as Christopher Lloyd rightly observes, undermined by Julien's ultimate refutation of social artifice.[5] Nevertheless it is very hard not to see an echo of Sorel's own reading in the images in the bedroom shared by Georges and Madeleine at his parents' home: Paul and Virginie, and Napoleon I on horseback. In part 1 chapter 7 of *Bel-Ami* the duel between Georges and Louis Langremont plays out a classic scenario in satirical fashion. Georges repeats the words of his second, who bears the self-parodic name Rival, 'comme les enfants apprennent leurs leçons' (p. 318). Just to reinforce the infantile quality of this supposedly ennobling scenario, they toss a coin 'comme des enfants qui s'amusent' (p. 319), and the ludic nature of this potentially grave situation is maintained in the culmination when both duellists miss with their pistol shots. This echoes the way in which the military mode of the swordsmen in *Les Huguenots* is ironized by the unheroic Octave Mouret whose duel with Auguste Vabre ends up with dinner in the restaurant Foyot. Once again potential tragedy is reduced to bathos. Maupassant's reader is not even left with the illusion of moral ambiguity offered by that least deluded of texts, *Les Liaisons dangereuses*, which allows the reader to wonder whether Valmont (as one of those *Angels with Dirty Faces*) chooses or welcomes death in his duel with Danceny.

In a notably modern moment, the weapons of honour and war become the equipment of sport at the display of shooting and fencing arranged by Jacques Rival on behalf of the orphans of the sixth *arrondissement*. Charity is the generosity of spirit offered by the new aristocrats (and as Zola's *Paris* suggests, this can be the most backhanded of gifts, as we shall see in chapter 6). The irony is that Georges, who has already been adopted by Madeleine, is using the charity event to court Mme Walter. What Madeleine calls a 'nom de guerre' is in a literal sense anything but as the mythology of the male body in bellicose action is demystified by Maupassant's cynical account of human motivation. As Georges realises only too well, his colonial adventures are no preparation for honourable combat: 'il avait tiré sur des Arabes, sans grand danger pour lui, d'ailleurs, un peu comme on tire sur un sanglier, à la chasse' (p. 313). After the scene in which he tells his mistress, Clotilde de Marelles, that he is to marry Madeleine, Georges is free to release his boyish tensions: 'il se mit à boxer contre le mur en lançant de grands coups de poing, dans une sorte d'ivresse de succès et de force, comme s'il se fût battu contre la Destinée' (p. 348). The force of destiny is only ever a metaphor (*comme si*) and George is rendered punch-drunk merely by shadow boxing. It is fitting that he should box against a wall as he will never accept the limits of domestic life, even though he has explained to Clotilde, 'Il faut que je me pose dans le monde, et je ne puis le faire tant que je n'aurai pas d'intérieur.'

Duelling dramatizes the logic of rivalry and jealousy which dynamizes the triangular narratives into which Georges is drawn. During the display of Marcowitch's painting of *Jésus marchant sur les flots* in part 2 chapter 7 the reader is shown a social system of compulsory triangularity where the swapping of partners appears quite natural. It is thus appropriate that Marcowitch's showing of the work should eschew the privacy of the home – with its bourgeois overtones – by aspiring to the elite sociability of the salon as a semi-public domain where guests stroll around 'comme dans un musée' (p. 440). When Clotilde's husband thanks Duroy for the tip off about the Morocco affair, Georges uses this as a lever to procure Clotilde's company: 'En échange de ce service, mon cher, je prends votre femme, ou plutôt je lui offre mon bras. Il faut toujours séparer les époux'

(p. 441). (Etymologically, 'to seduce' means 'to separate', i.e. *seducere*.) Georges himself, though, must endure a string of jealousies in this scene when faced with Walter's immense wealth, the sight of his wife in the company of Laroche and the marquis de Cazolles entertaining Suzanne (p. 438–9). As we shall see, it is this social experience of sexual life as a form of perpetual miscegenation which the incestuous love of *Le Docteur Pascal* confronts. What *Bel-Ami* also shows is the rivalry that Georges experiences not only towards other men but also towards women, both in general and also in particular cases such as Madeleine, as revealed above. He is jealous not only of the sexual achievements of men but also of the women he seduces. His alignment with Forestier is so complete that once married to Madeleine he is indignant at the 'presque certitude qu'elle avait trompé son premier mari' (p. 373). His epistemophilic 'désir de savoir' leads only to the homosocial fury of misogyny, 'cette colère qui couve[ ] au cœur de tous les mâles devant les caprices du désir féminin' (p. 374). It is clear that homosociality reflects self-interest since the law of perpetual displacement which defines the life of a Don Juan (as a series of women fulfil the role of being his lover, and he fulfils the sexual role of a series of men) means that paranoia sets in: 'Puisqu'elle avait trompé l'autre, comment pourrait-il avoir confiance en elle, lui?' He cannot resist the demon of analogy between his life and that of the man he has replaced. Now that he has literally and figuratively got his feet under the table (at Forestier's desk), he finds that he is simply filling a dead man's shoes (or foot-muff!): 'Sous la table, la chancelière du mort attendaient les pieds de Du Roy' (p. 365).

This rivalry between male and female sexual drives is inscribed in the display of Walter's art collection which pits against each other the desiring male and female gaze. On the one hand he takes particular pleasure in showing Jean Béraud's painting of the archetypal 'jolie Parisienne' mounting the stairs on a moving tram 'tandis que les hommes debout sur la plate-forme du bas considéraient les jambes de la jeune femme avec une expression différente de dépit et de convoitise' (p. 294). Walter's categorization is resonant, 'Ici les fantaisistes'. On the other hand though, the display concludes with Maurice Leloir's watercolour *L'Obstacle* which depicts the admiring gaze of a woman watching from a sedan-chair the herculean struggle between two 'hommes du peuple' (p. 295). The attempt to absorb the desiring female gaze is distinct – 'On voyait sortir par la fenêtre de la chaise un ravissant visage' – but the male viewer's gaze is not reciprocated; the triangle is already in the painting. Even if what is possible for Georges and Madeleine on a train remains merely a fantasy on a tram, Béraud's image of the opportunistic male gaze of modern desire is overridden by Leloir's far more elemental account of the triangularity of rivalry and desire. This time Walter offers no gloss.

Marriage is represented in the case of Madeleine and Duroy as a form of mutual suspicion rather than a bond of authentic reciprocity, as the story of Vaudrec's will reveals. When Georges stutters in shock at Vaudrec's privileging of heterosexual transgression over homosocial *convenance* (for as Madeleine observes, he was himself hoping to be named in the will), it is as if she sees her husband clearly for the first time:

> Madeleine, à son tour, le regardait fixement, dans la transparence des yeux, d'une façon profonde et singulière, comme pour y lire quelque chose, comme pour y découvrir cet inconnu de l'être qu'on ne pénètre jamais et qu'on peut à peine entrevoir en des secondes rapides, en ces moments de non-garde, ou d'abandon, ou d'inattention, qui sont comme des portes laissées entrouvertes sur les mystères dedans de l'esprit. (pp. 426–7)

Hypostatized by the narrator's quasi-philosophical reflections, this privileged moment of perspicacity echoes the language of domestic space so vital in novels of sexual transgression; Georges and Madeleine have entered the conjugal realm only to discover that their spouse is as it were another locked room into which they may rarely enter. Ironically enough, it was Forestier who first explained to him in precisely such diction the nature of his job at the newspaper as an explorer for political gossip: 'pénétrer partout malgré les portes fermées' (p. 237). It is little surprise when Georges is promoted to the role of chief *échotier*, for Forestier's description also describes the sexual invasiveness of this Don Juan type. The irony is that in his most intimate of relationships (with his wife) the doors remain shut, and he can hardly invade what he already in theory possesses:

> ils demeurèrent de nouveau quelques instants les yeux dans les yeux, s'efforçant d'aller jusqu'à l'impénétrable secret de leurs cœurs, de se sonder jusqu'au vif de la pensée. Ils tâchaient de se voir à nu la conscience en une interrogation ardente et muette: lutte intime de deux êtres qui, vivant côte à côte, s'ignorent toujours, se soupçonnent, se flairent, se guettent, mais ne se connaissent pas jusqu'au fond vaseux de l'âme. (p. 427)

The narcissism of Duroy is repeatedly confirmed as he seeks out his own reflection on the stairs on his way up the novel's symbolic structure of verticality, and it is an affirmation of this self-reflection which he seeks in the reciprocating female gaze, for instance when Georges and Suzanne's eyes meet early in the penultimate chapter as they plan how they might gain consent for their marriage: 'Leurs yeux se rencontraient, semblaient se concentrer, se comprendre, échanger secrètement une pensée, puis se fuyaient' (p. 460). Leo Bersani deconstructs this heterosexual gaze by suggesting that love can be a matter of looking in the same direction rather than looking at each other.[6] But even this homoerotic pattern is subject to Maupassant's vicious irony when Georges meets up with Mme Walter in the Eglise de la Madeleine in part 2 chapter 4. This not only echoes the meeting of Emma and Léon in Rouen Cathedral, as Louis Forestier points out (p. 1415) but also rehearses the ironically blasphemous erotic power imparted to this location in *Pot-Bouille*. The heterotopic church, 'bonnes à tous les usages' serves as an 'entremetteur' (p. 394) and paves the way for seduction precisely because Mme Walter does not have to look at the object of her desire. Georges joins her as she kneels before the altar in a grotesque parody of the wedding ceremony, and what is confessed is adulterous desire. But the taboo on the reciprocal gaze which allows the language of love to flow is threatened by Georges's next move when he suggests that they meet the next day in the parc Monceau. It is as if this arresting moment of candour is suddenly deflated by its insertion into the narrative of this capital of desire. The church is just one more scene of seduction. At this moment she asks him to leave her alone for a few minutes, he looks at her, and this spectacle silences him, as if verbal and visual revelation were mutually exclusive, lest the word be made flesh. She in turn must screw up her eyes to resist the possibility of letting her gaze follow him. However, the confession with the priest which follows is, as Georges realises, merely another twist in the inevitable tale of seduction (or a way of postponing the consummation of the reciprocal gaze).

Outside the polite society of married life the Don Juan figure finds his genuine female counterpart and rival in the figure of the prostitute, as we saw in our comparison of *Pot-Bouille* and *Nana*. The freedom that Octave has consists in large part in his capacity to move between the analogical realms of intimate and commercial desire. Whereas Nana is dealt a fatal blow at the end of her novel, Octave lives to fight another day, transposing the ruses of seduction from the privacy of the bedroom to the public world of the department store. In *Au bonheur des dames* Octave uses his talents to run the department store of the same name and seduce its female clientele. As we come to learn very soon after Octave's arrival in Paris, 'le commerce le passionnait, le commerce du luxe et de la femme, où il entre une séduction, une possession lente par des paroles dorées et des regards adulateurs'.[7]

In *Bel-Ami* the mirroring of male and female promiscuity is fore-grounded in a more explicitly comical vein in Georges's affair with Clotilde de Marelles. Clotilde pays to be entertained by Georges who takes her in part 1 chapter 5 on a low-life tour (again a threat to honour which he ultimately accepts).[8] She plays the game of carnivalesque inversion, bathing in the fantasy of role-play and the analogy between sexual and social transgression at the *marchand de vin*'s establishment, whilst the somewhat embarrassed Georges is racked by jealousy (not for the last time as we have seen) at the thought that she has had other lovers and knows this *demi-monde* only too well. Once more characters get their wires crossed in the discrepancy between playful and grave modes of response. She laughs; he is shocked, not least by the rivalry he feels in this revelation of an *histoire secrète* to which he has not yet been privy:

Certes elle avait eu des amants, déjà, mais de quelle sorte? de quel monde? Une vague jalousie, une sorte d'inimitié s'éveillait en lui contre elle, une inimitié pour tout ce qu'il ignorait, pour tout ce qui ne lui avait point appartenu dans ce cœur et dans cette existence. Il la regardait, irrité du mystère enfermé dans cette tête jolie et muette et qui songeait, en ce moment-là même peut-être, à l'autre, aux autres, avec des regrets. Comme il eût aimé regarder dans ce souvenir, y fouiller, et tout savoir, tout connaître . . . (pp. 269–70)

Expert in what Charles Cros ironically calls the *science de l'amour*, Georges shares with that other Naturalist hero, Octave, a voracious episte-mophilia which is threatened by the otherness of feminine desires. Bel-Ami's hypocrisy is exposed when Clotilde persuades Georges to take her to the Folies-Bergère where she discovers that Georges has slept with a prostitute, Rachel. All that Georges can offer is the rhetoric of Valmont discussed above in the context of *Pot-Bouille*: 'Ce n'est pas ma faute . . . J'ai connu cette femme-là autrefois.' Clotilde jumps out of their cab and pays the coachman with the words: 'C'est moi qui paye . . . Et recon-duisez-moi ce salop-là' (p. 280). For 'salop' read 'salope'. The comedy of Maupassant's scene finds its audience in the crowd which gathers because the temporary privacy of the *fiacre* has been broken by Clotilde's literal and figurative outburst. Mapped by Clotilde's fury onto the very subject-position of the woman from the Folies-Bergère he has seduced, Georges travels home with the cries of the crowd: 'Bonsoir, Bibi', ringing in his ears; the game of role reversal is complete. There are, of course, female characters who do make their way in the world, widows such as Mme Forestier/Du Roy and Mme Hédouin, but the tragedy for so many of the women in such fiction is that Clotilde's carnivalesque inversion of

roles and this collapsing of public and private categories are nothing
more than an analogy, and to live through metaphors, however potent,
is still to live through Bovaryesque dreams.

Within the space of one chapter, however, the *arriviste* Georges
becomes accustomed himself to the analogy which has just embarrassed
him. Before his visit to Clotilde in part 1 chapter 6 he goes for a stroll in
that *ne plus ultra* of lost innocence, the Bois de Boulogne, then by the Arc
de Triomphe and down the *grande avenue* where he inspects a rogues'
gallery of the sexually and financially corrupt. It is not until he sees a
courtesan in her carriage that Duroy finds his true analogue and in this
spectacle of Parisian public life it is all he can do not to burst into
applause: 'Il sentait peut-être vaguement qu'il y avait quelque chose de
commun entre eux, un lien de nature, qu'ils étaient de même race, de
même âme, et que son succès aurait des procédés audacieux de même
ordre' (p. 304). For 'cette parvenue de l'amour' also mocks the very
classes whose wealth she desires, and it is this, Georges might imagine,
which sets him apart from the crowds which cheer the appearance of
Nana on stage.

This only serves to corroborate a sympathy set out in the opening
street scene in the novel:

Il aimait . . . les lieux où grouillent les filles publiques, leurs bals, leurs cafés, leurs
rues; il aimait les coudoyer, leur parler, les tutoyer, flairer leurs parfums violents,
se sentir près d'elles. C'étaient des femmes enfin, des femmes d'amour. Il ne les
méprisait point du mépris inné des hommes de famille. (p. 199)

This is not the strange sympathy felt by Octave toward M. Pichon before
he seduces his wife. Georges sides with the honesty of sexual purpose
represented by the vendors rather than their clients, but this immersion
in the joys of public space is eclipsed by a feeling of superiority as he
nudges people out of the way when he strolls down the street in this
exposition: 'Il avait l'air de toujours défier quelqu'un, les passants, les
maisons, la ville entière, par chic de beau soldat tombé dans le civil' (p.
198). When he takes Mme Walter back to the room paid for by Clotilde,
he persuades her to enter by evoking the bourgeois nightmare of the
crowd scene: 'Venez. Vous voyez bien qu'on nous regarde, qu'on va se
rassembler autour de nous. Dépêchez-vous, dépêchez-vous . . . descen-
dez' (p. 404). When she allows herself to be dragged into his bachelor
pad (or what Bourget calls an 'aimoir' or a 'paradis en garni'),[9] the
reader is not clear why she is 'saisie de terreur'. Is this a fear of the crowd
which is embodied by the inquisitive wineseller? Or fear of the seduction which will fatally ensue? In other words, is this fear of private or

public exposure? Certainly Georges, this enemy of the people, hates and fears the crowds in a way that recalls the antipathy felt by des Esseintes. For the crowd reminds the Don Juan character of the mythical nature of a romantic ideology which grounds individual identity in the uniqueness of a particular reciprocal desire.[10]

As he rides through the Bois de Boulogne with Madeleine, Georges observes the idiocy of such an ideology before 'le défilé des voitures ramenant au logis, au lit désiré, l'éternel couple' (p. 374):

C'était un immense fleuve d'amants qui coulait vers le Bois sous le ciel étoilé et brûlant . . . Ils passaient, passaient, les deux êtres de chaque fiacre . . . perdus dans l'hallucination du désir . . . Tous ces gens accouplés, grisés de la même pensée, de la même ardeur faisaient courir une fièvre autour d'eux. Toutes ces voitures chargées d'amour, sur qui semblaient voltiger des caresses, jetaient sur leur passage une sorte de souffre sensuel, subtil et troublant. (pp. 371–2)

The capital whose maxim is *fluctuat nec mergitur* is perceived as a sea of desire, experienced not as an affirmation of ennobling individuality but, as in Zola's crowds, as a dehumanizing bestial eroticism where sameness overpowers difference. Even in that semi-private location of the carriage, consecrated as the mobile home of transgression, crowd psychology prevails, and even Georges and Madeleine are drawn in by 'la contagion de la tendresse'. It is fitting that this reminds Madeleine of their initial sexual encounter in the train compartment on the way to Flaubert's Rouen, for now they have made that return journey only to find that a hundred couples who might be Emma and Léon are circling around the playground of the metropolis. In a sense the final disillusionment occurs when a carriage which could be Emma's as much as anybody else's does reach the Paris she so desires. The Don Juan narrative provides by its multiplication of the scene of seduction a syntagmatic demystification of the unique amorous moment; what the city stages is a paradigm of uniqueness undermined. But this uniqueness is what Georges somehow expects from married life with Madeleine (and yet which he knows she cannot offer him), hence the nagging antagonism borne of 'le rappel incessant de l'autre' (p. 369). And as they leave the Bois and return home in the final scene of part 2 chapter 2, the gap between what husband and wife say to each other and what they really think is exposed by the narrator's excavation of Georges's thoughts which strip life of its 'robe de poésie' (p. 375). (By the end of chapter 6 they appear to each other as mere apparitions, only ever partially present.) At best this sense of thoroughgoing sameness is nuanced by the sexual Darwinism (identified as such by contemporary reviewers) which leads Georges to prefer Clotilde over Mme Walter although they both voice the clichés of affection, 'Mon chéri, mon petit, mon chat' (p. 419). As the narrator explains, 'les paroles d'amour, qui sont toujours les mêmes, prennent le goût des lèvres dont elles sortent' (p. 419), as if the interlocutionary relationship can reinvigorate the stereotypes of love. It is a strategy of such a cynical text to challenge the reader to dare to put such faith in the possibility of escaping the dead hand of the *idée reçue*, at the risk of sounding pathetically naive. As Tony Tanner notes, it is such a risk which Rodolphe fails to take in *Madame Bovary*: 'Il ne distinguait pas, cet homme si plein de pratique, la dissemblance des sentiments sous la parité des expressions.'[11]

The analogy between Don Juan and prostitute suggests the extent to which the seducer belongs to what Zola termed 'un monde à part', but within the logic of narrative focalisation Georges is keen to resist any threat to his central position. Though magnetised by his hero's perpetual sexual motion, Maupassant's narrator retains a certain ambivalence in spite of their homosocial contract which is voiced during Madeleine's flirting with Georges: 'elle lui jeta un de ces regards rapides et reconnaissants qui nous font leurs esclaves' (p. 284). And even if it is to flatter Maupassant to call the process Proustian, we can see his narrative development as an *éducation* in writing as he eventually acquires a certain journalistic facility. Still, it is hard not to see a degree of satire in the gap between the narrator's fluency and Duroy's stumbling compositions, initially staged as a gap between script and speech. As Duroy struggles with his *Souvenirs d'un chasseur d'Afrique*: 'Il sentait vaguement des pensées lui venir; il les aurait dites, peut-être, mais il ne les pouvait point formuler avec des mots écrits' (p. 224). It is, of course, Madeleine who bridges this gap. Indeed, it is quite feasible for the unintended reader to reconstruct the plot lines of the novel as a tale of the fate of female *volonté*, both sexual and textual, in a world which requires the mediation of men. It is in the private realm of seduction rather than the public text of journalism that Georges's verbal magic works wonders, seducing Rachel in the Folies-Bergère with one word, 'Parbleu' (p. 210), just as much as we might say that he is seduced by her.

Madeleine's ideals are presented as snobbish when she is disappointed by her meeting with Georges's parents, and this is generalized by the contract between narrator and hero, 'Est-ce que les femmes n'espèrent point toujours autre chose que ce qui est!' (p. 360). But the end of part I culminates with a set speech in which Madeleine details her views on marriage in a programmatic and idealistic thesis which reflects (and perhaps stretches) many of the aspirations of conservative feminism in the *fin de siècle*:

Le mariage pour moi n'est pas une chaîne, mais une association. J'entends être libre, tout à fait libre de mes actes, de mes démarches, de mes sorties, toujours. Je ne pourrais tolérer ni contrôle, ni jalousie, ni discussion sur ma conduite. Je m'engagerais, bien entendu, à ne jamais compromettre le nom de l'homme que j'aurais épousé, à ne jamais le rendre odieux ou ridicule. Mais il faudrait aussi que cet homme s'engageât à voir en moi une égale, une alliée, et non pas une inférieure ni une épouse obéissante et soumise. Mes idées, je le sais, ne sont pas celles de tout le monde, mais je n'en changerai point. (p. 340)

If this reply in the wake of her husband's death to Georges's marriage proposal seems particularly unromantic, it is perhaps because Madeleine's discourse on 'free association' refuses to background the ultimately political nature of such a bond. The fact that the setting out of these conditions is but a prelude to her consent makes it possible to imagine that the end of part 1 could serve as the denouement of a long Maupassant novella. Maupassant underlines the point by offering us a doubly classical closure – with both a marriage and a death. *Bel-Ami*, however, continues beyond this classical ending, and it does so because of the extended narrative possibilities offered by the divorce law of 1884. In other words, a change in family law begets a change in family fiction. Looked at in another way, this state-sponsored refashioning of narrative shapes reveals a philosophical shift in how the teleologies of life are viewed by the secular republic, and it is these shifts and refashionings which Bourget's conservative tale, *Un divorce*, will try to absorb and suppress. In Maupassant's pessimistic vision part 2 of the novel offers an alternative vision to the liberated modernity demanded by Madeleine.

Madeleine therefore undoes the gendered divide of private and public space, for if her thoughts project outwards to a wider social and political universe, the narcissism of Duroy threatens to exclude any authentic engagement with the explicitly politicized public domain on which he reports. As mentioned above, Duroy is captivated by interiors, so much so that he delights in associating women with the domestic spaces they inhabit. The Forestiers' drawing room 'enveloppait doucement, il plaisait, mettait autour du corps quelque chose comme une caresse' (p. 219) and when Madeleine dictates his first article, Duroy marvels at the correlation between character and space, 'Il lui semblait que tout ce qui l'entourait faisait partie d'elle, tout, jusqu'aux murs couverts de livres' (p. 232). His encounter with Clotilde de Marelles at home is, however, far more disconcerting because of the 'désaccord de cette élégance soignée et raffinée avec l'insouci visible pour le logis qu'elle habitait', in other words, the dysmmetry between character and space (p. 254), and when he expresses embarrassment at the thought of her visiting his room, she reminds him that it is him she would be visiting and not his room (p. 263). Georges simply cannot understand this decontextualisation of character which we are invited to interpret as provocative authenticity.

It is Georges who perceives the analogy between politics and sexuality when Madeleine returns with news from the Chamber of Deputies and compares his naivety about the issue of Morocco with Charles's political naivety. For Georges is furious at such a comparison with 'ce cocu de Forestier', both innocents before this same figure of dramatic irony (p. 388). Ironically Georges has just returned from his flirtatious encounter with Mme Walter at Rival's charity event of duelling and shooting. Madeleine's political acumen sees beyond the sexual motive in her exposure of the financial scandal behind the plan to send troops to Morocco. As she notes, 'Aujourd'hui, mon cher, dans les combinaisons politiques il ne faut pas dire: "Cherchez la femme", mais: "Cherchez l'affaire."'

The metaphorical relationship between military and sexual conquest is well-mapped terrain, but it enjoys particular piquancy in the context of this Age of Empire.[12] It is underscored in *Bel-Ami* by a wealth of colonial references, in particular to Georges's own military past in his reworked article on the *Souvenirs d'un chasseur d'Afrique* and the political question of North Africa. Though it is an inconspicuous detail, the tapestry in his entrance hall which depicts the tale of Mars and Venus already invoked in *Nana* could be construed as Marcowitch's true 'masterpiece' (p. 436). But it is the metaphor of flowers in a vase which maps out this connection. When he returns home to his new wife with a bouquet of roses at the start of part 2 chapter 2, Georges discovers three places set at the table and Madeleine putting exactly the same type of flowers in a vase on the mantelpiece, as if his idea has been stolen. This proves particularly galling when he realises that these flowers have been bought because Vaudrec, her long-term lover, is coming round for dinner, as is Madeleine's custom. She puts her husband's flowers in the other vase and takes delight in the appearance of her mantelpiece, and the evening goes off without a hitch. This image is echoed in part 2 chapter 5 when the right-wing deputy, Lambert-Sarrazin, cynically doubts the capacity of the new regime to resist the temptation of sending an army to Tangiers 'en pendant à celle de Tunis, par amour de la symétrie, comme on met deux vases sur une cheminée' (p. 405). Thus the decor of domestic space represents foreign policy. Within the logic of this metaphor, paradoxically, the decorative/invasive function of 'on' is executed not only by colonialist France but also by Madeleine. Hence at the beginning of chapter 7 after the invasion of Morocco, France is referred to as 'la maîtresse de Tanger' (p. 432), and the image of male sexual invasion – of both the female body and the cuckold's domain – is inverted as Madeleine arranges the vases to her own liking. At the announcement of Vaudrec's will in chapter 6 she manipulates the meta-phorical force of flowers and embarrasses Georges by stressing the erotic overtones of the homosocial bond between admirers and husbands:

Il m'apportait des fleurs, chaque lundi. Tu ne t'en étonnais nullement et il ne t'en donnait point, à toi, n'est-ce pas? Aujourd'hui il me donne sa fortune par la même raison et parce qu'il n'a personne à qui l'offrir. Il serait, au contra-ire, extrêmement surprenant qu'il te l'eût laissée? Pourquoi? Que lui es-tu? (p. 428)

Within the classic triangular structure Vaudrec can only offer gifts to Madeleine, and under the dictates of compulsory heterosexuality all that the husband can in effect give to this admirer is his wife. By hinting that the only alternative would involve a revectorization of relations within the adulterous triangle and thus an unthinkable homoeroticism, she asserts the necessity (and thus the innocence) of her role in the transmis-sion of gifts. For men, it seems, can only give to each other via women.

Georges experiences a 'léger trouble moral que produit un change-ment à vue' when he first sets eyes on the daughters of the newspaper proprietor, Walter: 'Il n'avait jamais songé aux filles de son directeur que comme on songe aux pays lointains qu'on ne verra jamais' (p. 293). By the end of the novel, though, Georges will have married Suzanne, and the quasi-colonial dream of the seducer will be fulfilled. By returning to this family scene at the end of the novel (even in an ironic mode) and thus refusing his readers the catharsis of apocalypse, Maupassant brings into question the rhetoric of decadence with which his novel engages. A conservative cultural diagnosis of degeneration belongs to the stock of stereotypes which a writer as untalented as Georges must use: 'comme il prit une peine infinie à découvrir des idées, il prit la spécialité des décla-mations sur la décadence des mœurs, sur l'abaissement des caractères, l'affaissement du patriotisme et l'anémie de l'honneur français' (p. 323). What Maupassant implies is that the urban space is by its very definition engaged in the 'decadent' confection of the natural. When Forestier and Georges meet at the start of the novel and stroll together, the reader is struck by the aimless quality of their *flânerie* which anticipates a narrative shape counter to the developmental structure of *éducation*. In Forestier's words:

On prétend qu'à Paris un flâneur peut toujours s'occuper; ça n'est pas vrai. Moi, quand je veux flâner, le soir, je ne sais jamais où aller. Un tour au bois n'est amusant qu'avec une femme; et on n'en a pas toujours une sous la main; les cafés-concerts peuvent distraire mon pharmacien et son épouse, mais pas moi. Alors, que faire? Rien. (p. 205)

It will be Duroy's aim never to be so alone and so purposeless. He is determined to find the playground which the city seems to offer, and he does so hand in hand with that experienced *citadine*, Clotilde. Forestier's mistake is to be trapped by the urban fantasy of nature confected: 'Il devrait y avoir ici un jardin d'été comme le parc Monceau, ouvert la nuit, où on entendrait de la très bonne musique en buvant des choses fraîches sous les arbres.' And in an absolutely vital distinction, Forestier asserts, 'Ce ne serait pas un lieu de plaisir mais un lieu de flâne.' Pleasure itself has been degraded in the eyes of this world-weary character, but there is no alternative. Only pleasure can fill the 'rien' around which Forestier's mind circles, and he lets Duroy persuade him to visit the Folies-Bergère, whose very name suggests the kitsch adulteration of a natural idyll. Even during Georges's *enlèvement* of Suzanne, the scene of nature is but a playground: 'Elle avait joué à la bergère' (p. 470), not unlike Molière's Angélique.

It is not only in public settings that the decadent simulation of self-consciously artificial nature is to be found. One of the archetypal fictional locations of transgression in the bourgeois novel is that simulacrum of nature, the conservatory (*la serre*), with its configuration of exotic fertility.[13] It is amidst the 'nature factice' of Marcowitch's conservatory that Georges hatches the notion of marrying 'cette petite marionette de chair', Suzanne (p. 438). The Forestiers' salon, however, offers a simulacrum of that simulacrum, as Georges notices:

En entrant dans le salon, il eut de nouveau la sensation de pénétrer dans une serre. De grands palmiers ouvraient leurs feuilles élégantes dans les quatre coins de la pièce, montaient jusqu'au plafond, puis s'élargissaient en jets d'eau. Des deux côtés de la cheminée, des caoutchoucs, ronds comme des colonnes, étageaient l'une sur l'autre leurs longues feuilles d'un vert sombre, et sur le piano deux arbustes inconnus, ronds et couverts de fleurs . . . avaient l'air de plantes factices, invraisemblablement, trop belles pour être vraies. (p. 219)

Just as in Wilde's dictum that life imitates art, so nature (in the form of genuine plants) imitates manufacture, and when the referent itself is *invraisemblable*, the realist-naturalist literary system must come under severe pressure.

As we have seen, the convolutions and *fausses fins* of Maupassant's narrative (the death of Forestier, the marriage of Madeleine and Georges, Vaudrec's will) undo the traditional order of family narrative, but only to replace it with a cynical vision of recycled narratives at odds with Madeleine's prescriptions. The resolution in which Georges divorces Madeleine and marries Suzanne is engineered by staging the melodramatic commonplace of the *flagrant délit d'adultère*.[14] The rhetorical shock of this set scene lies in its reversal of the situation of dramatic irony. No longer the victim, the savvy husband ironizes the ironists by exposing their deception and invading *their* intimacy. Duroy simply laughs when the naked Laroche-Mathieu is shy about dressing in front of him and the police chief because he is quite naked. Duroy has had the last laugh, and when they leave he insists on following the *commissaire* as 'Je suis presque chez moi, ici' (p. 458). He has almost recovered his patriarchal ground (though this 'politesse ironique' can also be read as merely a tacit avowal to the reader of his own acquaintance with such sordid scenarios of seduction). The triumph is also in a sense a verbal one, for Georges manages to pass on that damning sexually ambivalent epithet of 'Salop' which was given to him earlier by Clotilde. He throws the Légion d'honneur procured for him by Laroche-Mathieu into the fireplace with the words: 'Voilà ce que vaut une décoration qui vient de salops de votre espèce' (p. 457). This is the closest we come to a genuine duel in the entire novel as the *commissaire* is forced to come between the two men who are standing toe to toe.

At the end of the novel we return to the Eglise de la Madeleine, which is invoked at the start of the novel and in the wedding scenario. Marriage, however, no longer claims the same definitive status as death, hence the nod and a wink between those birds of a feather, Georges and Clotilde de Marelles, whose 'A bientôt' suggests that this ending is actually only a beginning. In this demystification of the ideal wedding day their reciprocal gaze offers the reader a glimpse of an inverted sublime, not unlike the knowingness of Octave and Valérie at the end of *Pot-Bouille*, though the latter's 'relationship' remains unconsummated. This gaze returns in circular motion to the imprint made on Georges by their initial encounter:

Il en garda le souvenir, les jours suivants, plus que le souvenir, une sorte de sensation de la présence irréelle et persistante de cette femme. Il lui semblait avoir pris quelque chose d'elle, l'image de son corps restée dans ses yeux et la saveur d'un être moral restée dans son cœur. Il demeurait sous l'obsession de son image, comme il arrive quelquefois quand on a passé des heures charmantes auprès d'un être. On dirait qu'on subit une possession étrange, intime, confuse, troublante et exquise parce qu'elle est mystérieuse. (p. 253)

This baroque immersion brings the reader closer to our hero's perspective only to discover the regendering of those archly eroticized terms 'pris' and 'possession' such that Duroy is taken and possessed.

The metaphorical system of the novel culminates in the ironies of the wedding scene (in the Eglise de la Madeleine of course!). In keeping with the colonial subplot Georges and Suzanne are married by the Bishop of Tangiers, who delivers a pompous speech on fidelity and points out to Bel-Ami that he has 'un bel exemple à donner' (p. 478). When the couple kneel towards the altar, the reader is reminded of the adulterous scenario in the Eglise de la Trinité where Georges and Suzanne's mother, Mme Walter, once met. And if Georges, like Jesus in Marcowitch's painting, walks on water then it is on the 'mer lointaine, le grouillement du peuple' which he has always despised (p. 476). In case we miss the point, after the service we read how 'la foule coulait devant lui comme un fleuve' (p. 480). For Georges, along with Octave, is a survivor who unlike other versions of the Don Juan figure, resists the narrative closure of death, which Varenne calls 'la gueuse' (p. 299), but cannot resist that other classic ending, marriage. The irony of this is that Georges, like Octave, has continually threatened the marital system, though not in the same way as Molière's Don Juan. For Georges and Octave prey on married women, whereas their earlier incarnation seems keener to upset the courting plot. In Felman's terms, 'The scandal of seduction seems to be fundamentally tied to the scandal of the broken promise . . . in particular, promises of marriage.'[15] Rather than allowing the plot, its itinerant hero and mobile metaphors to retain their polymorphous quality and enjoy what, in the wake of Deleuze and Guattari, we might term sexual and formal nomadism, Maupassant's rather heavy-handed irony cannot resist rehousing Georges within the realist-naturalist literary system. As Felman suggests, the performative scandal of donjuanism alienates the seducer from the realm of action. When Molière's Don Juan decides to 'risk "performances" other than those of speech and to use physical force to carry his lady love off to sea, he experiences failure, "infelicity", a shipwreck.' Nevertheless, the 'healthy' if unstable conclusion offered by Zola and Maupassant, however ironic and pessimistic they may be, is that Octave and Georges are projected forth into the respective domains of commercial and political activity (the former in *Au bonheur des dames* and the latter as he looks out across the place de la Concorde towards the Palais-Bourbon). The irony is that rhetorical seduction is central to both 'activities'.

Felman also suggests how the Don Juan figure's perpetual return to the scene of seduction undoes the primacy of the paternal figure. Any notion of progression from an originary point is upset by the way in which 'the Donjuanian belief in arithmetic . . . deconstructs, above all, the hierarchical value of the "first"'.[16] This implies 'a general deconstruction of beginning as a basis for identities. In this way Don Juan subverts the principle of genetic reasoning and the institution of paternity.' As such

Don Juan emblematizes the rupture and the gap between paternal conscious-ness and paternal performance, the discontinuity between intention and act: the lack of self-knowledge of the very act of production of meaning; the 'infelicity' or failure of the Father in his role as constative, cognitive authority.

The expectation of a 'relation of consistency and of resemblance of son to father' means that 'the paternal promise is, in other words, a promise of metaphor'. This promise is deconstructed 'by the very figure of [the Don Juan's] own life, which is that of the *anaphora*, of the act of begin-ning ceaselessly renewed through the repetition of promises not carried out, not kept.' But the multiplication of scenes of seduction as a series of carriages pass Georges and Madeleine in the Bois de Boulogne undermines not only the uniqueness of romantic reciprocity, as we have seen, but also Georges's own claim to *singularity*.

The element of male fantasy in this tale of women seduced is never-theless potentially considerable. What a novel such as *Nana* (and indeed the social history of bourgeois sexual mores) also reveals is the commonality beween patriarchy and donjuanism; many a 'good' husband (that is, socially and economically if not morally 'good') is cast in the role of seducer. These are, it seems, merely roles which may coin-cide in the same life and the same person. On the one hand the uncer-tainty of paternity (not only biologically but also in law) relieves the dangers of the woman falling pregnant as far as the Don Juan figure is concerned. If she is married, then by law her husband is deemed to be the child's father (in other words, law has its say over biology). If the fallen woman is unmarried, she and her child must simply suffer the ravages of penury and prejudice.

This is brought out most clearly by Rachel Fuchs who persuasively depicts the period from 1804 to 1912 as an age of paternal irresponsibil-ity.[17] As she explains:

An unwed mother could not name the father of the child on the birth certificate
unless he legally recognized his offspring . . . If the father did not legally recognize the child, as was usually the case, the child's birth certificate provided the
mother's name, but instead of the father's name was the simple phrase 'father
unknown.'

Unlike the married woman whose child would be automatically recognized in law as the progeny of her husband even if she fell pregnant by
another man, there was no similar protection for the *fille mère*, whose
child would have no rights to 'social paternity'. This system has its
origins in Article 340 of the Napoleonic Civil Code on *recherche de la paternité*, enacted in 1804, which prohibited the mother from seeking child
support for any of her children born out of wedlock. Fuchs traces this
beyond Napoleon's chauvinism back to Rousseau's 'antifeminist philosophy' which bases male legal authority in the uncertainty of paternity
(which is so central to traditional arguments about the novel of adultery's patriarchal motivations). As well as reflecting dominant attitudes
towards women's sexuality, Article 340 'accommodated the bourgeoisie's
desire to protect marriage, the family, and inherited property. They
feared that "legitimate" sons would have to share the patrimony with
children the men bore out-of-wedlock and thus lead to the breakdown
of the family.' In other words, the uncertainty of paternity is not simply
the Great Unconscious of the bourgeois century and its literature; it is
rather a conscious element in the construction of a bourgeois ideology
of the family, and just as Napoleonic law can be seen as a corrective to
this notorious uncertainty, so fictions of the abandoned *grisette* in particular can be seen as articulations of paternal fantasy (and not fear). This
system is exposed by feminist novelists of the Third Republic such as
Lucie Delarue-Mardrus who depicts the sorry tale of Marie who wants
to marry the wealthy man who initially raped her but is forced to leave
for Paris in order to escape her father. There she marries a man whose
brutality (despite his initial promises) leads to a tragic end for her and
her son.[18] Philip Nord also identifies 'a deeper level of anxiety about
paternal absenteeism' and notes more generally that 'the child in search
of a father was a stock figure in republican literature'.[19]

Only with the advent of the Third Republic did the pro-natalist
nationalist ideology of regeneration (symbolized on the eve of the Great
War by the title of Fernand Boverat's *Patriotisme et paternité*) dictate a
grudging sympathy with unwed mothers, especially after the Franco-
Prussian War of 1870 and the census results of 1891 which revealed that
for the last five years deaths had outnumbered births in France. Thus

anti-German nationalists such as Camille Rabaud began to question the law on paternity suits. On the other political wing, socialists such as Sicard de Plauzoles also called for paternal financial responsibility for the out-of-wedlock child. Few though wanted a return to the law of 1670 which allowed the mother to seek financial remuneration from any putative father. In Fuchs's terms, 'Most late nineteenth-century politicians wanted to protect married men and feared scandals harmful to the "legitimate family" if married men were pursued for child support for the offspring of an adulterous relationship.'[20] It was left to women such as Julia Bécour to voice the most heartfelt admonitions of the male seducer, and reformists such as Marie Béquet de Vienne to critique *la grève de la paternité*. Pressure emanated from the Second International Congress of Feminine Organizations and Institutions of 1900, but the result of the debate, Gustave Rivet's compromise bill of 1912, failed to address the responsibility of the married seducer. In Fuchs's words, 'married men would not likely have been liable for a paternity search under any of the conditions set forth by the law, except for the possiblity of rape and kidnapping.' It was only that problematic figure, the *célibataire*, who might be forced to feel the faint breeze of change.

On the other hand, the cuckolded husband who must assume the legal responsibility of paternity in which he may have played no biological role, is perhaps not as innocent as patriarchy's fears would have us believe. Although Maupassant fails to foresee the Campardon case and anticipates the wrong kind of *ménage à trois* in his article 'L'Adultère', Maupassant does highlight the ambivalence of the cuckold: 'Et toujours l'éternel doute se produit. Le mari est-il complice, témoin timide et désolé, ou invraisemblablement aveugle?'[21] This element of wishful cuckoldry is consecrated in Molière's bitter refrain, 'Vous l'avez voulu, Georges Dandin.' This connivence is exposed by Marie Maclean's psychoanalytically informed theory of an Amphitryon Complex which accounts for literary versions of that 'yearning to produce something better, more perfect than oneself or than the originary biological partners' by invoking the myth of Zeus (the divine natural father) seducing Alcmene by impersonating Amphitryon (the earthly social father) and thus producing the immortal bastard, Heracles.[22] 'Like the child [in Freud's 'family romance']', we are told, 'the parent may be prepared in imagination to sacrifice biological certainty to the promptings of desire', the philoprogenitive desire for the perfect child. It is interesting for our purposes that Maclean should cite as an example Anatol Karenin's love for the baby daughter. In such a theory the Don Juan figure may well play the role of the supernatural seducer who is manifestly superior to a rather banal social father (in other words, the husband). One purpose of the yet more supernatural tale of the statue which appears at the end may be to demystify this seducer's magical force (usually seen as charisma).

As Georges moves from woman to woman, the reader may start to feel that it is Georges who is being passed between women, and that his high pleasure dividend is simply the effect of his exchange value in the market of seduction. For Mmes Forestier, Walter and Marelles are not simply strangers played off against each other as Georges would have it, and clearly he is himself (ironically for a gossip columnist) the subject of female conversation, in which his code name is Bel-Ami. When he and Madeleine entertain their clique in part 2 chapter 3, Georges seems to be in his element, surrounded by the objects of his desires. Du Roy places on his right Mme Walter, whom he is now courting. From time to time he looks at Clotilde and thinks to himself 'Elle est vraiment plus jolie et plus fraîche', and he even finds his wife 'pas mal' in spite of the anger he feels towards her (p. 391). This is the fantasy of the harem which is taken to almost farcical extremes. At the end of the evening Georges accompanies Mme Walter home in a carriage where he declares his passion with 'cette banale musique d'amour' (p. 392) and arranges a tryst for the next day at the Église de la Trinité. He then returns to escort Clotilde home, before presumably returning to his wife. But ironically, Madeleine's admirer, Laroche-Mathieu, has also attended the party.

Maupassant's drama of seduction finds its complement in *Pierre et Jean* which plays out the question of the uncertainty of paternity from inside the family structure. It is not the legal father but the other son, Pierre, who fears the illegitimacy of his brother: 'il fallait que ce soupçon si léger, si invraisemblable, fût rejeté de lui, *complètement*, pour toujours. Il lui fallait la lumière, la certitude, il fallait dans son cœur la sécurité *complète*, car il n'aimait que sa mère au monde' (p. 763, our italics). So the son in the role of detective reconstructs a fantasy narrative of his mother being seduced by the Maréchal. What he fears is not so much the deception of his father but the desublimation of the maternal icon (the mother who is supposedly always certain). Pierre's attempts to objectify this crisis are shown in his rather naive affirmation that this is not a matter of jealousy but of knowledge and belief. As his suspicions grow though, it is knowledge itself which he fears: 'Plus il songeait, moins il doutait. Il se sentait traîné par sa logique, comme par une main qui attire et étrangle vers l'intolérable certitude.' (p. 769), for the desire for knowledge within the family cannot be truly objectified precisely because it is internal. This desire, however, turns Pierre into an alienated ethnographer of his own circumstances, and amidst his own family, 'il les regardait en étranger qui observe, et il se croyait en effet entré tout à coup dans une famille inconnue' (p. 778). So the obsessive desire for cognitive completeness implies that the seduction of the mother represents a gap in family history which undoes all manner of family relations, not least between (half?-)siblings. It is this sort of convoluted crisis of knowledge to which Zola's *Le Docteur Pascal* responds.

CHAPTER 4

Incest in 'Les Rougon-Macquart'

Les arbres sont aussi des monumens [*sic*], et ils imposent le respect
au même titre que l'ouvrage sorti des mains de l'homme.[1]

Published in 1893, *Le Docteur Pascal* enjoys a manifest structural
significance as the closing text in the *Rougon-Macquart* series, but critical
interest in Zola has tended to favour the other novels. Though one can
understand Zola's complaints about having to reread the whole of his
series in preparation for its concluding composition, Pascal's reflections
on the family do offer a highly literal as well as symbolic *relecture* of the
Rougon-Macquart family tree.[2] The account of the 'inceste' (Zola uses
the term) between the doctor and geneticist, Pascal, and his niece,
Clotilde, acquires a particular consequentiality when viewed in terms of
the spatial disposition of desiring relations and the issue of paternal
knowledge. The very foundations of the series in *La Fortune des Rougon* set
up the interplay of legitimacy and illegitimacy which is played out in the
ramifications of the family tree. The threat of illegitimacy and uncertainty threatens every union, be it conjugal or otherwise, for even the
union of legitimate marriage relies on a bond with another family and
hence a susceptibility to the secret history of its illegitimacies and seduc-
tions. Families usually perpetuate themselves by seeking bonds outside of
their own ranks, but the *renouement* (rather than *dénouement*) of *Le Docteur
Pascal* ties up the ever burgeoning family tree by crowning the plot of
progeny with this fertile incestuous bond. Within the context of Zola's
cycle, *Le Docteur Pascal* must terminate the extensions of this family tree.
Whereas des Esseintes is the final representative of a consanguineously
degenerating aristocratic family, *Le Docteur Pascal* suggests both a provi-
sional termination of the family as a principle of narrative structure and
a biological regeneration at odds with these æsthetic imperatives of
closure. In accordance with his developing ideology of *Fécondité*, the
family novel can never be wholly conclusive; it must imply its own partial

nature by the production of another child as a token supplement to the future. There is clearly a problem for the Naturalist project in the notion that reality is an interminable process to which literary plots can hardly do justice, for narrative closure provides a necessarily artificial termination in the flux of ongoing existence. The importance, however, of supposedly 'real experience' in Naturalist aims is manifest in its theoretical rhetoric. So novels reach their end even though a bourgeois version of history must imagine its own perpetuation. *L'Education sentimentale* accommodates history in the shadow of its plot by a circular journey which testifies to a disabling *décalage* between the personal and the political. But Pascal and Clotilde's son, otherwise known as the 'messie attendu', reaches out into the future in a final gesture of blithe positivism, and therefore allows this terminal moment to imagine its own perpetuation.[3]

The cyclical nature of Zola's project implies a vision of the historical process in terms of spirals of biological and social degeneration and regeneration (in a manner which recalls Vico's model of the *corsi i ricorsi* of history), and imposes an imperative of structural coherence at the level of writing. Just as the plot summaries, the retelling of family history, and the evocation of a myth of the origins of writing suggest a retrospective motion in *Le Docteur Pascal*, so *La Fortune des Rougon*, which was written before the demise of the imperial regime, prefigures this concern for terminations of different kinds. The cycle begins by describing a crisis of political denouement in the Plassans of 1851: 'le seul sentiment général était qu'un dénouement approchait. Et c'était l'ignorance de ce dénouement qui tenait dans une inquiétude ahurie ce peuple de bourgeois poltrons' (1, p. 97). It is thus clear that the apocalyptic rhetoric of the *fin de siècle* is but a special case of a continual cultural gesture towards a historical demise often couched in theological terms. In a telling inversion of the direction of influence within the family tree between father and son, Eugène warns Pierre Rougon in his letters of an imminent 'catastrophe finale', 'cette catastrophe, dont elle [Félicité] ne devinait pas bien le genre ni la portée, devint pour elle une sorte de fin du monde: Dieu rangerait les élus à sa droite et les damnés à sa gauche, et elle se mettait parmi les élus' (1, p. 94). Such apocalyptic discourse conceals a sense of political crisis and change to which Félicité must respond. A theological rhetoric which might imply an end to History actually foregrounds the historical process at its most acute point. Félicité's presence in *Le Docteur Pascal*, however, will intensify the cyclical motion commonly identified with *Les Rougon-Macquart*. By mapping the end of the cycle onto the end of the century, Zola manipulates an echo of the origins of tante Dide's resources. She inherits 'vers la fin du siècle dernier, un vaste terrain situé dans le faubourg, derrière l'ancien cimetière Saint-Mittre' (1, p. 41). As we know, reflections of that revolutionary *fin de siècle* will come to haunt the end of the nineteenth century. In *Les Rougon-Macquart* the shift from legitimate to illegitimate political regimes is refigured in the mythology of the family. It is surely no coincidence that Rougon, Adélaïde's legitimate husband and father to Pierre, dies in 1788, and that it is precisely in 1789 that she takes Macquart as her lover and gives birth to the illegitimate Antoine.[4]

Though incest might appear to be a more radical form of the same category of illicit sexual behaviour to which adultery also belongs, the spatial implications of these bonds suggest an oppositional model which allows us to view Zola's novel as a reactionary response to his own narratives of sexual uncertainty (and to the novel of adultery as a whole). Though both threaten the order of family life, adultery does so by explosion, whereas incest threatens the family unit with implosion (this unit is created in spatial form when, as a young girl, Clotilde is sent by her father, Aristide, to live with uncle Pascal under the same roof). As such these contrary transgressions represent the critical extremes of the regular systole and diastole of the social organism. In the words of Letourneau which Zola notes down in his preparatory writings at the very start of the series, 'La vie se peut définir un double mouvement d'assimilation et de désassimilation, dont les lois de l'endosmose et de l'exomose régissent les conditions principales' (5, p. 1677). The concern for what might be termed the adulterine porosity of the family cell, which allows for the migration of desire, is countered by that apparently most transgressive of relations, incest. Whereas the carnal knowledge of adultery undermines the cognitive authority of the cuckold by piercing the supposed self-enclosure of the family, the apparently transgressive motif of incest attempts to reassert the self-contained nature of desires held within the domestic arena. Incest appears to offer the father what we may term hæmic certainty, in other words the supposedly secure knowledge that his partner's family history is as respectable as his own. So Pascal appears to learn what fathers want to know – the sexual as well as intellectual *connaissance* that embodies the hæmic truth of the family tree. Even legitimate, non-incestuous, non-adulterous marriage involves another family tree, another field of potential illegitimacies and uncertainties (as Coupeau discovers in *L'Assommoir* when he marries into the illegitimate Macquart line and fathers Nana, only to see her echo the appearance of Gervaise's first lover, Lantier). So, paradoxically, the very fact of incest seems to ensure the rights of paternity, as the otherness of Woman is defused by the consanguinity of Clotilde and Pascal. The 'reconnaissance' (5, p. 1067) or gratitude which inspires Clotilde's love includes that other sense of *reconnaissance* as anagnorisis which underpins the consanguineous identification of self in other and other in self. The degree of 'appearance' and 'supposition' in such a denial of exterior relations is merely testament to the delusory nature of this quest for paternal self-assertion. For Pascal and Clotilde are not biological twins, after all; their genetic histories are linked but not identical. Moreover, Zola's invocation of the nineteenth-century science of genetics stresses the fragility of the fidelity/adultery opposition, for in any case the genetic bequests of family history visit the crimes of the past upon succeeding generations in the Rougon-Macquart line. This desire for genetic knowledge central to Zola's Naturalist enterprise multiplies upwards the stakes in the desire for paternal knowledge reflected in the novel of adultery.

In Zola's new repopulationist narrative (in a somewhat bizarre cohabitation with the nationalistic politics of *revanche*) the tension beween fertility and sterility replaces the oppositional pairing of legitimacy and illegitimacy. This virtual cult of reproduction, which underpinned Zola's support for the 'Alliance nationale pour le relèvement de la population française' and the 'Société maternelle parisienne', has grave implications for the possibilities open to women. This ideological fervour, defended previously in 'Aux mères heureuses' which was published in *Le Figaro* on 18 April 1891,[5] will of course reach its full extent in *Fécondité* where (in Serres's terms quoted above in chapter 1) milk flows above and beyond the fluid dynamics of blood and gold. The contrary pole of sterility is glorified in the vision of des Esseintes, as we shall see in the next chapter. As Zola writes in *La Revue blanche* on 1 March 1902, 'Le mariage n'est qu'un mot prononcé par le code . . . c'est de l'union qu'il s'agit'.[6] This valorisation of fertility in spite of any transgression of official values on the part of the parents is inscribed in the paratextual tale of *Le Docteur Pascal*'s dedications. Genette opens his chapter on 'Les dédicaces' in *Seuils* by drawing a distinction between 'deux pratiques':

l'une concerne la réalité matérielle d'un exemplaire singulier, dont elle consacre en principe le don ou la vente effective, l'autre concerne la réalité idéale de l'œuvre elle-même, dont la possession (et donc la cession, gratuite ou non) ne peut être, bien évidemment, que symbolique . . . les verbes distinguent fort heureusement ces deux actions: *dédier* pour la dédicace d'oeuvre, *dédicacer* pour la dédicace d'exemplaire.[7]

He also notes the reticence of realist and naturalist authors in this regard, for instance: 'Zola, sauf omission, n'a dédié que *Madeleine Férat* à Manet, et, *in extremis* et comme par remords, *Le Docteur Pascal*, dernier volume des *Rougon-Macquart*, à sa mère (*in memoriam*) et à sa femme.' In the latter case Zola offers to his public readers the following official dedication: 'A la mémoire de MA MERE et à MA CHERE FEMME je dédie ce roman qui est le résumé et la conclusion de toute mon œuvre' (5, p. 915). The rarity of Zola's dedications suggests that this textual event embodies more than mere habit or *politesse*. Indeed, this tale of remorse is not the whole story, as Genette fails to mention Zola's handwritten *dédicace d'exemplaire*:

A ma bien-aimée Jeanne, – à *ma Clotilde, qui m'a donné le royal festin* de sa jeunesse et qui m'a rendu mes trente ans, en me faisant *le cadeau* de ma Denise et de mon Jacques, les deux chers enfants pour qui j'ai écrit ce livre, afin qu'ils sachent, en le lisant un jour, combien j'ai adoré leur mère et de quelle respectueuse tendresse ils devront lui payer plus tard le bonheur dont elle m'a consolé, dans mes grands chagrins. (5, p. 1573, our italics)

This vocabulary of the gift can also be read transparently from the novel itself in a manner which reinforces to some degree this identification of actual mistress and fictional heroine: '[Clotilde] lui [Pascal] fit *le royal cadeau de son corps* . . . Elle avait ouvert les bras, elle *se donnait* toute . . . "Si tu savais comme je suis contente que tu me trouves belle, puisque cette beauté, je puis t'en faire *le cadeau*"' (5, p. 1128, our italics).

Alain Decaux tells us that the dual dedication to mistress and illegitimate children, dated 20 June 1893, replaces in Jeanne's copy the printed dedication to wife and mother which was torn out by Zola.[8] The violence of this adulteration which replaces one erotic relation with another might well be interpreted as a compensatory response to Alexandrine Zola's appropriation of the letters that her husband had sent Jeanne Rozerot, when Alexandrine was informed of the adultery by anonymous letter in November 1891. By this time, of course, Zola had fathered two children by Jeanne whereas his marriage had been barren, and what needs to be foregrounded is the link between the incest narrative in *Le Docteur Pascal* and this paratextual narrative of adultery it harbours. For Zola's private tale of adultery articulates his relation to the order of family life and to the encoding by bourgeois culture of the dramatic ironies inherent within marital transgression. Zola replaces the epistolary texts Jeanne has lost by offering her this key novel which completes the *Rougon-Macquart* series in an affirmation of the fertility of transgressive sexual practice. It is the fertility common to Zola's private adulterous relationship and this fiction of incest which allows Zola to equate Jeanne and Clotilde in the handwritten *dédicace d'exemplaire*. The dedication as an apparent gift in fact conceals a system of exchange which crystallizes the contractual nature of author-reader relations implicit within the mimetic writing project. The *page d'amour* of the *dédicace d'exemplaire* appears to set up a tension with the *dédicace d'œuvre*, in other words a tension between the private and the public, fertility and sterility, the adulterous relation with Jeanne and the conjugal bond with Alexandrine, the uniqueness of handwriting and the mechanical reproduction of print. Yet in both a grammatical and an intimate sense, Jeanne is the third person . . . or the Other Woman, propelled by the act of naming, in this supposedly private dedication, beyond a 'je-tu' reciprocity. This theoretically private manuscript dedication from the wayward husband to his lover is itself displaced by another, public and oral dedication to his wife. At the banquet held on 21 June 1893 to celebrate the completion of the series, the short speech by Zola's publisher, Charpentier, concludes by offering a toast to Zola's wife, Alexandrine, 'la compagne courageuse et dévouée des jours d'autrefois, des jours heureusement lointains de chagrin et de misère'.[9]

To an extent Zola clearly projects Pascal as a fictional alter ego who constructs the genetic records of the family recounted in the previous nineteen novels. But unlike the Naturalist narrator who bathes in the material complexity and sensory intensity of modern life, the doctor only connects with the outside world through intellectual paradigms (via genetic history and medical diagnosis), whilst his emotional life is framed within his own domestic realm. The particular irony is that doctors in this period enjoyed an unusual access to the corseted female body and thus provided an index of the very porosity which Pascal's incestuous love seeks to deny. As the self-concerned Bellombre discovers, absolute denial of the external world is in Zola's view bound to fail (as des Esseintes also learns). The baby who replaces Pascal at the end of the novel reaches out into the world in a gesture of 'healthy curiosity' already permitted within the encoding of domestic space in the novel. For at the very start of the novel light filtering through the shutters allows Pascal to read: 'Dans la chaleur de l'ardente après-midi de juillet, la salle, aux volets soigneusement clos, était pleine d'un grand calme. Il ne venait des trois fenêtres, que de minces flèches de lumière, par les fentes des vieilles boiseries' (5, p. 917). Similarly, illuminating the image of Madonna with child at the start of the final chapter, 'les volets, soigneusement clos, ne laissaient pénétrer, à travers les fentes, que de minces flèches de soleil, dans l'ombre assoupie et tiède de la vaste pièce' (5, p. 1024).

In terms of Naturalist theory, the representation of spaces, private and public, is equated with a determinant milieu. As Zola explains, 'l'homme ne peut être séparé de son milieu . . . il est complété par son vêtement, par sa maison, par sa ville, par sa province'.[10] In particular, Jean Borie illuminates the 'système de la maison' in Zola's writing where 'le monde se partage entre une clôture de forteresse et une irrésistible béance'.[11] The 'élément constitutif' of his houses is 'la cloison, . . . trait qui découpe et donc qui définit. Système de cloisons mobiles ou immobiles, la maison est bien pour l'imagination matériau linguistique.' At a metatextual level, we might note how Zola conceptualizes the writing of the series in terms of architectural construction. In his *Discours au banquet de l'Association générale des étudiants*, he reflects:

Je suis un peu comme l'ouvrier qui termine la maison où il compte abriter ses vieux jours, et qui s'inquiète du temps qu'il fera désormais. La pluie va-t-elle lui endommager ses murs? Si le vent souffle du nord, ne lui arrachera-t-il pas son toit? Et, surtout, a-t-il construit assez solidement pour résister à la tempête? N'a-t-il épargné ni les matériaux résistants ni les heures de rude besogne?[12]

By playing on the notion of *le temps*, Zola expresses his fear that the house of his family history will be adulterated by adversarial cultural forces.

Indeed, the initial taboo between Pascal and Clotilde is set out in spatial terms. On the one hand, she is forbidden access to his work, in particular 'jamais elle n'entrait dans cette chambre, où il aimait à cacher certains travaux, et qui restait close, ainsi qu'un tabernacle' (5, p. 939); and on the other, her bedroom (with its wall hanging depicting busts of the sphinx) is out of bounds to the master of the house: 'cette chambre, où il n'entrait jamais, avait la douceur des lieux sacrés, qui contentent les soifs inassouvies de l'impossible' (p. 1060). This spatial exclusivity reflects an intellectual gap between their respective preoccupations, for this religiously fervent young woman cannot accept the scientific positivism of her uncle and he is rightly suspicious of the influence of Félicité and Martine. In particular he denies Clotilde access to his genetic records of the family: 'quand tu rangeras, ne touche pas aux dossiers là-haut . . . C'est défendu' (p. 77). It is only by her gradual immersion in the intellectual endeavours of Pascal that their affection grows, and as the layout of the house shows it is only possible to walk from his bedroom to hers by crossing the scientist's study. Thus an analogy is engineered between the private taboos of sexual morality and the cultural taboos which demarcate the cultural space of the *fin de siècle* (and this house in

Plassans). Critics have traditionally characterized Pascal and Clotilde as markers of alternative philosophies who ventriloquize none too obliquely the dominant voices of the epoch. Pascal represents science, naturalism, materialism, reference, reason, maturity, in short, the phallocentric. He has Clotilde produce botanical sketches for his work, and we find 'dans ces sortes de copies, une minutie, une exactitude de dessin et de couleur extraordinaire' (p. 920). In an act of artistic revolt, she angers Pascal by producing 'sur une autre feuille, toute une grappe de fleurs imaginaires, des fleurs de rêve, extravagantes et superbes'. She symbolises Symbolism, and embodies mysticism, the irrational, transcendentalism, youth, and an endoxalised femininity. The union of the dialectical moments in the text represented by the positivistic scientificity of Pascal and the mystical utopianism of Clotilde signifies in a kind of cosmic marriage the utopia of the text as *bilan*. Though often dismissed as a *roman à thèse*, *Le Docteur Pascal* should perhaps be classed as a *roman à synthèse*. This synthesis is, of course, incestuous. In *Totem and Taboo* Freud notes how, 'anything that diverts the patient's thoughts to the forbidden object, anything that brings him into intellectual contact with it, is just as much prohibited as direct physical contact'.[13] This implies an active link between sexual and intellectual taboos. One tragic effect of *Le Docteur Pascal* seems to lie in the fact that the ideal taboo of intellectual synthesis is only ever transgressed metaphorically in terms of the physical taboo that Clotilde and Pascal defy, as if the body's value were but rhetorical. Yet as a fiction of the origins of writing *Les Rougon-Macquart*, *Le Docteur Pascal* mitigates this tragedy given that it is Clotilde, perhaps with her child, who shall write the family history that Pascal has prepared.

The act of seduction is based on a fictionalized narrator–audience relationship when Pascal tells her (and reminds the reader) of the previous plots which constitute their common family history. This is their own *texte de plaisir* which they feel compelled to prolong as sexually active characters rather than merely by speaking and listening. Their sexual union is repeatedly idealized by an erasure of place which marks a regression to a utopia of presocietal organization: 'ils allaient passer la nuit dans cette passion de savoir, sans besoin de sommeil, en dehors du temps, et des lieux' (p. 1005); then 'la nuit entière s'était écoulée à cette terrible leçon de vie, sans que ni Pascal ni Clotilde eussent conscience du lieu où ils étaient, ni du temps qui fuyait' (p. 1024); and 'le lieu, le temps, les âges avaient disparu' (p. 1061); and as their love blossoms, 'c'était bien vrai qu'ils s'aimaient hors du monde, si loin, si haut, que pas un des bruits ordinaires de leur existence ne leur parvenait' (p. 1108), by contrast with the musical polyphony of apartments which seems to invite Octave Mouret when he is first taken upstairs to his room.

In wider epistemological terms the *interdit* of incest offers a fitting challenge to the naturalist fantasy of 'tout dire' also voiced in the novel by Pascal. This fantasy of an absolute inclusiveness (or what has been termed a 'naturalisme pervers')[14] in which all dare speak their name should therefore recognize no taboos. Within the genetic science that Zola draws upon, the mythology of the virgin is reworked in the notion that a woman never escapes the biological imprint of her first lover. As a result, Nana bears a 'ressemblance physique, par influence, avec le premier amant de sa mère, Lantier', according to the 1893 version of the genealogical tree. Although Nana's father is Coupeau, she appears to be related to Lantier.[15] Gervaise functions as a genetic vessel connecting the two. This physical resemblance has perturbing overtones for the relationship between Nana and Lantier. In chapter 11 of *L'Assommoir* we learn what the hatmaker knows: 'Lantier voyait Nana bien souvent. Oh! elle n'en aurait pas mis la main au feu, il était homme à faire pire, quand une jupe lui trottait dans la tête' (2, p. 747). The implication is almost made that Nana inherits her mother's lover, and that a quasi-incestuous link connects them, even though Lantier is not her biological father. This casts a dubious retrospective light on Lantier's offer to Gervaise, at the time of Maman Coupeau's death, that Nana may sleep in his bed. In a prefiguration of her future career, Nana exhibits 'son air bête, son air du jour de l'an, quand on lui donnait des pastilles de chocolat. Et on n'eut pas besoin de la pousser, bien sûr' (p. 654). Hence, incest acts not only as a theme of family history but also as a figure of other sexual relationships which are deemed inappropriate. Far from being unrepresentable because it is taboo, incest comes to represent a range of transgressions which dynamise Zola's family plots. As such, it functions as the covert centre of a web of ideologically charged frames of interpretation which touch upon questions of privacy, property and legitimacy.

Indeed the final novel only succeeds in an idealistic evocation of a reciprocity ultimately sure in its exclusivity after overcoming the threats from Félicité's nosy interventions and Raimond's romantic rivalry for Clotilde's affections. Félicité interprets Pascal's research (which focusses on the story of *Les Rougon-Macquart*) as an illegitimate *fuite* of private information. Félicité fears that social form of investigation and policing known as gossip, hence her anger over the threat presented to 'la légende des Rougon' by the rumours being spread in Plassans about the presents Pascal buys for Clotilde. This is the sign of a certain impotence in the face of the absorption of romance into the economic nexus (as Pascal cannot escape the intersubjective encounter of shopping – not wholly unlike the exclusive des Esseintes, even if the latter does as it were bring the market to his own home). For the gift is never purely a gift; hitherto it has been an object of exchange. Gossip – another social currency – foregrounds the porous interface of home and town, of private and public, which undermines the domestic enclosure. Félicité is equally anxious to censor Pascal's attempts to write the *Rougon-Macquart* series, 'résolu à ne laisser debout que les beaux documents, cette légende qui la faisait saluer comme une majesté tombée'. She exhibits a pyromanical aversion to Pascal's warts-and-all version of the family tale. She wants only an Official History to be told, sanctioning the narrative closure of family history, the dictation of social perception. She hates nothing more than the disclosures of the novel cycle to which she belongs, and the novel qua novel is testament to the ultimate failure of her plot.

The idealized sexual bond between uncle and niece (as figures of science and imagination) also bespeaks Zola's own fantasy of an intellectual mastery which could accommodate the diverse strands of a *fin de siècle* culture whose avant-garde had already turned its back on naturalism. This redirection by incest of the vectors of reproduction which are seen most clearly on the family tree also suggests a particular model of reading which cuts across the essentially linear unfolding of the series through historical time and biological process. Within the series the figure of incest acts as a structuring principle which links branches of the tree and novels which might otherwise remain disparate. Such a transgressive 'zigzagging' effect takes us, literally and laterally, across the terrain of the family, from novel to novel, and thus allows us to read the series qua series. As such trees, bodies and books form a symbolic chain.

This echoes the image of the body represented as a tree which we find, for example, in the Enlightenment's *Encyclopédie*.[16] Similarly Tante Dide appears as a 'squelette jaunie, desséchée là, telle qu'un arbre séculaire dont il ne reste que l'écorce' (5, p. 973). In Pascal's upbringing of Clotilde, 'Dans sa croyance que les arbres poussaient droit, quand on ne les gênait point, il lui avait permis de grandir à sa guise' (p. 984). In a reciprocal metaphor, as he shows her the family tree, 'son doigt se mit à indiquer les cas, sur la vieille feuille de papier jaune, comme sur une planche anatomique' (pp. 1006–7). When Pascal realises that his ill health means that he will be unable to write his family history, he imagines his heart to be the 'couleur de feuille morte' (p. 1179). The *feuille* can, of course, be both a leaf on the metaphorical family tree and the sheet of paper upon which that family history is written. Such wordplay betrays an economic logic. The relation of tree to book describes a process of material production: for paper is, of course, a product of the tree and the medium of a book. Zola's use of the family tree as the skeleton on which to hang his novelistic corpus is an actualization of what might be termed the arboreal logic of classic fiction whose plot shoots forth organically in sequential (and consequential) patterns of causality. The cultural theory of Gilles Deleuze and Felix Guattari provides a wider context in which to situate the figure of the tree. Zola's writing fits into their first category of cultural artefacts, the 'livre-racine' where 'l'arbre est déjà l'image du monde, ou bien la racine est l'image de l'arbre-monde. C'est le livre classique, comme belle intériorité organique, signifiante et subjective'.[17] The vertical, hierarchical and paternalist order of the tree describes a model of 'classical' writing at odds with avant-garde practice. It is precisely this conflict which the *fin de siècle* witnesses. So epistemologically, *Les Rougon-Macquart* can be defined as a 'livre-arbre', whose founding thematic and narratological structure is also that of a tree.

The metafictional concerns of Zola's novel are filtered through the reading tastes of Clotilde: 'son continuel étonnement, sa continuelle indignation, étaient de voir que, dans les romans d'amour, on ne se préoccupait guère de l'enfant . . . Le sexe des héros, dans les romans distingués, n'était plus qu'une machine à passion' (p. 1086). This is echoed in an article on 'Dépopulation' in *Le Figaro*, 23 May 1896, in which Zola criticises the novel of adultery for its failure to represent the new-born child:

Dans notre littérature aussi, on ne fait plus d'enfants . . . L'éternel adultère y règne en maître, et le pis est qu'il est infécond; car, si l'amant, au lieu du mari, fécondait la femme, ça compterait tout de même, pour la nature; mais l'enfant n'apparaît presque jamais, parce qu'il est encombrant et sans élégance; l'enfant a cessé d'être littéraire.[18]

Clotilde's repudiation of the erotic self-indulgence of major novels of the time allows Zola to associate purified emotion with the perversion of incest, whilst underpinning Zola's own preoccupation with the reproductive results of sex. She is neither Emma Bovary nor Marie Pichon. Though Zola plans to conclude the series in a tone of doubt as well as hope (1602), the confidence embodied in the unnamed child (originally given the name, Victor, with its Wagnerian overtones) provides a conspicuous response to the *fin de siècle*'s sense of historical crisis, as the stakes of the future have only been raised by this use of the incest motif. As Durkheim points out:

Là où il existe des tares organiques, même simplement virtuelles [la consanguinité] les aggrave parce qu'elle les additionne. Mais, par la même raison, elle renforce les qualités que présentent également les parents. Si elle est désastreuse pour les organismes mal venus, elle confirme et fortifie ceux qui sont bien doués.[19]

This idealization of incestuous love is at odds with other depictions of incest, as the epitome of decadent artifice in *La Curée* and of brutish nature in *La Terre* in particular.

The uncle–niece relationship in *Le Docteur Pascal* is not unique in *Les Rougon-Macquart*. In part 2, chapter 4 of *La Terre* we learn how Suzanne Lengaigne has run off with a *clerc de notaire* to Chartres so as to escape the 'débandades d'hommes' to which country girls are prey:

Est-ce qu'un vieux de quarante ans, un oncle à elle, ne l'avait pas eue déjà, avant qu'elle partît à Châteaudun, un jour qu'ils épuchaient ensemble des carottes? Et, baissant la voix, Berthe dit, avec les mots, comment ça s'était passé. Françoise, pliée en deux, riait à s'étouffer, tant ça lui semblait drôle. (4, p. 477)

The comedy of articulating the *interdit* is transferred to the level of narrative by the reference to the self-parodically phallic carrots. In *Pot-Bouille* the overtones are clear when Berthe and Hortense Josserand try to get their uncle, Narcisse Bachelard, so drunk that he will give them both twenty francs (3, pp. 40–5). We read how 'elles s'étaient jetées à son cou, lui prodiguaient des noms de tendresse, baisaient son visage enflammé, sans répugnance pour l'odeur de débauche canaille qu'il exhalait'. M. Josserand has no doubts about the connotations of such behaviour and shows 'une révolte, lorsqu'il vit les grâces vierges de ses filles se frotter à ces hontes ramassées sur les trottoirs'. The ambivalence of 'filles' is amplified by the novel's analogy between bourgeois adultery and prostitution in general. 'L'oncle [Bachelard]', we read, 'disait . . . que, lorsqu'on voulait vingt francs, il fallait les gagner. Et ces demoiselles, lasses et contentées, soufflaient à sa droite et à sa gauche, les lèvres encore tremblantes, dans l'énervement de leur désir'. The dubious nature of this avuncular affection is further suggested by Bachelard's revelation at the café Anglais of his pædophilic relationship with Fifi, which he defines in familial terms: 'je suis un papa pour elle . . .' (p. 191).

La Curée (1872), the second novel in the *Rougon-Macquart* cycle, describes how stepson and stepmother, Maxime and Renée, fall in love. At the level of character, Clotilde provides a connection between this novel and *Le Docteur Pascal*. She is introduced in chapter 2 of *La Curée* as the daughter of Aristide and Angèle (1, p. 365). The circumstances which draw Pascal and Clotilde together are also elucidated. Several times he asks Saccard if she could stay with him 'pour égayer la maison silencieuse de savant'. Finally Saccard agrees. Homosocial bonds within the family between Pascal and Saccard are confirmed, as Clotilde is passed between men, just as Renée will be. As her mother lies on her deathbed, Clotilde cradles her doll gently so as not to disturb Angèle (p. 378). It is thus that the conditions for the last novel in the cycle are set. This maternal image returns with the birth of Clotilde's child and the scenes of motherly attention in the final chapter of the novel series. Pascal may have died but the son replaces the father.

The incestuous if not consanguineous passion between Renée and Maxime is foregrounded in chapter 4 of *La Curée* by their embrace in the salon blanc at the café Riche. This 'faute suprême' is explained as a verbal transgression, 'et tout fut dit' (p. 456). A 'reborn' Renée is transfixed by the verbal articulation of the strictly *interdit*. She can tell herself, 'j'ai mon crime' (p. 494), just as Emma Bovary finds delight in the very language of adultery when she exclaims: 'J'ai un amant! un amant!'[20] Words rather than actions become the site of transgression. From the start it is clear that Renée and Maxime do not blame themselves (p. 459). When stepson and stepmother consummate their passion, the husband Aristide is being doubly cheated, both by his second wife, Renée, and by his son by his previous marriage, Maxime. Incest in this case is therefore also adultery and for Maxime this *amour* actually satisfies the *amour-propre* of adultery: 'c'était la première femme mariée qu'il possédait. Il ne songeait pas que le mari était son père' (p. 482). The internalised narrative of adultery postpones the return of the repressed at the level of language even though the taboo has already been broken. Ironically the passion of Renée and Maxime transgresses the calculating norms of adulterous behaviour. They meet nightly 'd'une impudence parfaite, se cachant à peine, oubliant les précautions les plus classiques de l'adultère' (p. 483). They use the language of adultery to displace this sense of guilt whilst failing to conform to the cultural patterns of such a model of behaviour.

For Zola's narrator their love is without doubt a product of a decadent milieu: 'L'acte brutal ne fut que la crise aiguë de cette inconsciente maladie d'amour. Dans le monde affolé où ils vivaient, leur faute avait poussé comme sur un fumier gras de sucs équivoques; elle s'était développée avec d'étranges raffinements, au milieu de particulières conditions de débauche' (p. 481). This is perversion in an Offenbachian mode where any ennobling *gravitas* dissolves in the Bacchanalian frenzy of imperial society. What appears in Lévi-Strauss's terms to be a return to nature is actually facilitated by a particular culture, indeed by the very artifice of culture, symbolised by the vestimentary code of the 'tunique' and the 'habit de garde'. In chapter 4 we learn how:

L'incestueuse s'habituait à sa faute, comme à une robe de gala, dont les raideurs l'auraient d'abord gênée. Elle suivait les modes de l'époque, elle s'habillait et se déshabillait à l'exemple des autres. Elle finissait par croire qu'elle vivait au milieu d'un monde supérieur à la morale commune, où les sens s'affinaient et se développaient, où il était permis de se mettre nue par la joie de l'Olympe entier. Le mal devenait un luxe, une fleur piquée dans les cheveux, un diamant attaché sur le front. (pp. 510–11)

Nudity is clothed in the culture of the period. The narrator perceives in this culture an inverted sense of values. Culture (or, in Lévi-Strauss's terms, the taboo) does not suppress nature (or incest); clothes become a veil which safeguard the perversities of the body from the self-reflexive gaze. The perfect form of the diamond suggests how culture might find an image of its own self-conception within nature. For the terms of the taboo and its transgression are confused in this exemplar of æsthetic wholeness. Docteur Edouard Toulouse, we may note, claims that, '[Zola] aime . . . beaucoup les bijoux et les machines à vapeur; c'est-à-dire le fini et la solidité du travail. Une machine à vapeur en diamant serait pour lui la plus belle des choses'.[21] The image of the diamond as nature perfected deconstructs the nature/culture binarism which, in Lévi-Strauss's terms, is at the heart of the incest taboo. This image also functions as a metaphor of artistic closure. Indeed, in *Le Docteur Pascal*, Pascal showers Clotilde with jewellery. In return, she must, in theory, complete the family history that he is unable to finish.

Though the incest in *La Curée* is not consanguineous, the appearance of sibling bonds functions as a sign of a proximity which excludes the older Aristide. When they first meet, a fourteen-year-old Maxime tells a twenty-one-year-old Renée, 'vous pourriez être ma sœur' (p. 405). This exclusion of the father is reversed by the homosocial bond between father and son which emerges after the revelation of this incest in chapter 6. Saccard stands in the doorway listening to Renée who is asking Maxime to elope with her. Saccard is gripped by 'ce coup suprême qui faisait enfin crier en lui l'époux et le père' (p. 570). As a divided subject, Saccard must select one of these roles. He chooses paternity, and takes Maxime with him to say goodbye to Louise and her father. Renée looks on in astonishment at such an enduring friendship between father and son. The axis of generations is displaced by the axis of gender. She stares at herself in the mirror only to see father and son mocking her. This realisation of her status as an object of exchange between generations of men coincides with a lucid appraisal of the relation between the twin plots of flesh and of gold: 'Saccard l'avait jetée comme un enjeu, comme une mise de fonds, et . . . Maxime s'était trouvé là, pour ramasser ce louis tombé de la poche du spéculateur. Elle restait une valeur dans la portefeuille de son mari' (p. 574). She tries to split up father and son by telling Saccard the details of their incestuous affair and how Maxime had once visited her, seen another man (actually Saccard himself) and thus abandoned her.

The novel concludes, however, with Renée's ruin, as she returns full circle to her childhood home at the hôtel Béraud. She climbs to the top of the stairs to look down over Paris but this panoramic gaze is one of resignation, not mastery. Renée is quite aware of the circularity her name implies. She recalls an earlier premonition, in the parc Monceau, of Saccard driving her insane. She cries in anguish at having ignored 'les grandes voix des arbres' (p. 575). The voices of the trees in the parc Monceau, suggest in metaphorical terms the laws of the family tree, denoted in contemporary diction by 'la voix du sang'. The latter have been ignored and transgressed, and Renée pays with her life. She dies that winter. The end of the novel coincides with this sacrificial demise, as the cyclical resonances of her name are finally erased. It is Maxime who escapes this equation between the end of the novel, the end of the incestuous affair, and the end of a life. For Renée, the exposure of incest creates a deflating sense of an ending: 'alors le drame était fini?. . . Tout cet amour maudit qui l'avait brûlée pendant des mois, aboutissait à cette fin plate et ignoble' (p. 572). Within this context of inverted values, it is not incest but its exposure and termination which extinguish character and plot: 'c'était la fin d'une femme' (p. 588).

It is worth contrasting the relationship between, on the one hand, sexual transgression and textual or historical closures in *La Curée*, and, on the other, its dramatised form, *Renée* (adapted around 1880 and performed in 1887). In Act 1 Scene 2 Béraud interprets Renée's loss of innocence as a sign that 'notre race est finie'.[22] He does not realise that Renée has been raped and that Saccard is not her seducer. His premonition of a circular plot ('la faute recommencera, tu trahiras ton mari') is displaced by a different pattern of return. In the final scene of Act 5, Renée exposes Saccard to her relationship with Maxime as her husband demands to meet her lover and kill him. In the event Renée shoots herself. In accordance with melodramatic conventions, Béraud enters, only to hold his daughter in his arms as she passes away. His premonition underestimates her actual crime which is both adultery and incest, but he kisses her gently on the forehead. So Renée is returned to her natural father in this symbolic gesture which testifies to the failure of all other relations she has had with men, as the forbidden kiss is legitimated in its displacement from lips to forehead.

If the power of paternity is recuperated in *La Curée* by the homosocial bonding of father and son, and the demise of Renée, then the dramatisation of the novel offers an alternative version of paternal hegemony. The preface to *Renée* illuminates some of Zola's reflections on 'cette jouissance aiguë, l'inceste'.[23] He begins by distinguishing between the possibilities of fictional and dramatic representation: 'le sujet de *La Curée*, l'inceste, me semblait radicalement impossible à la Comédie-Française'. This explains the play's use of 'l'expédient, la tricherie, pour dire le mot, qui esquive l'inceste réel, en établissant que Saccard n'est que de nom le mari de Renée'. Zola quotes a letter from Emile Perrin dated 20 June 1881 which confronts the effectiveness of such *tricherie*:

Le public de la Comédie-Française ne supporterait pas la Phèdre moderne possédée par son fils, presque sous les yeux de son époux. Je sais bien que ce fils n'est point son fils, qu'elle n'a jamais été à son mari, mais n'importe, pour le public, Renée est, en même temps, épouse et mère.

What mattered, it seems, was not the system of biological relations as such, but the status or role of sexual transgressions within the symbolic order of the family. The shocked reactions of Perrin, Korning, Porel and Sarah Bernhardt were couched in terms of a crisis of closure: 'tous ceux qui la [*Renée*] connaissait prophétisaient que le public ne l'écouterait pas jusqu'au bout'. Perrin warns, 'la représentation de votre drame, tel qu'il est à cette heure, serait à partir du troisième acte, un continuel danger.' Zola recounts a dinner where Sarah Bernhardt explains her worries about the 'dénouement de cette abominable scène où Renée jette le fils à la colère du père; elle m'en parla avec un frisson, en comédienne qui entend déjà les sifflets dans la salle. Pour elle non plus, la pièce ne finirait pas.'

When the play eventually appeared at the Théâtre du Vaudeville, the *Journal amusant* published Stop's caricature of the play, a dozen cartoons and captions, the last of which describes Renée's desire for Maxime as 'une névrose qui ressort beaucoup plus de la clinique du docteur Charcot que de l'art théâtral'.[24] Though we may be tempted to interpret such plots in the psychoanalytical terms which immediately present themselves, we might recall that contemporary interpretations used the psychological case (as opposed to the literary type) as a way of marginal-ising the incest plot.[25] In his review for *Le Gaulois* dated 17 April 1887, Albert Delpit asks:

Qu'est-ce que Renée? Une femme domptée par la fatalité, comme Phèdre? Non: c'est une névropathe que devrait soigner M. Charcot . . . Comment puis-je m'intéresser à cette pauvre créature hésitante et déséquilibrée, qui éprouve et qui ne sent pas?. . . Toujours une femme atteinte d'accidents physiologiques, et non de sentiments purement humains.[26]

Yet the author himself could manipulate the question of the taboo to defend his work against a dubious reception. Whereas 'dans *Phèdre*, il n'y a pas du tout d'inceste', Zola tells us that 'l'inceste [est] accompli dans le livre, sur le point de l'être dans la pièce'. Certainly, after the Commune, censorship was tightened and the café Riche scene in which Renée and Maxime yield to their desires was enough to allow the Parquet to suspend publication of the novel.

As suggested above, this incest motif could be explained in terms of an epistemophilia strangely analogous to the tenets of Naturalist writing itself. Yet from early in his career Zola was aware of the dangers of 'cette folie de notre siècle, de tout savoir, de tout réduire en équations, de tout soumettre aux puissants agents mécaniques qui transformeront le monde'.[27] It is clear from this observation in his article on 'M. Taine, artiste', reproduced in *Mes Haines*, that Zola is quite aware of the limits of such a rhetoric of total knowledge. In her 'insatiable besoin de savoir et de sentir', Renée considers lesbian pleasures in *La Curée*, as she searches for 'une jouissance unique, exquise, où elle mordrait toute seule' (1, p. 422). This clearly contradicts Zola's ideology of fertile hetero-sexuality and signals his implicit distinction between the perspective of the ethical writer and, from this perspective precisely, the writing of the unethical. Zola's moral positions are intended to constitute an immun-isation against the contagion which his subject matter threatens and which contemporary critics continually diagnosed.

Also as explained above, the relationship between narratives of incest and of adultery are often focused by the architecture of domestic and social space in the bourgeois novel. In chapter 7 of *La Curée* we see Saccard and his colleagues observing demolition work in preparation for the new boulevard du Prince-Eugène. This representation of Haussmannization symbolises the dismantling and reconstruction of domestic space within the historical development of urban existence. The triangular configurations of the novel of adultery, echoed ironically in narratives of incest, are even suggested by the 'delta' at the apex of

Saccard's *hôtel* (pp. 330–31). Chapter 1 of the novel describes this 'réduc-
tion du nouveau Louvre', a pale imitation, as 'un des échantillons les plus
caractéristiques du style Napoléon III, ce bâtard opulent de tous les
styles' (p. 332). The illegitimacy of an eclecticism which denies any single
lineage of influence produces a crisis of recognition. As M. Hupel de la
Noue exclaims, 'imaginez-vous que moi, qui suis un vieux Parisien, je ne
reconnais plus mon Paris. Hier, je me suis perdu pour aller de l'Hôtel de
Ville au Luxembourg. C'est prodigieux, prodigieux!' (p. 342).

This crisis of recognition within the eclectic maze of the architec-
turally reconfigured city is reflected in the reorganisation of familial
bonds by the incestuous scenario. Chapter 3 describes the sight of
Saccard, Maxime and Renée around Paris, arm in arm, Maxime in a
relationship of sibling *familiarity* with both parents. Maxime and Saccard
even share prostitutes just as they will ultimately share Renée (p. 426).
'L'idée de la famille' is lost in this crisis of recognition (just who has
authority over whom? just who is in love with whom?) that is also a crisis
of indifferentiation (as the delta of parents and child implodes). Hence
the architecture of family life threatens to collapse. As Zola writes in 'Les
Notes générales sur la marche de l'œuvre':

La caractéristique du mouvement moderne est la bousculade de toutes les
ambitions, l'élan démocratique, l'avènement de toutes les classes (de là, la famil-
iarité des pères et des fils, le mélange et le côtoiement de tous les individus). Mon
roman eût été impossible avant 1789. Je le base donc sur une vérité du temps:
la bousculade des ambitions et des appétits. (p. 1572)

This description of the disorganisation of family life after 1789 culminates in the symbolic depiction of incest as a rabid dissemination of the
political rhetoric of *fraternité*. As such, this metaphor of political egalitar-
ianism returns to disestablish its very origins within the family. As we
shall see in chapter 6, in certain Naturalist novels politics is more than
merely metaphorical, threatening at the level of plot (if not of form) to
explode the family romance.

Incest's symbolic petrification of the boundaries between domestic
space and the outside world is concentrated in *La Curée* in the conservatory in Saccard's *hôtel* where Renée and Maxime meet on 'les jours
mauvais': 'c'étaient là qu'ils goûtaient l'inceste' (p. 484). This 'nef close,
où bouillait la sève ardente des tropiques' offers a decadent redefinition
of the confines of the Romantic *prison heureuse* (p. 357). The incest-cum-
adultery of Renée and Maxime enjoys the regressive *volupté* of this
edenic scenario. In terms of Lévi-Strauss's equation of incest and
nature, the garden represents nature enclosed and subjected to the

demands of cultural organisation. In chapter 1 of the novel the Chinese hibiscus, which covers the side of the *hôtel*, not only suggests the constant threat of nature to culture (or incest to the taboo), it also connotes 'des bouches sensuelles de femmes qui s'ouvraient, les lèvres rouges, molles et humides, de quelque Messaline géante, que des baisers meurtrissaient, et qui toujours renaissaient avec leur sourire avide et saignant' (p. 356). This botanical description of an infinite female desire which undermines male certainties reappears in *A Rebours*. The specificity of this connotation is rendered explicit in chapter 4 of *La Curée* when Renée is depicted as 'une Messaline géante' (p. 489). She is nature incarnata, toward which the decadent Maxime regresses.

This depiction of incest as nature, along the lines of Lévi-Strauss's nature/culture divide, is informed by an intertextual reading necessarily apprised, as in the case of *A Rebours*, of the requisite cultural knowledge. In contrast to the Racinian version of the Phædrus myth, which she sees at the Théâtre-Italien, Renée notes 'comme son drame était mesquin et honteux à côté de l'épopée antique!' (p. 509). It is precisely this self-conscious difference from a classical cultural model which registers the degeneration of a society which can no longer replay its own tragic scenarios without an inversion of genre. In terms of the general debate, this novel would seem to corroborate Raymond Williams's description of a modern rewriting of tragedy rather than George Steiner's notion of *The Death of Tragedy*. In a letter to Ulbach dated 6 November 1871, Zola indicates: 'j'ai voulu, dans cette nouvelle *Phèdre*, montrer à quel effroyable écroulement on en arrive, quand les mœurs sont pourries et que les liens de famille n'existent plus' (p. 1605). Ironically, the relevant intratextual reference, M. Hupel de la Noue's playlet, *Amours du beau Narcisse et de la nymphe Echo*, is performed at Saccard's *hôtel* in chapter 6. The self-parodic theatricality of this almost farcical allegory offers the other term in the compass between genres in which *La Curée* swings. The 'style bâtard' of this novel transgresses the generic norms of writing.[28]

As Zola's preface stresses, one sign of degeneration in *La Curée* is hermaphroditism. The marquise d'Espanet refers to Maxime as 'un garçon qui aurait dû naître fille' (p. 412). Indeed, he has to dress up as a woman to attend Renée's Monday salon from which men are normally excluded. This context of 'plaisanteries équivoques' implies a relation between sexual and semantic equivocations. Maxime's ambiguity offers a metonymy of the demise of family life: 'cette famille vivait trop vite; elle se mourait déjà dans cette créature frêle, chez laquelle le sexe avait dû hésiter . . .; hermaphrodite étrange venu à son heure dans une société qui pourrissait' (p. 425). The hermaphrodite is echoed as a figure of decadence through an inventory of characters in the nineteenth-century novel which includes Emile Blondet, Lucien de Rubempré, Henri de Marsay, Maxime de Trailles, Octave de Parisis and Charles Demailly.[29] If the century can be interpreted as a series of political revolutions, then this also implies a series of *fins d'époque* relativised *ex post facto* by the intense self-consciousness of the *fin de siècle*. *La Curée* forms a part of that interweaving of historical terminations and sexual perversions which *Le Docteur Pascal* and *A Rebours* exploit. In Maxime's sexual encounters with Renée, she plays the role of the leading male: 'Renée était l'homme'. In the same scene, Maxime compares her to a marble sphinx: 'Renée avait la pose et le sourire du monstre à tête de femme, et, dans ses jupons dénoués, elle semblait la sœur blanche de ce dieu noir' (p. 485). This hermaphroditic fusion of god and goddess is focussed on the sphinx as a figure of interpretative doubt. It is Renée, we should recall, who carries Maxime off to bed (p. 480).

The shifting relations of power between men and women in incestuous relationships are also explored in *La Terre* where Palmyre, 'une grande femme d'une trentaine d'années, qui en paraissait bien cinquante', lives with her cleft-lipped brother, Hilarion, in an abandoned stable. She offers him 'des soins passionnés, une tendresse vaillante de mère' (4, p. 411–12). Rumours spread until Jean confronts Palmyre in chapter 4 of part 2. Her refusal to deny Jean's allegations incites his interest and that of Françoise: 'dame! dans l'étable en ruines où ils logaient, elle et son frère, il n'y avait guère moyen de remuer, sans tomber l'un sur l'autre. Leurs paillasses se touchaient par terre, bien sûr qu'ils se trompaient la nuit'. An erotic relationship is imagined to be an accident determined by the spatial arrangements of rural domestic life. Palmyre, however, defends her behaviour in terms of the autonomy of private life: 'et quand ce serait vrai, qu'est-ce que ça vous fiche? . . . Le pauvre petit n'a déjà pas tant de plaisir. Je suis sa sœur, je pourrais bien être sa femme, puisque toutes les filles le rebutent' (pp. 483–4). Jean is silenced by this assertion of the rights of the family as an enclosed cell at the expense of the social exchange we call gossip and rumour. The barrier Palmyre erects between her stable and the outside world maintains a distinction not only between fields of desire but also between fields of discourse.

Palmyre's defence reveals, however, 'le déchirement de sa maternité pour l'infirme, qui allait jusqu'à l'inceste'. She is at once sister, wife and

mother to Hilarion, attempting by a form of polymorphous hetero-
sexuality to make up for other people's callousness. Just as *Les Rougon-
Macquart*'s project of 'tout dire' could be read at one level as an inventory
of polymorphous perversity, so the demands of the subject (in this case,
Hilarion) are seen to require a multiplicity of amorous forms which
renders this exclusive object of affection, Palmyre, necessarily 'perverse'.
This complex sexual function is reduced within Zola's mythology of the
bête humaine to a primitive reciprocation, 'une approche instinctive sans
consentement réfléchi, lui tourmenté et bestial, elle passive et bonne à
tout, cédant ensuite l'un et l'autre au plaisir d'avoir plus chaud, dans
cette masure où ils grelottaient' (p. 484).

The authority of the maternal figure is undermined in part 3 of *La
Terre* in terms of this primitive distinction between male dominance and
female passivity. Hilarion starts to tyrannise and beat Palmyre. Once
more she has to defend the privacy of their bond, this time before her
great aunt, Rose: 'est-ce que ça les regardait, les autres? est-ce qu'ils
avaient besoin d'entrer espionner chez nous?'. Rose argues that, 'si vous
couchez ensemble, comme on le raconte, c'est très mal'. Palmyre retorts,
'ah! très mal, est-ce qu'on sait? . . . Le curé m'a fait demander pour me
dire que nous irions en enfer. Pas le pauvre chéri toujours . . . Le jour où
il m'étranglera . . . je verrai bien si le bon Dieu veut me pardonner'
(pp. 539–40). Rose changes the subject; once more, Palmyre has
defended the autonomy of the incestuous bond. By a fine distinction
between forms of knowledge, the experiential imperative of 'tout con-
naître' underpins the projects of both Naturalist writer and sexual trans-
gressor. For this transgression is defended in terms of the relativism of
moral knowledge ('ah! très mal, est-ce qu'on sait?').

Eventually Palmyre works herself literally into the ground to pay for
Hilarion's bouts of drinking. Reduced to another primitive scenario, she
nearly dies in the fields 'sous des besognes de bête surmenée' (p. 575).
That night Françoise listens to Hilarion clinging to Palmyre's body, 'refu-
sant de lâcher ces restes, sa sœur, sa femme, son tout' (p. 578). Rather
than experience 'everything', Hilarion has in fact known very little.
When Palmrye dies, he is thrust back into the realm of social interaction. Abbé Godard sends him to work for Marianne la Grande, who
exploits him mercilessly. We glimpse his 'regard furtif sur sa grand-mère,
un regard d'animal battu, épouvanté et soumis' (pp. 595–6). He has
inherited his sister's submissive characteristics. Contrary to Palmyre's
wishes, the privacy of incest does not in this case define a utopian space
beyond the determinants of a social milieu; it describes a tragedy of pre-

social desires and of female submission. *Le Docteur Pascal* will, as we have seen, recast in a scenario that is neither decadent nor brutal the terms of these tragic plots found in *La Curée* and *La Terre*.

The shift from feudalism to private ownership in *La Terre* is character-ised as a displacement of figures between adulterous desire and incestu-ous genealogy.[30] Fouan recalls the sense of injustice created by working the land for a 'seigneur', 'la terre, fécondée de son effort, passionnément aimée et désirée pendant cette intimité chaude de chaque heure, comme la femme d'un autre que l'on soigne, que l'on étreint et que l'on ne peut posséder' (pp. 433–4). The second chapter in the novel introduces the theme of property transmission, as Fouan prepares to share his land amongst his progeny: 'il devait céder cette maîtresse à ses fils, comme son père la lui avait cédée à lui-même, enragé de son impuissance' (p. 383). Mother Earth is to be passed between fathers and sons. In contrast to inheritance upon death, this *démission de biens* by parents who are simply too old to tend the land invites Œdipal strife. As the *notaire*, Baillehache, warns, 'beaucoup de bons esprits blâment la démission de biens, qu'ils regardent comme immorale, car ils l'accusent de détruire les liens de famille' (p. 384).

Fouan's 'adulterous' desires for another man's property have been internalised within this property-owning family in the form of 'incestu-ous' urges and rivalries amongst his children (including Buteau, whose desire to possess, as we have seen above, leads to the rape of his cousin). In Fouan's case, this resignation of authority is symbolically eroticized: 'il avait aimé la terre en femme qui tue et pour qui on assassine'. Mother Earth is at once an object of exchange between fathers and sons, and a sadistic tyrant: 'combien . . . elle était indifférente et ingrate, la terre!' This ambivalent attitude towards the maternal figure corresponds to alternative visions of history. On the one hand, Jean is proud to relate the euphoric narrative of *Les Malheurs et le triomphe de Jacques Bonhomme* which culminates in Napoleonic *gloire*; on the other, Fouan depicts a pes-simistic vision of political stasis reflected in the intransigence of the earth: 'est-ce que le malheur est jamais fini? Ça ne met pas de viande dans la marmite, n'est-ce pas? leur suffrage universel' (p. 435). Thus the reading of sexual metaphors in *La Terre* turns upon the form of histori-cal narrative. One effect of Fouan's *démission* is the division of a reason-ably sized property. Clearly, marriage within the family would be one way of resisting this dissolution of family power. A more complex nego-tiation is involved in exogamy where the benefits of inheritance are counterbalanced by the benefits of an advantageous marriage. In place of incestuous permanence, a rhythm of separation and addition is generated: 'de père en fils, on avait partagé ainsi; et les acquisitions, les mariages venaient ensuite arrondir de nouveau les pièces' (p. 34).

In terms of the internal shape and symmetry of the novel series, *La Débâcle* reflects the position of *La Curée* just as *Le Docteur Pascal* reflects that of *La Fortune des Rougon*. *La Débâcle* also describes French history around the time of the writing and publication of *La Curée*. In that sense it concludes this history of the Second Empire. As Zola himself had observed in 1870, 'la chute des Bonaparte dont j'avais besoin comme artiste et que toujours je trouvais facilement au bout du drame . . . est venue me donner le dénouement terrible et nécessaire de mon œuvre' (1, p. xx). History coincides with the æsthetic imperatives of the series as the illumination of an epoch. *Le Docteur Pascal* is thus a supplement which lies beyond the historical parameters of the series (after the fall of the Second Empire). As the tale of the series's myth of its own origins, it offers a history of writing rather than a writing of history and thus institutes the vital difference of self-awareness between *histoire* as fiction and History as such.

The debauchery of the decadence portrayed in *La Curée* is echoed in the depiction in *La Débâcle* of 'l'Empire vielli . . . pourri à la base, ayant affaibli l'idée de patrie en détruisant la liberté, redevenu libéral trop tard et par sa ruine, prêt à couler dès qu'il ne satisferait plus les appétits de jouissances déchaînés par lui' (5, p. 413). This terminal vision culminates in the image of Paris ablaze, 'le spectacle de la Babylone en flammes'. This evocation of the 'barbares conquérants' who have come from the East to purify latin decadence triggers a chain of obsessive reference to such a vison, which is expressed as gallic defeatism (p. 433). As early as chapter 2 we learn via *style indirect libre* of Maurice's sense of the war's abortion of the historical epic: 'ah! c'était bien la fin de tout! A peine avait-on commencé et c'était fini' (p. 435). The rapid defeat of French troops reflects 'l'envie d'en finir tout de suite, avant d'avoir commencé' (p. 426). This historical version of the end in the beginning seems to abort the Aristotelian model of narrative whereas the 'cercle fini' concluded by *Le Docteur Pascal* positions the novel series itself in the fictional space between a beginning and an ending mapped one onto the other in cyclical fashion.

The end of political regimes and the ambience of the Decadence offer a threat to figures of paternity of various kinds. The threat to legitimate orders is revealed in *Les Rougon-Macquart* as an erasure of the *nom de famille* which is also the *nom du père*. We should note how both Aristide and Pascal Rougon drop the patronym of conjugal legitimacy, Rougon.

In chapter 2 of *La Curée* we learn how Aristide has come to adopt the name Saccard. On his arrival in Paris, Eugène informs him that they should have different names (1, p. 364). In a scene laden with psychological reverberations these two sons play with different versions of suitable patronyms until a choice is made upon the grounds of euphony and connotation. In some sense delegitimised by this onomastic shift, Aristide fails to exert the power of the father. His continual absence means that 'Renée était aussi peu mariée que possible', whilst for Maxime, 'son père ne semblait pas exister' (pp. 420, 428). Absent father, absent husband and absent name, Aristide loses control within the incestuous convolutions of his family. He loses the Rougon name and loses his wife to his son. Pascal Rougon also loses his *nom de famille* and is known in Plassans simply as docteur Pascal. His onomastic shift, however, is to a professional title rather than a fictitious name, and this title becomes the title of the novel he dominates. Whereas Aristide loses out in the incestuous scenario, Pascal's loss of the Rougon name symbolises the lifting of the taboo, and it is this which might be said to facilitate his relationship with Clotilde. At the level of naming, when Pascal and Clotilde combine, this is in one sense no longer a fusion of Rougons. This difference between Pascal and the family he documents is underlined in genetic terms by his *innéité*.

Zola's novels, like children, are born into the lineage of the family tree. It is, therefore, particularly fitting that the hereditary reproduction of similar characteristics can be described as a diachronic mimesis of the human subject. In such terms, the *innéité* of Pascal's traits renders him *invraisemblable*. In his *Traité philosophique et physiologique de l'hérédité naturelle dans les états de santé et de maladie du système nerveux*, from which Zola worked, Prosper Lucas draws a distinction that will haunt the Naturalists with the charge that they are mere *copistes*.[31] On the one hand, he compares imitation with heredity, and on the other, invention with *innéité* which is said to explain the kind of radical difference inside the family realm that Pascal exhibits. (It is worth asking in this case whether incest is an attempt to 'cure' that difference by a dose of the same.) In what is for Zola an advantageous *mise en abyme* of authorial practice, Pascal works under the sign of creativity that is *innéité*. Lucas draws this pertinent distinction between invention and imitation:

La première de ces lois est *l'invention*: c'est celle où notre esprit ne suit aucun modèle, où il improvise, où il compose de soi, où il imagine, en un mot, où il *crée*. La seconde de ces lois est *l'imitation*: c'est celle où notre esprit se soumet à l'exemple, celle où il copie, celle où il se souvient, celle où il *répète*.

The relationship of influence between the science of genetics and the art of mimesis seems to be recursive. Lucas goes on to explain:

Dans cette transition de la CRÉATION à la PROCRÉATION, la loi d'INVENTION devient l'INNÉITÉ, qui représente ce qu'il y a d'originalité, d'imagination, et de liberté de la vie dans la génération médiate de l'être. La loi d'IMITATION devient l'HÉRÉDITÉ qui représente ce qu'il y a de répétition et de mémoire de la vie, dans la même nature de génération.

The *innéité* of Pascal distances him as an individual. Thus *innéité* is a radicalisation of the principle of identification 'par lequel l'existence physique de chaque être est distincte et différente en soi de l'existence physique de tous les autres êtres, des plus rapprochés de lui, des plus semblables à lui, de celle de ses père et mère, de celle de ses frères et sœurs.'

The historian Adeline Daumard notes a discourse at the end of the nineteenth century on 'les trois composantes qui façonnent les destinées hors du commun: «miracle du génie», l'influence du père et de la mère, «aboutissement» d'une lignée'.[32] Innateness is a refutation of parental influence that echoes the Romantic figure of *le génie*. Pascal is, however, unlike des Esseintes, not the end of the line. We may extend the use Daumard makes of Henry Bordeaux in order to foreground the perturbing function of *innéité* within the genetic discourse on family lineage. In the context of Pasteur and Barrès, Bordeaux notes:

Notre dépendance, c'est la certitude de notre continuité. Elle explique et justifie la durée des familles, des races, des nations . . . Un Gœthe sera l'aboutissement d'une lignée bourgeoise élargie, un Mistral à la fleur d'une famille paysanne. Un grand homme commande sans le savoir l'armée de ses morts. Il n'est grand qu'à la tête de cette troupe invisible qui demeure anonyme.[33]

Pascal's independence ruptures this continuity. It is ironic, moreover, that his professional life culminates in an obsessive examination of the family which his personal biology hitherto 'ignores'. It is only by escaping such genetic determinism that Pascal can attain the objectivity necessary to plan his family history. At the same time, it is only by the most radical immersion in the vicissitudes of family biology, as offered by incest, that the completion of this history is assured within the novel's myth of textual genesis.

Pascal's own appearance in the first and last novels of the cycle underpins its circular structure. In *La Fortune des Rougon* he conceives of the family tree in terms of a tension between sameness and difference, 'ces poussées d'une famille, d'une souche qui jette des branches *diverses*, et dont la sève âcre charrie les *mêmes* germes dans les tiges les plus lointaines' (1, p. 301, our italics). Incest embodies the extreme form of sameness returning to itself, whereas *innéité* incorporates a radical notion of biological difference. The science of genetics recast in *Le Docteur Pascal* does not merely explicate the self, it also articulates a crisis of selfhood caught within the intricacies of the family: 'la ressemblance peut aller jusqu'à faire illusion sur l'identité ou jusqu'à déceler, au premier coup d'œil, l'origine des personnes.'[34] This is a problem, it would seem, for the policing of the individual along the lines of the 'conjectural paradigm' presented by Carlo Ginzburg.[35] So incest and innateness place Pascal at the heart of the family history and yet also exterior to it. This ambivalence, amplified as perspectives of sympathy and detachment in the novel, stands ultimately as a condition of the very possibility of writing fiction, not least in the Naturalist mode.

PART 3

The blindness of passions: Huysmans, Hennique and Zola

CHAPTER 5

The conquest of privacy in 'A Rebours'

Like Taine and Nietzsche, [Huysmans] craved for some haven of refuge to escape the whirring wings of Wotan's ravens.[1]

The tension in family fictions between consanguinity and illegitimacy, adumbrated in the previous chapters, is amplified in certain novels which question in extreme form the status of individuality amidst the sociopolitical mælstrom of modernity. The intersubjective network on which the density of Naturalist plots often rely (and which is finally parodied to death by Gide's 'sotie', *Les Caves du Vatican* (1914)) ultimately threatens the coherence of the family plot, as we shall see in chapter 6 in the cases of Hennique's *Un accident de Monsieur Hébert* and Zola's *Paris*. Both infer by the evocation of radical politics the dangers of narcissism in the self-concerned family romance in both its adulterous and incestuous forms. What both novels reflect is the political irresponsibility of a narrative form (and of a lifestyle) whose focus on private desires ignores the demands of public life, or fails to register the political dimension of private life. The decadence of modernity is pathologized by these Naturalist novelists as a form of social blindness, an unwillingness to engage with the political. Nowhere is this quest for privacy voiced more audaciously than in *A Rebours* (1884) by Joris-Karl Huysmans. His suspicion of the commercial metropolitan centres of modernity and their very public culture of spectacle, presided over by the likes of Octave Mouret, is addressed elsewhere in a warning about the social effects of the *grands magasins*:

Ce sera la fin de la famille, éparse, du matin au soir, dans les galeries éloignées de manufactures pareilles, se joignant juste la nuit, pour enfanter, un soir de mégarde, un gosse voué à un destin semblable et auquel, en fait d'éducation l'on inculquera la peur du Code, si l'on est pauvre . . . Joignez à cela, des épouses dont les tout puissants patrons s'adjugeront l'entame et la facilité du divorce, laissant un petit chien abandonné qui court, d'un chenil à l'autre, de la niche de la maman, à celle du père . . . Ah! l'avenir familial, dans cette société qui se décompose à vue d'œil, est effrayant.[2]

As a farewell to the family and its fictions, *A Rebours* meditates on what type of novel is writable in the social context of urban modernity and in the wake of the nineteenth-century literary tradition to which Huysmans has hitherto contributed. As Martiarena observes, the 'Notice' which precedes the first chapter of the novel functions as 'un roman naturaliste abrégé'.[3] It races through the family history which has produced des Esseintes as the last in this long line of consanguineously degenerating aristocrats, which was 'au temps jadis, composée d'athlé-tiques soudards, de rébarbatifs reîtres'.[4] The decline of the family is accelerated by two centuries of inbreeding:

La décadence de cette ancienne maison avait, sans nul doute, suivi régulière-ment son cours; l'effémination des mâles était allée en s'accentuant; comme pour achever l'œuvre des âges, les des Esseintes marièrent, pendant deux siècles, leurs enfants entre eux, usant leur reste de vigueur dans les unions consan-guines. (p. 80)

The sterile perversity of des Esseintes (which appears to signal the *fin de la famille* as a biological as well as social construct) is presented as the endgame of this passage from normative sexual relations to consanguin-ity:

De cette famille naguère si nombreuse qu'elle occupait presque tous les terri-toires de l'Ile-de-France et de la Brie, un seul rejeton vivait, le duc Jean, un grêle jeune homme de trente ans, anémique et nerveux, aux joues caves, aux yeux d'un bleu froid d'acier, au nez éventé et pourtant droit, aux mains sèches et fluettes.

The decadent novel begins where the Naturalist novel ends, in the move from the château de Lourps to Fontenay-aux-Roses (and from the 'Notice' to chapter 1 proper). It is as if, in a state of fatigue, desire cannot summon the energy to pierce the bounds of the family by making a bid towards otherness. This narratological as well as spatial enclosure is marked by an atavistic circularity akin to Charles's echo of tante Dide in *Le Docteur Pascal*: 'par un singulier phénomène d'atavisme, le dernier descendant ressemblait à l'antique aïeul'.

For des Esseintes, consanguinity is the only way of marrying regres-sion and lust, and thus resolving the constitution of the self in terms of narcissism and alterity.[5] The solipsist's anger at the impossibility of denying the need for the otherness of Woman engenders the aggressive misogyny which the narrator exhibits in his reference to 'la sottise innée des femmes' (p. 185). One way of disposing of women in this traditional society, so it seems, is to deny their reproductive agency and to proclaim the closure of the family. Consanguineous love is the son's route to such domestic apocalypse, his way of nullifying the mother's biological relation to the future. As Kristeva writes, 'Œdipe est *agos* du fait d'avoir, par le meurtre du père et l'inceste avec la mère, perturbé et interrompu la chaîne de la reproduction. La souillure est l'arrêt de la vie: (comme) une sexualité sans reproduction'.[6] Incest, from this perspective, necessitates the end of the line. According to this anti-reproductive code, des Esseintes will always be the young man in the family portraits of a moribund genealogy. This is the closest he can come to the perpetual youth of Narcissus.

Faith in inheritance is undermined in *A Rebours* where the reader is told that syphilis alone provides the common thread of transmission through history: 'tout n'est que syphilis . . . Depuis le commencement du monde, de pères en fils, toutes les créatures se transmettaient l'inusable héritage, l'éternelle maladie qui a ravagé les ancêtres de l'homme' (p. 197). This decline culminates in the demise of this aristocratic lineage with des Esseintes's relatives discarded as 'les dernières branches des races feódales' (p. 84). As Maclean observes in her discussion of Flora Tristan's *Méphis* (1838), 'the love children of the nobility were often seen as bringing a secret transfusion of energy to exhausted stock'.[7] Marius-Ary Leblond strikes a sobering note, however, when he warns:

La sélection par unions consanguines aboutit à une extrême débilité, et les apports de robustesse que fait de temps à autre la bourgeoisie, d'ailleurs le plus souvent déjà anémiée par la richesse, ne peuvent que précipiter la déchéance physiologique de l'aristocratie, comme il va d'un vin fort pour des nervosités trop sensitives.[8]

It is precisely this exhaustion of consanguineously purified stock which produces des Esseintes. He appears in one sense as the anti-bastard, neither needing nor able to find the energy of Napoleonic proportions required to conquer the social universe.

References in *A Rebours* to consanguinity are not just contrasted with adultery; they can also intersect. In his relationship with the ventriloquist, Miss Urania, des Esseintes enjoys only the limited awareness of the self-centred child: 'Doucement, il étreignait la femme silencieuse, à ses côtés, se réfugiant, ainsi qu'un enfant inconsolé, près d'elle, ne voyant même pas l'air maussade de la comédienne obligée à jouer une scène, à exercer son métier, chez elle, aux instants du repos, loin de la rampe' (pp. 215–16). The fiction of a mother–son bond is generated in des Esseintes's refusal to recognise the crucial distinction between inside and outside (between Miss Urania's privacy and the public role of performance). This refusal to accept as an absolute the distinction between inside and outside is, as we have seen, central to the adulterous scenario, and when the threat of impotence arises, in his search for stimulation des Esseintes turns to the simulation of the risk of being caught in the adulterous act. Miss Urania throws her voice such that 'une voix de rogomme éclatait derrière la porte: «Ouvriras-tu? je sais bien que t'es avec un miché, attends, attends un peu, salope!»'. 'De même que ces libertins excités par la terreur d'être pris en flagrant délit', what des Esseintes actually experiences are the pleasures of Don Juan: 'il éprouvait des allégresses inouïes, dans cette bousculade, dans cette panique de l'homme courant un danger, interrompu, pressé dans son ordure'. Within this fiction of adultery, of course, Miss Urania is both adulterous wife and cuckolded husband. In the bedroom des Esseintes may possess her body, but her voice is outside.

In chapter 6 of *A Rebours* the narrator recounts des Esseintes's success in encouraging his friend, d'Aigurande, to get married. Des Esseintes realises that the marriage will never succeed, and, indeed, d'Aigurande ends up finding his pleasures elsewhere and his wife, unable to satisfy her materialistic desires and tired of 'sa vie pluvieuse et plate', resorts to 'les expédients de l'adultère' (p. 167), which leads to the couple's separation. However, Huysmans's hero is not involved in the adulterous situation. No longer embroiled, the hero is but an agent of despair who can trigger and observe this situation from an ironic distance. He does not engage personally in the duplicitous world of marriage and adultery, but makes of it yet one more subject for observation and study, hence his possession of a book on 'la mœchialogie' (p. 129), as explained by Fumaroli's note, 'Mœchialogie: de *moïcheïa*, mot grec signifiant adultère, et de *logos*, discours; c'est le titre d'un ouvrage du R. P. Debreyne (1786–1867) traitant des aspects moraux des questions sexuelles' (p. 420).

As such, Huysmans adulterates the novel of adultery, as the treatment of colour in the decor at Fontenay implies. In the opening chapter the reader is told how, 'les boiseries immobilisèrent leur bleu soutenu et comme échauffé par les oranges qui se maintinrent, à leur tour, sans s'adultérer, appuyés et, en quelque sorte, attisés qu'ils furent par le souffle pressant des bleus' (p. 99). This language of adulteration and separation is continued in chapter 4 where des Esseintes's goal in the decoration of his tortoise is to find 'les moyens de concilier ces mésalliances, d'empêcher le divorce résolu de ces tons' (p. 132). The clash of colours is described in terms which evoke marital disharmony, and this diction of adulteration returns in the final pages of the novel when the corruption of priests is criticized: 'Depuis des années, les huiles saintes étaient adultérées par de la graisse de volaille; la cire, par des os calcinés ... Mais ce qui était pis, c'était que les substances, indispensables au saint sacrifice, les deux substances sans lesquelles aucune oblation n'est possible, avaient, elles aussi, été dénaturées' (pp. 356–7). To be adulterated, it seems, is to be denatured, as if adulteration represents a falling away from an original state of innocence and fidelity (and thus a form of decadence). In the terms of Lévi-Strauss reinterpreted by Derrida, the time of incest is, of course, the time of nature, and so the 'denatured' signals the advent of civilisation.[9] The process of 'adulteration' seems to take us ever further from that natural state where incest is not deemed guilty.

Severed from the future by his sterility, des Esseintes is caught within an inescapable present which is alienated from the past of family history. The 'Notice' states:

Un trou existait dans la filière des visages de cette race; une seule toile servait d'intermédiaire, mettait un *point* de suture entre le passé et le présent, une tête mystérieuse et rusée, aux *traits* morts et tirés, aux pommettes *ponctuées d'une virgule* de fard, aux cheveux *gommés* et enroulés de perles, au col tendu et *peint*, sortant des cannelures d'une rigide fraise. (p. 79, our italics)

Between past and present, health and decadence, representation itself is inscribed in its grammatical, scriptural and pictorial contexts within the lacunæ of historical discontinuity. The canvas acts as a mediation in diachronic as well as spatial and visual terms. The implicit and manifest metaphors of representation produce a saturated image which appears to be the only way out of the prison of the present. For Huysmans, indeed, the body is always already written. If for his Naturalist heroine, Marthe, 'Léo fut vraiment son premier amant', his desire for her is already mediated by an æsthetic culture and 'motivated' by the intellectualized signs of beauty, 'bouche en *o*, jambes en *i*', as if the body were always textualised.[10]

Just as des Esseintes is to be written about rather than painted in spite of the long line of family portraits, so Huysmans is a writer who concludes a genealogy of painters. As Christopher Lloyd reminds us in his fine account, 'Huysmans seems not to have had any personal talent for the visual arts. In the autobiographical essay he wrote under the pseudonym "A. Meunier", he notes that he has thus ended a family tradition; "de père en fils, tout le monde a peint dans cette famille".'[11] It is worth noting in this regard that in *A Rebours* the narrator explains des

Esseintes's admiration for the painting of Moreau in terms of the relation between writing and painting, 'cet art qui . . . empruntait à l'art d'écrire ses plus subtiles évocations' (p. 154).

The diction of the family also provides a set of terms by which Huysmans self-consciously negotiates his response to Zola, the dominant father figure of French Naturalism. The language of paternity, affiliation, and their subversion is not some *ex post facto* Bloomian imposition but a rhetoric set out in *A Rebours*'s discussion of literary and artistic models. As such the question of biological reproduction is displaced in the novel by the enigmas of cultural productivity. The distinction between inside and outside also colours the relationship between Huysmans and Zola, with the former (like des Esseintes) claiming not to hanker after the acclaimed status of the *intellectuel* with which the self-publicist Zola is so clearly associated. At one level, *A Rebours* can be read as a text obsessed with æsthetic models, yet at another those models cited are often cherished precisely because they undermine the very notion of modelling and of influence. Of Moreau the narrator notes: 'Sa filiation, des Esseintes la suivait à peine; . . . la vérité était que Gustave Moreau ne dérivait de personne. Sans ascendant véritable, sans descendants possibles, il demeurait, dans l'art contemporain, unique' (p. 153). This æsthetic principle is represented in the chapter on 'profane' literature as an ideal toward which criticism should gesture and yet can never reach:

Pour [des Esseintes], les écoles n'existaient point; seul le tempérament de l'écrivain importait; seul le travail de sa cervelle intéressait quel que fût le sujet qu'il abordât. Malheureusement, cette vérité d'appréciation, digne de La Palisse, était à peu près inapplicable, par ce simple motif que, tout en désirant se dégager des préjugés, s'abstenir de toute passion, chacun va de préférence aux œuvres qui correspondent le plus intimement à son propre tempérament et finit par reléguer en arrière toutes les autres. (p. 305)

Yet there are moments when this principle of an 'anti-genealogy', or an 'anti-school', seems to offer little more than cultural disorientation, as registered by Huysmans's critique of a fresh generation of writers:

En littérature, les écrivains qui débutent nous habituent maintenant à d'inénarrables désillusions, s'ils se sont tout d'abord révélés comme étant de vrais artistes. Un livre paraît, signé d'un nom inconnu; par extraordinaire il ne pastiche point les proses antérieures, divulge des qualités de détails ou d'ensemble, *arbore* un style *sans filiation adultérée qu'on reconnaisse*; aussitôt des avances sont faites, dans le monde des lettres, au débutant; l'on attend avec impatience son second livre. Il paraît et s'effondre.[12]

So Huysmans perceives a *fin de siècle* literary scene where a genealogical narrative of developing careers and recognisable influences, that borrows the arboreal hierarchy of the family novel which has provided its traditional subject matter, is replaced by a form of *innéité*. The cult of particular texts displaces that of individual authors.

This anti-genealogical æsthetic principle is developed twenty years later in the preface of 1903 where Huysmans explains the importance of Flaubert to his generation. *L'Education sentimentale* is cited as 'un chef-d'œuvre qui a été beaucoup plus que *L'Assommoir* le parangon du naturalisme':

Ce roman était, pour nous tous, «des Soirées de Médan», une véritable bible; mais il ne comportait que peu de moutures. Il était parachevé, irrecommençable pour Flaubert même; nous en étions donc, tous, réduits, en ce temps-là, à louvoyer, à rôder par des voies plus ou moins explorées, tout autour. (p. 56)

Precisely because he is so dominant, Flaubert disestablishes the very notion of literary paternity which informs traditional versions of literary history. No œdipal tension seems viable, for there is no space left within which literary progeny can overthrow this figure of alternative paternity. The analogy with des Esseintes is clear; the family (of cultural production as well as of biological reproduction) seems to have come to a close. The novelist, it seems, is left in the isolation of his personal 'temperament'. The fantasy in writing is, according to Huysmans, no longer traditional literary fatherhood but a dominance so unquestionable as to do away with the recursive transmission which allows for the creativity of the son.

The ruse of this preface is to negotiate with Flaubert a relationship of transference which is not one of genealogy. Huysmans thus casts Zola as chief antagonist in this paratextual drama of the reception of *A Rebours*. According to the preface, Zola accuses *A Rebours* of the very limitation which, in Huysmans's reading of *L'Education sentimentale*, is cause for praise, namely 'unrewritability': '[Zola] me reprocha le livre, disant . . . que je brûlais . . . mes vaisseaux avec un pareil roman, car aucun genre de littérature n'était possible dans le genre épuisé en un seul tome' (p. 71). Zola as father of a genealogy of novels is ironically manipulated as the tool of what might be termed an anti-genealogy. By the time of the preface Huysmans had already abused Zola's status as the icon of Naturalism in *La Cathédrale*, where Zola's *Lourdes* is read within a deterministic fiction of divine necessity as the inevitable antidote to the religious zeal of Henri Lasserre de Monzie. Zola's denial of the supernatural is perceived as insignificant within the field of literary relations that swallows up his discourse. The supposed ineffectiveness of Zola's novel is itself seen as fuel to the Catholic cause: 'l'escandre soulevée par cet ouvrage fut profitable . . . Lasserre et Zola furent deux instruments utiles'.[13] Hence Catholicism becomes for Huysmans a way of imposing upon Zola a kind of 'meta-mastery' that subverts the *maître*'s own imperious gestures. Between 1884 and 1903, that is, between the publication of *A Rebours* and the writing of its preface, this novel is indeed subject to rewriting. As Huysmans informs Jules Destrée from Paris on 29 April 1891, he hopes to 'rewrite' *Là-Bas* as well as *A Rebours*:

Je vais me débarbouiller de toutes les nécessaires horreurs du Satanisme, pour voir à balbutier un peu, si je puis, dans le blanc, dans l'A rebours [*sic*] de ce livre. Ça serait bien nécessaire, car j'ai écrit dans ma vie bien des sottises. Quand je songe que dans *A Rebours* j'ai à peu près mis Schopenhauer au dessus de l'*Imitation*.[14]

This ambivalence towards a genealogy of novels accompanies a similar sentiment towards Zola's novels of genealogy and the form to which they subscribe. Meanwhile an implicit analogy is drawn in *A Rebours* between the revision of novelistic closure in *L'Education sentimentale* and that founding text in Huysmans's history of the novel, Petronius's *Satyricon* (also foregrounded in Tanner's account of adultery in fiction):

Ce roman réaliste . . . sans préoccupation . . . de réforme et de satire, sans besoin de fin apprêtée et de morale; cette histoire sans intrigue, sans action, mettant en scène les aventures de gibiers de Sodome . . . en une langue splendidement orfévrie, sans que l'auteur se montre une seule fois, sans qu'il se livre à aucun commentaire, sans qu'il approuve ou maudisse les actes et les pensées de ses personnages, les vices d'une civilisation décrépite, d'un empire qui se fêle. (p. 118)

The original *fêlure* which haunts *Les Rougon-Macquart* is postponed within Huysmans's scheme as the closural *fêlure* of a civilisation in radical decline, depicted by a novelistic form which nuances ironically the linearity of the teleological structure. For it is quite clear that Huysmans becomes dissatisfied with the Aristotelian notion of a plot as an action leading from beginning to end via the middle. Nevertheless, it would be misleading to argue that *A Rebours* is a Modernist novel.

The well-documented formal innovations of *A Rebours* involve not merely the problems of mimetic representation but also the question of the construction of plots in continual progression towards a point of closure. Huysmans's attempts to refashion both the referential function and what Barthes terms the proairetic code are clearly linked; realist fiction depicts the recognizable scenarios in which completed actions may unfold. Just as Huysmans subverts the object–copy relation in mimetic representation whilst remaining within the bounds of recognizable scenarios, so *A Rebours* undermines the progressive plot structure typical of realist narrative whilst luring the reader into such structures in another key. Memories and dreams, or – in broader terms – histories and fantasies provide the frames of narrative action in *A Rebours*. 'Events' as such rarely surface in the present of historical time and the presence of consciousness. Ultimately however, escape from the chronology of plots proves impossible. For reasons that will be explored, des Esseintes must return to society, and the novel must end. It is no surprise that these returns to reality – both reality in the plot and the reality of plots – should coincide.

The shift from *A Rebours* to Catholicism is illuminated in the context of Huysmans's relationship to Barbey d'Aurevilly. Huysmans concludes his preface of 1903 by praising Barbey's perspicacious review which had appeared in *Le Constitutionnel* on 28 July 1884 and been reprinted in Barbey's *Le Roman contemporain* of 1902. Barbey had reached the conclusion that, 'après un tel livre, il ne reste plus à l'auteur qu'à choisir entre la bouche d'un pistolet ou les pieds de la croix' (p. 77). Huysmans replies: 'c'est fait'.[15] Huysmans undermines the logic of narrative action leading from beginning, through the middle, to the end, as he prefers in art generally an æsthetics of the unfinished and the imperfect as opposed to the notion of the 'well-made' work. Barbey, however, converts the alternatives left open by *A Rebours* into Hobson's choice, the choice that was for Huysmans really no choice at all, between faith and suicide. In reality, Barbey tells Huysmans, he must choose between the closure in death and the teleology of Christianity. This relationship extends back to Huysmans's ambivalent praise of Barbey via the idiosyncratic tastes of des Esseintes:

Deux ouvrages de Barbey d'Aurevilly attisaient spécialement des Esseintes, le *Prêtre marié* et les *Diaboliques*. D'autres, tels que l'*Ensorcelée*, le *Chevalier des Touches*, *Une Vieille Maîtresse*, étaient certainement plus pondérés et plus complets, mais ils laissaient plus froid des Esseintes qui ne s'intéressait réellement qu'aux œuvres mal portantes, minées et irritées par la fièvre. (p. 279)

Barbey's offer of Hobson's choice could be read as a double-edged response to this paradoxical praise. On the one hand, Barbey may perceive in *A Rebours* the same incompleteness which earns him des Esseintes's praise; on the other, he implicitly questions such an æsthetic by answering the questions which the apparently inconclusive ending of *A Rebours* begs. Moreover, to the extent that des Esseintes was identified with Huysmans, there is a particular acidity in Barbey's observation that, 'le héros de M.Huysmans . . . est un malade comme tous les héros de cette époque malade . . . Il est de l'hôpital Charcot'.[16]

At one level, it appears that the end of the novel returns us to silence. Yet the conclusion to *A Rebours* returns des Esseintes to the polyphony of the city that this novel finds unwritable. In fact, silence is only appreciated in this novel in terms of an analogy with the non-silence of sound. Hence the synæsthetic effect of des Esseintes's famous mouth organ of liqueurs which only produces 'sound' in the mind of the player and so invites no audience: 'il était parvenu . . . à se jouer sur la langue de silencieuses mélodies, de muettes marches funèbres à grand spectacle' (p. 139). Silence would seem to be the logical conclusion of the pessimism which pervades the writing of the Decadence.

Des Esseintes's interpretation of evolution as demise inverts the son's incestuous love for the mother into hatred . . . or rather a sense that to be born is to be rejected by the womb. The child, it seems, is expelled as *déchet*. Observing 'la cruelle et abominable loi de la lutte pour l'existence', as children fight, 'il ne put s'empêcher . . . de croire que mieux eût valu pour eux que leur mère n'eût point mis bas' (p. 292). The nihilistic corollary of this attitude is des Esseintes's belief in abortion (p. 295). In defiance of Catholicism, and Zola's ideology of *Fécondité*, des Esseintes's cynicism about the virtues of reproduction figures in a tradition which includes most conspicuously Schopenhauer and Beckett. The child becomes a symbolic counter in arguments between positivism and nihilism, between faith (in God, in the future) and an empirically grounded despair, as well as the site of growing debates over women's rights in the *fin de siècle*.

This tension between the abortive or decadent on the one hand, and the procreative or positivist on the other, articulates an historical crisis over the fate awaiting the Third Republic. As we have stressed, the myth of the 'end of the family' was one version of the end of history which struck a particular chord in a society based on property and inheritance and obsessed by the question of its own legitimacy. In *A Rebours* a critique of what Huysmans elsewhere terms 'l'inflexible figure de la Certitude' is couched in terms of a Schopenhauerian pessimism where doubt and despair collude.[17] In the preface of 1903 Huysmans explains how the denial of the closure in logic that is conclusiveness distinguishes Schopenhauer from Christianity:

Les prémisses sur le Pessimisme sont les mêmes, seulement, lorsqu'il s'agit de conclure, le philosophe se dérobe . . . Les observations de Schopenhauer n'aboutissent à rien; il vous laisse, pour ainsi parler, en plan; . . . l'Eglise, elle, explique les origines et les causes, signale les fins, présente les remèdes . . . Le besoin de conclure ne me tentait pas. (pp. 61–2)

Schopenhauer, whose *Aphorisms* had been translated into French in 1880, provides a philosophical basis for a formal eschewal of conclusions, both novelistic and philosophical.[18] Registering the passage from the education of the senses to the exhaustion of the senses, the attempted closure in *A Rebours* of the textual pleasure to be found in the unfolding of a plot describes a hero on the verge of pleasure's end. In the 'Notice' the reader learns: 'Ce fut la fin: comme satisfaits d'avoir tout épuisé, comme fourbus de fatigues, ses sens tombèrent en léthargie, l'impuissance fut proche. Il se retourna sur le chemin, dégrisé, seul, abominablement lassé, implorant une fin que la lâcheté de sa chair l'empêchait d'atteindre' (p. 87).

According to a male libidinal scheme, impotence separates desire from pleasure. In des Esseintes's case impotence appears to be a consequence of perversion, defined here as that saturation which leaves no animating gap between desire and pleasure. Ultimately des Esseintes's body, like the narrative which constructs it, knows no suspense as such. The fabrication of artificially induced pleasures procures fictions of anticipation that only appear to liberate the hero. The reader's response to such 'fabrications' involves the secondary anticipation that is the suspense of interpretation rather than the suspense of plot. This twinning of the exhaustions of plot and of perversion suggest a relationship between traditional narrative structures and a masculine regime of desire. Huysmans's will to non-conclusiveness is contradicted by the cult of the unique text (such as *L'Education sentimentale* and perhaps *A Rebours*) and yet supported by the imperative of its rewriting and rereading.

In *Le Pessimisme au XIXe siècle*, an influential guide to Schopenhauer, Hartmann, and Leopoldi, Elme-Marie Caro suggests the significance both of the incomplete in the construction of tragic irony, and of the endgame of nihilism: 'dans toutes les races, dans toutes les civilisations, des imaginations puissantes ont été frappées de ce qu'il y a d'incomplet, de tragique dans la destinée humaine'.[19] This vision of 'la suprême ironie des choses' is countered in chapter 6 of his study, entitled 'Le but de l'évolution du monde: le néant, dernier terme du progrès':

Le pessimisme seul, à ce que l'on nous assure, a pu saisir cette fin absolue des choses à lumière toujours grandissante de son principe . . . C'est un axiome posé

... par M. Hartmann, que la série des fins ne saurait être infinie, que chaque fin, dans la série, n'est par rapport à la suivante qu'un moyen, qu'il faut de toute nécessité qu'il y ait une fin dernière ou suprême à laquelle soient suspendues toutes les fins intermédiaires ... Si la série des fins est nécessairement finie, quelle est celle de toutes les fins proposées que l'on peut regarder comme l'explication dernière et le terme du mouvement de l'univers ?

By parodying his obsession with *la fin*, Caro exposes in Hartmann a nihilistic faith in the realizable nature of apocalyptic discourse, or what may be termed its ultimate non-fictionality. Writing itself becomes a questionable vocation for pessimists such as Maupassant and Huysmans who believe in the futility of endeavour. Caro, however, concludes in favour of a work ethic which corresponds to Zola's own: 'c'est le travail qui sauve et sauvera toujours l'humanité de ces tentations passagères et dissipera ces mauvais rêves'. Huysmans himself later retracts his affiliation to Schopenhauer. In a letter of November 1891 to an anonymous correspondent, he complains, 'le néant de[s] conclusions [de Schopenhauer] me gêne. Dans l'inintelligible abomination qu'est la vie, il ne peut pas ne rien y avoir'.[20]

Another contemporary critic, Albert Pinard, offers decadent authors another version of Hobson's choice:

Cher pessimiste, il faut ne plus écrire un mot, brûler vos œuvres complètes et anéantir votre nom, ou revenir à quelque confiance dans les choses, admettre une vague bonté de la Nature répondant sur les êtres de fugitives lueurs de contentement comme le soleil jette sur les mondes d'insouciants et délicieux reflets.[21]

As naive or pernicious as this confidence seems, Pinard is unwittingly close to one of the paradoxes of such decadent writing. As in this 'roman suicide', texts which predict the apocalypse necessarily harbour a dream of destruction, and in accordance with that dream any such text fantasises that it may have the last word, literally as well as figuratively.[22] Aware of the weight of cultural heritage, the artist's goal is no longer the originality of being the first but the prescience of being the last. At such an historical terminus texts and their readers (or both) are presumably destroyed.

It is just such a symbolic burning of the text which Zola toys with but ultimately rejects in *Le Docteur Pascal*. To dream of having the 'last word', as does *A Rebours*, contradicts the fantasy of cultural paternity which Zola entertains. Zola's dream of dominating the public space in terms of fame and success stands at odds with the claustrophilia of the pessimist. As Elme-Marie Caro writes of Lucretius in his classic analysis of pessimism, 'la sagesse est d'éteindre en soi tout désir et d'arriver à cette apathie qui ressemble assez au nirvâna boudhique, et dans laquelle rien ne pénètre plus, ni bruit du dehors, ni étonnement, ni émotion'.[23] It is precisely this 'wisdom' which des Esseintes cannot maintain. Alone in a compartment on a train bound for Paris on the first (and only) leg of his abortive trip to London, des Esseintes discovers: 'Cette solitude si ardemment enviée et enfin acquise, avait abouti à une détresse affreuse; ce silence qui lui était autrefois apparu comme une compensation des sottises écoutées pendant des ans, lui pesait maintenant d'un poids insoutenable' (pp. 239–40).

This silencing of civilisation is met by the logorrhea of the Decadence which generates discourse – if we may use the phrase – as if there were no tomorrow. Though *A Rebours* resists the end-determined structures of traditional narrative, the Decadence as such is obsessed by the imminent closure of a grand historical narrative. This 'culture of the penultimate' seems to accelerate towards its close. Counter to this apparent inevitability stands that logorrhea of the Decadence. Description proffers a fiction of resistance to the silence that may follow the end of the text (and the end of the culture it voices), and it does so without adding to the skeletal framework of the narrative. Another privileged means of resisting the end of one's encounter with the text is, of course, the art of interpretation itself. *A Rebours* does not simply invite interpretation; it is itself an extended act of cultural analysis. The critic adds to the logorrhea of the Decadence by 'reading between the lines', and, according to *A Rebours*, to invite such a reading is a mark of literary value. In praise of Edmond de Goncourt's *La Faustin*, the narrator tells us:

Cette suggestion au rêve qu[e des Esseintes] réclamait, débordait de cette œuvre où sous la ligne écrite, perçait une autre ligne visible à l'esprit seul, indiquée par un qualificatif qui ouvrait des échappées de passion, par une réticence qui laissait deviner des infinis d'âme qu'aucun idiome n'eût pu combler. (pp. 309–10)

Reading between the lines can be a matter of completing a text by reading against it. This tension between the silence after Armageddon and the logorrhea of description and interpretation is further stressed by *A Rebours*'s position between the silence of privacy and the act of rereading which the novel encourages.

It might be claimed that the suspense usually generated by the uncertainty of an ending is created in *A Rebours* by the reader's interest in des Esseintes's fate. Nevertheless, Huysmans's avoidance of the end-determined structure of the Aristotelian plot invites a reading more con-

cerned, as we have said, with the suspense of interpretation than the suspense of intrigue. The suspense of interpretation demands that the
novel be reread, and the preface of 1903 is clearly such a rereading. The
way in which texts may demand rereading is another mark of literary
value according to *A Rebours*. In praise of modern secular literature in
chapter 14, the narrator recalls how des Esseintes has reread Baudelaire,
Flaubert, Zola and Edmond de Goncourt, until he can open them no
more, 'à force de les relire, de s'être saturé de leurs œuvres, de les savoir,
par cœur, tout entières, il avait dû, afin de les pouvoir absorber encore,
s'efforcer de les oublier et les laisser pendant quelque temps sur ses
rayons, au repos' (p. 312). Mourning the rarity of the literary qualities
exhibited by Villiers de l'Isle-Adam, a little later in the chapter, des
Esseintes sighs, 'mon Dieu! mon Dieu! qu'il existe donc peu de livres
qu'on puisse relire' (p. 325). This desire to be reread functions at a metatextual level as an implicit aim in *A Rebours*.

Huysmans's nuanced attitude towards traditional narrative endings
is suggested at an early stage in the short story, 'Claudine', one of the
tales in *Le Drageoir aux Épices* of 1874. Claudine is pursued by two suitors,
Just and Aristide, who are in conflict precisely because they have so
much in common (and vice versa). Once again, the irony of this narrative bifurcation is that Claudine's alternatives actually offer her no real
choice at all. Yet, as Marie warns, 'cette situation-là ne peut durer'.[24] In
fact Claudine hesitates because of this very binary structure which
appears to propel the narrative forward. In fact this choice is avoided
when Maman Turtaine sends Claudine to the aptly named Plaisir
where she finds a husband. So the plot, which appears momentarily to
escape the conjugal paradigm, is recast in terms of a traditional
denouement.

The fact that Just and Aristide later marry other women teaches
Maman Turtaine about the inverse relationship between fidelity and the
bourgeois cult of Romantic love. 'Plus un homme aime', she concludes,
'moins longtemps il reste fidèle'.[25] The act of marriage is not merely a
rite of passage. It also represents an idealized stasis in the history of personal relations, which might in fact be termed an anti-passage, where at
least in theory emotional certainties may be anchored. The ideal of
Romantic love would be a situation where narrative development was
no longer necessary, where desires and pleasures coincided. In this
Romantic tradition to which Huysmans responds, narrative is experienced as a process of perdition. In a story which culminates in marriage,
the narrative recounts a loss of innocence, and in the novel of adultery

(typically the tale which ends in death) characters lose those emotional certainties promised by the rituals of the wedding day.

Huysmans's attitude towards narrative endings is also illuminated by his *mal de siècle* which involves a decadent fear of the future. Yet the dystopian rhetoric of apocalypse speaks of the power of the divine with an eloquence equal to the idealism of faith. As des Esseintes asks, 'est-ce que, pour montrer une bonne fois qu'il existait, le terrible Dieu de la Genèse et le pâle Décloué du Golgotha n'allaient point ranimer les cataclysmes éteints, rallumer les pluies de flammes qui consumèrent les cités jadis réprouvées et les villes mortes?' (p. 361). This fear of the future explains des Esseintes's disdain for 'les horreurs d'un jour de l'an' evoked by the smell of one of the flowers he orders, the 'Cattleya de la Nouvelle-Grenade' (p. 196). New Year's Day, of course, marks the progression of the calendar ever closer to the century's close. This fear of the future has an effect on the novel's construction – in both senses of the term, as structure and process. The narrative enjoys a structural circularity which takes des Esseintes back to Paris, and the writing of the novel is presented in the preface of 1903 as an act of radical freedom which takes its author beyond the enclosures of the literary school: '*A Rebours*, qui me libéra d'une littérature sans issue, en m'aérant, est un ouvrage parfaitement inconscient, imaginé sans idées préconçues, *sans intentions réservées d'avenir*, sans rien du tout' (p. 59, our italics).

Des Esseintes's return to Paris is prescribed by his doctor as a cure for his neurosis. As we have seen, *Les Rougon-Macquart* also concludes with the tale of a doctor, *Le Docteur Pascal*, and Christopher Lloyd ventures the hypothesis that, 'œdipally speaking, Zola was the father whom Huysmans had to kill in *A Rebours*, to be born as an author in his own right'.[26] Joseph Halpern also connects Zola and the ending of *A Rebours*: 'the doctor treats him like a child and he responds like a child; if Zola is the father assassinated in *A Rebours*, then God and the doctor are his replacements'.[27]

In *A Rebours* des Esseintes's mother, 'immobile et couchée', remained during her son's early years 'dans une chambre obscure du château de Lourps' (p. 81). Fontenay-aux-Roses represents an escape from Lourps and yet is distinct from Paris, which was his father's realm. To accentuate the isolation of des Esseintes's own domain, the narrator notes 'la difficulté des communications mal assurées par un ridicule chemin de fer, situé au bout de la ville' (p. 88). His father, so the 'Notice' says, would make regular trips to Paris. Paris is not just the public male world of business and politics, and the implication may be that his father's motives are amorous. So for des Esseintes to follow his father back to what in his *guide de l'adultère* of 1883 Pierre Veron had called *Paris vicieux* is, in a sense, to return to the capital of adulterous desires.

A Rebours claims to cure des Esseintes's neurosis in terms of the passage from maternal love to paternal identification, from Lourps to Paris, advised by that surrogate father, the doctor. Des Esseintes's appreciation of Schubert's *Lieder* locates the *banlieue* as that *terrain vague* between maternal bonding and paternal identification. It is the point where one amorous narrative ends and another may thus lawfully begin:

Il y avait dans ce lamento ['Les Plaintes de la jeune fille'[28]], quelque chose de plus que de navré, quelque chose d'arraché qui lui fouillait les entrailles, quelque chose comme une fin d'amour dans un paysage triste. Et toujours lorsqu'elles lui revenaient aux lèvres, ces exquises et funèbres plaintes évoquaient pour lui un site de banlieue. (p. 341)

This Romantic terminus is in fact but a stopping-off point between parental icons. The father's return to Paris through the son (before and after *A Rebours*), and the Marles's return to Paris, both testify to the impossibility of fully privatizing desire by excluding society, without extinguishing the terms of desire itself. The impediments of social interaction provide the necessary separations or animating differences at the heart of the conjugal bond (in *En rade*, as we shall see) and in the constitution of the subject (in *A Rebours*). Paris, as the goal of the Romantic hero, becomes unwritable (literally, beyond the text) precisely because it is all too writable. The *Bildungsroman* which treats the problem of how to begin in life receives ironic treatment from Huysmans in a cultural environment attuned to the imperatives of closure. Its ending's repression and postponement of the theme of death is haunted by a Baudelairean immersion in the funereal. To arrive in Paris is no longer the start of the hero's progression but an admission that the game is already over. Like the first chapter, the 'Notice', the 'Préface', and the title, which all lay claim to and yet subvert the very notion of inaugural status, Ruysbroeck's epigraph suggests the ultimate circularity of the apparent hierarchy of modalities; *falloir* > *savoir* > *vouloir*: 'il *faut* que je me *réjouisse* au-dessus du temps . . ., quoique le monde ait horreur de ma joie, et que sa grossièreté ne *sache* pas ce que je *veux* dire' (p. 54, our italics). The object of necessity, *jouissance*, is itself the aim of desire. *Falloir* and *vouloir* coincide, with the effect that the distance between necessity and will that animates Romantic ethical philosophy is short-circuited.

Clearly the intertextual parade does not simply refer the reader outwards to a seemingly infinite body of other texts beyond *A Rebours*, to other authors beyond Huysmans, and to other places beyond Fontenay. It also refers the reader inwards to the text's own use of language. The novel provides several metaphors of texts-within-texts. On days of unrelenting spleen, we are told, des Esseintes shakes the cage where he keeps a cricket and watches the cage 'se répercuter à l'infini dans le jeu des glaces' (p. 93). Similarly, in the next chapter, des Esseintes's dining-room at Fontenay, designed like a ship's cabin to fit inside the original dining-room, is compared to 'ces boîtes du Japon qui entrent, les unes dans les autres' (p. 103).

A key model for this kind of self-reflexive awareness in *A Rebours* is provided by Mallarmé. He is also a vital figure in the novel's account of 'telegraphic writing', which involves a particularly rigorous pruning of the descriptive excesses of verbal expression. As far as des Esseintes is concerned, *Les Amours jaunes* (1873) by Tristan Corbière inaugurates this style of writing (Huysmans includes Rimbaud in the canon of 'l'art profane' in the preface of 1903 (p. 68)). Of Corbière we read, 'c'était à peine français; l'auteur parlait nègre, procédait par un langage de télégramme, abusait des suppressions de verbes' (p. 316). This is yet one more process in the tension between forms of inflationary rhetoric, on the one hand, which postpone the absolute closure of a text (such as the copia of description, the acts of rereading and interpretation) and, on the other, the will-to-silence feared by this logorrhea and intuited by 'telegraphic writing'.

One of the poems cited from des Esseintes's copy of *Quelques vers de Mallarmé*, 'Les Fenêtres', invokes the very issues of æsthetic closure which are at stake in *A Rebours*.[29] Still attempting to write from and yet beyond traditional quatrains of *rimes croisés*, this poem suggests a way in which the tension between idealism and materialism might integrate the form of æsthetic closure and the theme of spatial enclosure experienced under the extreme conditions of hospitalisation ('Las du triste hôpital'). The rupture of the exclamation mark after 'souvenir' at the very centre of these ten stanzas – which signals in a brutal transference the shift from third- to first-person, from analysing to analysed – cracks the narcissistic mirror-stage by which the Idealist gestures towards an infinite openness. As we read in stanzas seven and eight:

> Je fuis et je m'accroche à toutes les croisées
> D'où l'on tourne épaule à la vie, et, béni,
> Dans leur verre, lavé d'éternelles rosées,
> Que dore le matin chaste de l'Infini

> Je me mire et me vois ange! et je meurs, et j'aime
> – Que la vitre soit l'art, soit la mysticité –
> A renaître . . .

This regressive theology of the transcendent human subject is immediately countered by the materialist present whose Flaubertian *bêtise* subverts the scene of beauty elsewhere. After the line, 'Au ciel antérieur où fleurit la Beauté!', the poem continues:

> Mais, hélas! Ici-bas est maître: sa hantise
> Vient m'écoeurer parfois jusqu'en cet abri sûr,
> Et le vomissement impur de la Bêtise
> Me force à me boucher le nez devant l'azur.

A Platonic ideal of æsthetic openness is reinscribed in negative terms by the shift from 'la bouche, fiévreuse et d'azur bleu vorace', which opens the third stanza, to the blocking of the nose which is a closure of the body to the realm of sensations. This is a transposition from *la bouche* to *boucher*, from mouth to nose, from the oral to the olfactory, from the substantive to the verb. The poem closes on a dream of openness, of exploding the crystalline model of æsthetic completeness by mobilising the hypnotised fixations of this molecular model. It dreams of smashing rather than merely opening the windows to which the title refers:

> Est-il moyen, ô Moi qui connais l'amertume,
> D'enfoncer le cristal par le monstre insulté
> Et de m'enfuir, avec mes deux ailes sans plume
> – Au risque de tomber pendant l'éternité?

Once again the question of æsthetic closure is filtered through the problems of spatial enclosure. Written in London in May 1863, 'Les Fenêtres' sets a poetic agenda for the second half of the century. By its necessarily *mauvaise foi*, however, couched in the enclosure of a metalanguage that gestures towards openness, the poem implies the futility of such an agenda. It registers therefore the stubborness with which a culture of æsthetic enclosures and 'well-made' readable artifacts posits a seductive fiction of its own universality by demanding – like *A Rebours*, paradoxically enough – to be read from the inside.

The tension between novelistic elaborations and poetic concision is resolved in the prose-poem which, as des Esseintes's favoured literary form, exhibit:

la puissance du roman dont elle supprimait les longueurs analytiques et les superfétations descriptives. Bien souvent, des Esseintes avait médité sur cet inquiétant problème, écrire un roman concentré en quelques phrases qui contiendraient le suc cohobé des centaines de pages toujours employées à établir le milieu, à dessiner les caractères. (pp. 330–1)

Yet twenty years later, Huysmans will defend *A Rebours* precisely in terms of its reaction to a stultifying Naturalism where 'le roman se pouvait résumer en ces quelques lignes: savoir pourquoi monsieur Un tel commettait ou ne commettait pas l'adultère avec madame Une telle' (p. 57). It is this fine line between reductivism and creative distillation which makes the telegraphic writing of the prose-poem so 'inquiétant'.

The ambivalence of this fantasy of distillation can also be explained in terms of a parody of reception. The Stendhalian elitism of 'une collaboration spirituelle consentie entre des personnes supérieures éparses dans l'univers' (p. 331) is subject to implicit irony in the dialogue between the chimera and the sphinx that des Esseintes has Miss Urania perform: 'il . . . se réfugia, ainsi qu'un enfant inconsolé, près d'elle, ne voyant même pas l'air maussade de la comédienne obligée à jouer une scène, à exercer son métier, chez elle, aux instants du repos, loin de la rampe' (pp. 215–16). Des Esseintes's fantasy alienates him from the socioeconomic realities of performance. The 'prostitution' of Miss Urania's body by his payment for her services signals the desublimation of the desired body. Caught within the self-universalising procedures of his solipsism, des Esseintes commits what in the bourgeois economy is the most heinous of crimes: blindness to the distinction between public and private, between performance and intimacy. For des Esseintes, the Happy Few are not sufficiently exclusive. All but 'I' are to be silently laughed out of a club which has a head but no body of members. Yet by this derisory collusion of hero and reader, this subject space is rendered yet more utopic still as a non-place where 'I' cannot be. It is as if, according to the text's self-idolization, neither des Esseintes nor the reader are fit to lay claim to a privileged knowledge that might reduce the radical otherness in Huysmans's writing. The hero's mirror is cracked, and the heuristic *telos* of the reader's traditional projection along the path of narrative logic is recharted.

Prior to Mallarmé in des Esseintes's inventory of literary tastes stands Baudelaire, the poet of apparently unwritable desires, and his figure of taboo is incest 'où l'un se livre encore quand l'autre se tient déjà en garde, où la lassitude réclame aux couples des caresses filiales dont l'apparente juvénilité paraît neuve, des candeurs maternelles dont la douceur repose et concède, pour ainsi dire, les intéressants remords d'un vague inceste' (p. 262). What this replaces is the literature of adultery:

A une époque où la littérature attribuait presque exclusivement la douleur de vivre aux malchances d'un amour méconnu ou aux jalousies de l'adultère, [Baudelaire] avait négligé ces maladies infantiles et sondé ces plaies plus incurables, plus vivaces, plus profondes. (p. 262)

Indeed it is quite clear from *A Rebours* that the imposition of a taboo is one of the very conditions of desire. At the end of the 'Notice' the narrator explains how the fact that des Esseintes can still reach Paris from his new home in the suburbs will ensure that he does not feel the need to return to society: 'il suffit qu'on soit dans l'impossibilité de se rendre à un endroit pour qu'aussitôt le désir d'y aller vous prenne' (p. 88). In chapter 6, for instance, the reader learns of des Esseintes's plot to lead the young Auguste Langlois into a life of crime by paying for his use of a brothel and then impeding the fulfilment of his desires by removing such financial support. 'Il prendra l'habitude de ces jouissances que ses moyens lui interdisent', des Esseintes rightly predicts (p. 169).

This male domain is at odds with a 'feminisation' of inhabited space, which can be tracked back by Huysmans (with the help of the Goncourt brothers) to the eighteenth century, and is invoked in the tale of d'Aigurande's marriage which, as we have already mentioned, des Esseintes encourages, unlike his other bachelor friends, because he sees in this mismatch 'une perspective infinie de ridicules maux' (pp. 166–7). First of all, d'Aigurande's wife wants to live in 'l'un de ces modernes appartements tournés en rotonde' for which d'Aigurande buys 'des meubles façonnés en rond, des consoles évidées par derrière, faisant le cercle, des supports de rideaux en forme d'arc, des tapis taillés en croissants'. Bored by this Greuzian feminized space, however, which bears, it is implied, the circular forms of her own body and desires, she has her husband move with her to 'un appartement carré, moins cher' where 'aucun meuble ne put ni cadrer ni tenir'. Now the round furniture in square rooms (or square pegs in round holes) represents the inability of marriage to *accommodate* the mobility of desire. For financial reasons d'Aigurande cannot change the furniture too, which implies the socioeconomic limits on the individual's self-expression through control of his environment. This echoes Folantin who is in a sense a des Esseintes without the money to indulge his whims. The closure of d'Aigurande's tale is the failure of the marriage, 'la séparation de corps'. Here the denouement of the tale literally means the untying of the knot.

So Huysmans's acceptance of the validity of marriage is at best grudging:

Le seul bonheur que l'on peut avoir, on se le donne soi-même. C'est folie que de tabler sur les autres – mais on peut les faire entrer en son jeu. Le mariage, avec efforts mais volonté, donne sans doute tout cela, mais il faut se classer avec soi-même.[30]

The marital bedroom is encountered in *En rade* as a metaphor for the incongruence of minds and bodies. For Jacques Marles, 'décidément, un bain de tristesse tombait de ce plafond trop haut, sur ce carreau froid. Louise pensa que son mari songeait à ses ennuis d'argent; elle l'embrassa'.[31] We might say that the Marles in fact 'inherit' the château from des Esseintes, who abandons it, according to the 'Notice' in *A Rebours*. As a bourgeois couple, they try to live where des Esseintes knows he cannot survive. The Marles in turn return to Paris from the château at the end of *En rade*. Images of conjugal self-enclosure are common to the imperatives of narratives of both adultery and consanguinity, hence the ambivalence of placing the married couple threatened by adulterous desires, Louise and Jacques Marles, within the château of consanguineous degeneration, Lourps. Before going to bed, Jacques attempts to shore up the gaps that perforate the conjugal cell: 'Il alla visiter les portes; les pênes ne marchaient pas et, malgré ses efforts, les clefs s'entêtaient à ne point tourner; il finit par adosser une chaise contre la porte d'entrée pour empêcher le battant de s'ouvrir, puis il revint à la fenêtre, sonda les ténèbres des vitres et harassé d'ennui, se coucha.' Yet, by a 'phénomène bizarre', the room is distorted in the mental space between consciousness and dream, 'le mur, devenu liquide, oscilla, mais sans s'épandre; bientôt, il s'exhaussa, creva le plafond, devint immense, puis . . . une brêche énorme s'ouvrit, une arche formidable sous laquelle s'enfonçait une route'. Material organisation is threatened by the reworkings of the transgressive imagination. Structure is 'de-realized' within the subject's fantasy realm by 'l'immesurable fuite des espaces'.

Hearing footsteps outside, Jacques goes to investigate but finds only a bird flapping. The house of the paranoid spouse is haunted in Ibsenian fashion. The detested yet desired Other of the adulterous scene is reincarnated in a degenerated version of the received passionate conceit of the nightingale. The husband-as-policeman can read from the tawdry remains of an Early Modern aristocracy in the salon and dining-room a portent of the demise of his own class. The history of Lourps bears implicit witness to the ephemerality of bourgeois power. What Jacques took to be an ordered space turns out to be 'une véritable folie de portes', 'ce labyrinthe', 'cet inextricable fouillis de cabinets et de pièces', leading to . . . the library.[32]

In contrast to the d'Aigurandes, des Esseintes can control his domestic environment by playing with its compartmentalisations. He divides the salon into a series of 'niches', each carpeted individually and yet bearing the traces of more general patterns. Des Esseintes's habit of reading specific books in certain parts of the room connotes the analogy between spaces and texts. His cult of privacy sets into relief the non-private nature of this bourgeois family unit which claims for itself the status of privacy. At the same time he connotes the anti-social extreme towards which the atomisation of the bourgeois family tends. The decadent recluse is not merely the opposite of the bourgeois individual; he also represents an extreme version of straitened middle-class lives. In 'Le pont du jour' (*Croquis parisiens*) the *ouvriers* are contrasted with the *petits bourgeois* who are 'plus enchaînés dans leurs boutiques qu'ils ne peuvent quitter et au fond de laquelle ils couchent; puis, ils prennent moins souvent l'air que l'artisan'.[33] The geometry of everyday living is intimately related to the value of privacy within bourgeois discourse. Such an idealization of privacy (which may be read as a delimitation of the encroachments of public space) suggests perniciously that there might be an apolitical sphere which brackets out relations of power. Indeed, Jennifer Birkett defines the Decadence perceptively as 'an attempt – and a very successful and entertaining one – to substitute fiction for history'.[34]

The isolation of des Esseintes as a member of an already isolated class poses the problem of just whom this text might inspire. *A Rebours* is a text which at one level requires reading from the inside, as we have seen, and yet, for the mass of the bourgeois readership, it must appear radically exterior to their experience. Indeed, it is only at the end of the novel that the hero returns to Paris and the realm of a reading public. Bourgeois readers can only approach this text by standing at a certain distance from themselves. Yet the issue of class relations does still function in the text, but only as the subtle index of a post-Naturalist nuancing of social questions. This explains the difficulties that social interpretations of *A Rebours* have encountered.[35]

In fact, the avoidance of 'cette basse distraction des esprits médiocres, la politique' (p. 111) may be a way for Huysmans to inscribe the political at the expense of politics as such (in a way which Roland Barthes would have admired).[36] Located in *A Rebours* outside the *polis*, this distinction between non-politics and the apolitical is exemplified by the reference to Tertullian whose relation to his Age is, the reader learns, one of 'antithèse': 'il préparait tranquillement ses sermons, ses écrits dogma-

tiques, ses plaidoyers, ses homélies, pendant que l'Empire romain bran-
lait sur ses bases' (p. 120). The maintenance of æsthetics in the face of
cataclysmic history can itself be implicitly political. Like those heroes of
the *fin de siècle*, Gilles de Rais and Dorian Gray, des Esseintes is, in Fritz
Schalk's terms, 'in Zwist mit der Zeit'.[37] The narrator expresses des
Esseintes's awareness of the threats posed to genius by utopianism in an
age of platitudes: 'il vient un moment où il s'évade violemment du péni-
tencier de son siècle et rôde, en toute liberté, dans une autre époque avec
laquelle, par une dernière illusion, il lui semble qu'il eût été mieux en
accord' (p. 308). The paradoxical imaginative freedom of the claus-
trophiliac exhibits a phosphorescent instability that the narrative cannot
maintain: des Esseintes must return to Paris and the novel must close.

Again Baudelaire offers a point of comparison and contrast. Both
Cramer in *La Fanfarlo* and des Esseintes leave their utopia to return to
reality. We should note, however, that Cramer returns explicitly to the
political, to the *polis*, where a multiplicity of social and erotic activities
compete. It is in fact the logic of contagion governing the figure of
antithesis which politicizes des Esseintes's solitude. According to 'la loi
des contrastes' his attempt to try to cure his neurosis by reading Dickens
only begets more erotic thoughts (p. 208). It is recalled several pages later
that antithesis has in fact already been an organising principle of his
erotic itinerary, 'la ventriloque . . . lui plut par le contraste même qu'elle
opposait avec l'Américaine' (p. 214). So a return to the centre of political practice that is Paris must also be a return to the milieu of sexual
encounters. Ultimately the doctor's diagnosis of neurosis mediates the
deconstruction (rather than the synthesis) of the antithesis between solitude and politics. Des Esseintes's paradoxical sense of liberty by
incarceration is itself a critical reading of freedom within Third
Republic society symbolised by a crisis in the body's dysfunctional relationship to the otherness of substance: 'par le temps qui court, il n'existe
plus de substance saine, . . . le vin qu'on boit et . . . la liberté qu'on pro-
clame, sont frelatés et dérisoires' (p. 235). As we shall see in the next
chapter, the characters of *Un accident de Monsieur Hébert* and *Paris* indulge
in the material pleasures of modernity to the point of intoxicating blindness, only to find a radical questioning of the social order emerge like a
return of the repressed and thereby bring into question the cultural
significance and acuteness of the received narratives of family transgressions and perversions.

CHAPTER 6

Painting, politics and architecture

Combien je vous plains, mâles épaissis,
Rongés d'Hébétude et bleus de soucis,
Dont l'âme se vautre en de viles proses![1]

The reactionary and regressive forces embodied in a figure such as des Esseintes stand at the opposite pole to those texts which embrace the imbrication of the private and the political, such as Hennique's *Un accident de Monsieur Hébert* and Zola's *Paris*. Both of these novels are informed by systems of analogy which suggest, in the first case, the politically corrosive force of adultery amongst the bourgeoisie, and in the second, a metaphorical link between the implosion of the decadent aristocracy by incest and the explosions of the anarchist movement in *fin de siècle* Paris. By taking us, in the first instance, outside the city, and in the second, into its subterranean depths, these novels refuse to allow the self reflections of indulgent erotic desires to expel marginal radical politics beyond a yet wider perimeter. Hennique's novel in particular highlights those moments of ideological blindness around which this bourgeois political map is charted. By the same token, though, this underlining of the psychosexual dynamics of what might be termed the politics of rupture ultimately serves to hold these marginal discourses within the figurative and formal self-satisfaction of bourgeois realism. As such they ultimately fail to rise to the provocative challenge set by *L'Education sentimentale*'s melding of sexual and political polarities.

DINING OUT BEYOND THE CITY LIMITS

ACCIDENT Toujours «déplorable» ou «fâcheuse»; comme si on devait jamais trouver un malheur une chose réjouissante.
CAMPAGNE Tout y est permis.[2]

Remembered mainly for his contribution to the *Soirées de Médan*, Léon Hennique (1851–1935) has never truly escaped the monumental shadow of Emile Zola. As O. R. Morgan notes 'little is known of this rather remote figure'.[3] However, one of his many overlooked texts, *Un accident de Monsieur Hébert*, belongs to the cluster of Naturalist texts completed in the 1880s in the wake of Gustave Flaubert's death, which reveal how the theme of adultery was subject to a particular critical retrospection on the part of the latter's admirers.[4]

Un accident de Monsieur Hébert recounts the adulterous liaison of the wife of a Versailles magistrate, Gabrielle Hébert, with the officer Robert Blanc de Ventujol. Morgan is rightly critical of both these characters as examples of bourgeois stupidity in this 'satirical work of considerable potency'.[5] It will be argued, however, that there is, as in the case of *Pot-Bouille*, a generic category error in critics' isolation of this social satire with little reference to literary parody as such. Morgan contrasts 'the documentary value' of *Un accident* favourably with *La Dévouée*. It is, he argues, 'more selective in [the] accumulation of detail' and 'free from the dull enumerations of irrelevant accessories'. Indeed, he claims, it 'qualifies completely for the title of "roman naturaliste"'. In the words of a more recent thesis, however, '*Un accident de Monsieur Hébert* est un moment important dans sa carrière, point de convergence d'une production apparemment naturaliste, même aux yeux de Zola, et d'aspirations essentiellement individualistes'.[6] Rousseau asserts that

Hennique n'est pas foncièrement engagé dans le mouvement naturaliste. C'est un bourgeois qui trouve dans l'écriture une occupation qui ne doit pas être contraignante, et s'il a choisi d'être un écrivain naturaliste, c'est davantage parce que le mouvement naturaliste était le plus apte à l'époque de l'accueillir, que par vocation.

This echoes the cynicism of Morgan: 'His financial situation became sound with the death of his father-in-law in 1886, and his association with Zola and his literary campaign began to emerge as what it really was: the flirtation of a *bourgeois révolté*, an aspirant to literary success, with the newest and most original theories of his day.'[7] This suggests that when Hennique is not with Zola, he is to be found some way behind rather than beyond his writing.

The novel's use of the adultery motif can be read at one level as an economical narrative device for twinning two legitimate objects of Naturalist inspection, the army and the law. What becomes clear on a closer reading, however, is the extent to which the paternalist authority symbolized by the army and the law (in a moral economy of self-legitimating power) is compromised by a principle of narrative economy whose logic runs thus: 'How can I write in one text the Novel of the Army *and* the Novel of the Law?' Of course, what represents narrative efficiency (bringing together the army and the law) also presents a moral threat, by bringing together the officer and the magistrate's wife.

Hennique appears to place his novel squarely within the Flaubertian tradition by stressing the stultifying sameness within both bourgeois marriage and bourgeois adultery. In the flashback in chapter 2 Monsieur Hébert's mother clasps a picture of her dead husband and tells her son, 'comme cela . . . il sera de ton mariage, lui aussi', and then we are told that 'le mariage avait eu lieu comme tous les mariages auxquels Gabrielle avait assisté'.[8] It soon becomes clear that the ritualized aspect of such historical continuity merely anticipates the routine of married life, and after the *déjeuner sur l'herbe* episode on which we shall focus Gabrielle asks herself, 'qu'étaient, en effet, les pauvres nuits, les nuits monotones, les nuits éternellement jumelles dont Hébert l'avait saturée?' (p. 145). Like Emma, of course, Gabrielle finds in adultery all the platitudes of marriage, and in a symbolic moment of mirroring as Gabrielle and Ventujol walk down the allée du Mail during the *fête* of Saint-Louis, they come across another soldier with a female companion. As Gabrielle observes their doubles she notes, 'Ils sont venus s'aimer ici, comme nous' (p. 82).

This theme of sameness at the level of experience (and also at the level of language) is anticipated in the crowd's response to the military procession at the start of the novel. In what is 'perhaps the most successful'[9] of the text's descriptive tableaux, 'de tous côtés, des mots, les mêmes, s'entendaient: entrain, discipline . . . nos soldats! bonne tenue! et tous étaient à la louange de l'armée' (p. 12). As such Hennique returns in *Un accident de Monsieur Hébert* to Flaubert's dilemma of how to write an interesting novel about essentially boring lives. What Gabrielle learns is that Hébert and Ventujol are two sides of the same coin, which is underlined by the homosocial bond developed between husband and lover in the course of the novel. Even on the evening of Saint-Louis when they embrace and Gabrielle declares her love, Ventujol fails to understand why she hates her husband so:

- Mais que vous a-t-il fait? finit par dire l'officier.
Gabrielle s'en tira par un de ces mots archi-féminins qui coupent court à toutes les interrogations.
- Rien, répondit-elle. (p. 80)

In this typical gesture of realist typology (where the reader is invited by the narrator to recognize 'one of those women') it becomes quite clear that the homosocial bond also includes Hennique's narrator.

As shall be shown, this bond between lover and husband is intensified in the *déjeuner sur l'herbe* scene. Indeed, Ventujol's very pretext for attending the *déjeuner* is that he remembers having gone to school at Louis-le-Grand with Hébert. As such there is no reason why he cannot be introduced to the husband of his mistress. Gabrielle's disconcerted reaction is to leave Ventujol's quarters. Once she is outside, the thematization of sameness and difference is highlighted before the reader in a moment of blinding clarity: 'la clarté de la rue lui causa un éblouissement. La disparité des couleurs, la dissemblance des êtres et des choses lui apparurent avec une intensité vibrante' (p. 102). What Gabrielle seems to ascertain in this perturbing scenario is that within the triangle of adultery it is she (as well as her husband) who is the victim of irony; far from forcing husband and lover into conflict, she throws them together.

Later in the novel when the adulterous encounters become infrequent, Gabrielle even calls her lover, Robert, by the husband's name, Raoul – much to the amusement of Ventujol (p. 271). 'La sympathie peu bavarde de son amant pour son mari' grows in the wake of the *déjeuner sur l'herbe* and whenever they meet thereafter there is a veritable 'assaut d'amabilités'. At the same time, though, Gabrielle feels quite isolated: 'elle aurait tout donné pour avoir une confidente attentive, dépourvue de préjugés' (pp. 148–51).

Clearly therefore the adulterous triangle in this novel generates a third, all-male couple as well as a second heterosexual one. The romantically minded heroine hopes that it is her adulterous passion that will enjoy a singular value, but it is in fact the paradoxical (and yet in a sense quite endoxalized) male friendship which is so particular. For this is a novel in which men and women seem bound to see things differently. In the 'seduction' scene Gabrielle laughs at the naivety of her husband: 'C'est si amusant un homme qui ne se doute de rien!' (p. 93). Ventujol, however, is less certain about the supposedly comic nature of the cuckold's ignorance: 'Amusant! . . . amusant! tout dépend du point de vue auquel on se place'. To suggest that analytical decisions about a story's genre depend on one's point of view ('is Hébert's tale a comedy or a tragedy?') is to highlight the challenges in reading a novel which stresses the humorous aspect in this narrative of adulterous deception.

The humour borne of social satire and literary parody seems at times to take us from a nineteenth-century bourgeois crisis over illegitimacy back to Mozart's world of comic infidelity. As *Così fan tutte* reminds us, however, 'tears are neighbours to a smile', and just as Ventujol has failed to share Gabrielle's sense of the comic, so she will fail to appreciate his. In this same chapter she claims that it is duty which prohibits her and Ventujol from indulging their desires. Ventujol smiles secretly but she spies him in the mirror and complains, 'vous ne me croyez pas . . . Vous ne croyez jamais à cela, vous hommes . . .' (p. 95). In a divisive admixture of genre and gender, one man's comedy is another woman's tragedy, and vice versa. Gabrielle may catch the soldier off his guard in the mirror, but the mirrored image is as always the wrong way round. This is Marx's notion of history repeating itself as farce registered in a personal mode, and the repetition lies in the cynical interpretation which follows the potentially tragic moment. After the abortion Gabrielle prays every morning and every evening, but for the narrator (with an attitude similar to Ventujol's) these are merely 'des tendresses d'opéra-comique' (p. 209). In the self-parodic banality of trivial bourgeois life, potentially tragic experience is already filtered through the farce of *répétition* (which bears comparison with the pattern of rehearsal without performance that we find in Céard's *Une belle journée*).

This reinterpretation of the genres of human experience highlights the cynicism of the Don Juan figure, and this episode precedes the 'seduction' scene toward which the early part of the novel has led.[10] I place 'seduction' in quotation marks for this is clearly represented as rape. According to the perturbing relativism of Ventujol, however, 'tout dépend du point de vue auquel on se place'. She has flirted with him by sitting on his knee, kissing him and then jumping off, but he throws her onto the bed and the narrator articulates coldly the fact of rape: 'soudain, lasse de se débattre, efforcée, Mme Hébert ne bougea plus. Alors Ventujol la viola' (p. 98). Ventujol leaves the room and returns with trepidation a quarter of an hour later, only to be embraced affectionately by his victim who apologizes for being silly. It is on such unromantic grounds that the adulterous relationship is founded. Mutual passion, it seems, can be confirmed by rape, and Gabrielle will return to Ventujol.

Indeed she will return to this problematic origin in chapter 7 after the *déjeuner sur l'herbe* scene:

«Elle se souvenait bien d'avoir annoncé à Versailles qu'elle était enceinte, le jour où, pour la première fois, elle s'était donnée! . . . donnée! . . . Donnée? . . . le jour où il l'avait prise plutôt, car elle ne s'était pas donnée! . . . A quoi bon biaiser ainsi? pourquoi vouloir s'abuser soi-même? . . . Elle s'était donnée après avoir été prise, peut-être en même temps . . . Et qu'importait, d'ailleurs! puisqu'elle aimait Ventujol, puisqu'elle l'adorait . . . Aimer n'était pas un mot assez fort . . . il avait trop servi, traîné dans les ruisseaux, dans la lie de toutes les fanges . . . Adorer! à la bonne heure! adorer, adorer!» Elle s'arrêta au mot *adorer*, se plut à le répéter. (p. 146)

This verbal fixation echoes Emma Bovary's famous assertion 'j'ai un amant!', which is itself refocused by the Don Juan figure in Zola's *Pot-*

Bouille who, as we have seen, cries 'j'ai mon crime!' That such a moment should be generated by the memory of rape is particularly perturbing, but this memory is itself not without a verbal play which is in keeping with the novel's often comic tone, such that 'A quoi bon biaiser ainsi?' can be recast by the playful reader as 'A quoi bon *baiser* ainsi?'

The reader should not therefore be surprised to discover that Gabrielle is the victim of a certain misogyny in this novel, not simply from Ventujol but also from the complicitous narrator. Gabrielle is represented in chapter 2 as a female type (and thus part of another pattern of repetition): 'orgueilleuse comme toutes les femmes, Mme Hébert ne se demanda pas un instant si Ventujol l'aimerait, lui! . . . elle allait sûre d'elle-même, dans la vanité triomphante de son sexe et de son inexpérience' (p. 47). It is as if the narrator is one of Ventujol's army pals who meet at the Café des Anglais.

It is at the Café des Anglais that Ventujol gets his friend Pointude to read aloud the anonymous love letter he has received, which is, of course, from Gabrielle. The author of the letter imagines the consummation of her apparently impossible (and thus tragic) passion: '«c'eût été romanesque et exquis! . . . Hélas! je suis tombée toute fris-sonnante de mon rêve»' (p. 27). Such fantasy is, we may note, already conceived of in the generic terms of literature as 'romanesque'. Indeed, in the flashback which recounts the composition of the letter, the narra-tor asks: 'allait-elle se dégrader comme une de ces femmes dont elle avait lu l'histoire dans des romans?' (pp. 32–3). Mme Hébert has, it seems, already read *Madame Bovary*. Ventujol's place on the rue Saint-Pierre in Versailles includes 'une bibliothèque de livres spéciaux et de romans' (p. 22) whilst the Hébert household includes 'le petit salon où Gabrielle, habituellement, un livre à la main, cherchait à éluder les rancœurs de sa languissante oisiveté' (p. 73). As she recovers from the abortion, Gabrielle disobeys the doctor and starts to read again in secret (p. 230), for this novel is a textual representation of a world of jaded sensibilities in which desire is always already textualized for women who find an inner exile in reading (and not just for the likes of Huysmans and des Esseintes, as we saw in the previous chapter).

Desire in this world is not the pre-civilized anarchic force which haunts Romanticism but a form of social experience which is already subject to literary artifice and to the conventions of genre. The narrator recalls the military parade at the start of the novel in which Gabrielle first saw Ventujol in explicitly novelistic terms: 'Et une après-midi, sous le soleil d'une revue, banal comme un héros de roman, en uniforme, à cheval, répondant aux aspirations de son adolescence, à l'ahurissement de son esprit capricieux, au prestige maladif qu'il fallait à ses vapeurs de femme ennuyée, Ventujol lui était apparu' (p. 43). And that parade is itself a mere simulacrum of military glory played out in the wake of humiliation by the Prussians (the novel is set in 1876–7). The charge of seven thousand men looks like the real thing but is, of course, pure theatre.

What the references to literary models suggest is that this novel is a parody of existing forms and not just a satire against social norms. One need only read Flaubert's analysis of Hennique's *Les Hauts Faits de M. de Ponthau* to surmise that he would probably not have overlooked the parodic aspect. As far as Flaubert is concerned, Hennique is a parodist as well as a satirist, and in his letter to Hennique dated 3 February 1880 Flaubert warns Hennique that Romanticism has already been ably parodied: 'Deux hypothèses: ou je suis un idiot, ou vous êtes un farceur. Je préfère la seconde naturellement . . . Sous prétexte de blaguer le romantisme, vous avez fait un très beau livre romantique.'[11] This nuances René Dumesnil's sense of sadness in reading this novel, which he describes as 'un des romans naturalistes les plus tristes'.[12] In spite of Monsieur Hébert's homosocial bond with Ventujol, he is still the dupe of the comedy, for in this triangular pattern of dramatic irony, the cuckold is for a long time ignorant of the guilty knowledge shared by lovers and readers alike. One sign of this ignorance is the way in which Hébert fails to perceive the irony of his own observations. When he loses his wife in the crowd at the *fête* of Saint-Louis, he laments, '«on aurait dû se donner rendez-vous quelque part, prévoir les désagréments possibles, se garer de l'imprévu»' (pp. 72–3). It is left to the reader to distance himself from the fool in the ironic gloss of interpretation. A further irony in this metaphor of moral disorientation is that the adultery is, in the terms of the genre of the novel of adultery, far from *imprévu*. [13]

What the novel shows, moreover, is that the language of innuendo and connotation (i.e. the underdetermined message) is characteristic not just of the novel of adultery's mediation of deceit through the figure of dramatic irony; it is also central to the social discourse of flirtation. A prime example of this is the barely coded conversation between Ventujol and Gabrielle during the *fête* in chapter 4:

- Pardon, dit Ventujol, je marche trop vite . . .
- Oui, répondit-elle . . . un peu trop vite . . . beaucoup trop vite même . . .
- Nous n'avançons plus?
- Si . . . mais voyez-vous . . . je crois n'avoir jamais trotté autant. (p. 78)

As such the allusive tone of both satire and parody are interwoven in this novel. For Hébert is the victim not just of the narrator's irony; he is also the victim of the characters' irony and sarcasm which he consistently fails to grasp. Hébert's naivety is made clear from the start of the novel. He is the only member of the party at the parade not to laugh at Morizot's satirical observation when he looks at Jancourt, Majorelle and Hébert: ' – Ont-ils assez l'air de magistrats! Regardez-les: trois paires de favoris' (p. 13). The friends and family of Gabrielle were surprised in the first case that she should agree to marry 'ce jeune homme sans fredaines, dont on riait parfois à mots couverts' (p. 36). Hence the comedy of adultery belongs to a social discourse as well as a literary form, and this fusing of the social referent and its literary textualisation is apparently symptomatic of a decaying society in which the order of signs and things is radically confused.

This is one meaning of the peculiar ending to chapter 5 when Gabrielle visits a friend to calm down after learning to her horror that Hébert and Ventujol were at school together. When she arrives at the home of one of Jancourt's cousins in order to establish an alibi, she finds that one colonel Thuilier is already there. Injured in 1870 and referred to as '*le fou*', he explains how he plans to destroy Germany. Wherever she turns, the world of homosocial bonding (embodied in the army) haunts her attempts to strike out against the banality of her existence. In her search for individuality she finds only exclusion. In this chapter, though, the madness of desire is replaced by madness alone, for the colonel exclaims, 'je prendrais une paire de ciseaux . . . et j'éliminerais la Prusse et ses alliés de toutes les cartes d'Europe' (p. 106). According to the Realist code, madness might be defined as a state in which the world of signs usurps the real world, and this is the position in which *revanchiste* France finds itself, as the semiotics of the map displace geographical reality within Thuilier's delirious imagination. Similarly, as the fusing of satire and parody reveals, the realm of personal relations (as well as the public domain) borrows from the ironic literary mode of the novel of adultery in the register of flirtation, innuendo and connotation.

As much as this world of delirium and *ennui* looks forward to the Decadence, so the novel also echoes other models, such as those of Flaubert and Naturalism. The self-delusion of Gabrielle clearly fits the pattern of *bovarysme*. Typical are her 'rêves de jeune fille' and the 'banalité intoxiquée de sentimentalisme' which pervades her fantasies: 'Elle aurait voulu encore qu[e Ventujol] chantât près d'elle, le soir, dans les salons, à l'heure où les pianos roucoulent les accompagnements des romances à la mode; qu'il fût une espèce d'esclave en perpétuelle adoration; qu'il s'appelât Henri' (pp. 16–17). As Rousseau asserts, 'l'histoire de Madame Bovary devient elle-même un roman que lira Gabrielle Hébert'.[14] He also contrasts Flaubert's influence with Zola's: 'Si Zola ne perçoit pas le caractère individualiste du roman de Hennique, il ne voit pas non plus que *Un accident de Monsieur Hébert* se réfère à des œuvres et des écrivains non naturalistes. Ainsi Hennique doit trop à Flaubert pour faire une véritable création. Madame Hébert, c'est Madame Bovary'. This echoes René Dumesnil's description of the novel as 'une paraphrase encore plus désenchantée de *Madame Bovary*'.[15] In a sense, Hennique's text is indeed a continuation of Flaubert's novel in which Emma dreams of going to Paris. Like Colonel Thuilier, she mistakenly believes that to run her finger along the map is in itself already an act of possession. In the flashback to her marriage in chapter 2 it is clear that Gabrielle was delighted to leave Brest when her husband was named *procureur de la République* in Versailles, 'enchantée de cette nomination qui la rapprochait de Paris, objet de ses continuels désirs, partie de toutes les élégances' (p. 42). But Versailles, of course, is not Paris, and the contrast is made explicit at the start of chapter 4 before the *fête* of Saint-Louis when life in Versailles is described, in an idiom that d'Annunzio would have recognized, as 'comme dans les cités mortes' (p. 64).

When she does finally manage to get to the capital, it is to meet up with Ventujol at the hôtel des Colonies near the gare Montparnasse (pp. 158–9). The name of this hotel is particularly ironic given the way in which this novel maps military disaster onto decadence in private matters, as we have seen above.[16] It is not until the end of the novel that the tedious Monsieur Hébert agrees to take her to Paris, but only on the advice of his mother who recommends a doctor there.[17] The novel closes in a moment of self-conscious circularity with the couple arriving at Versailles station to take the train to Paris. As in Céard's *Une belle journée*, the rain is coming down: 'Puis, la face morne, l'âme éteinte, – lui, d'aspect rébarbatif, elle, de plus en plus malade, – ils revirent leur arrivée à Versailles autrefois, par une après-midi de soleil, sous un ciel bleu tout vibrant d'hirondelles: Hébert venait d'obtenir un avancement inespéré; Gabrielle était grosse du petit Jules' (p. 316). This flashback to a previous flashback (pp. 41–2) makes Hébert sob as his sense of personal tragedy is confirmed.

Flaubert may figure implicitly as an ideal reader in the novel's conception, but Zola and Céard were actual readers, and their varying responses can be followed in the correspondence between the

Naturalists. Céard writes to Zola from Paris on 23 November 1883 and though he sees the novel's useful strategic function in the conflict between Charpentier and Kistemæckers, he criticizes the lack of any philosophy underpinning Hennique's text:

C'est très bien exécuté avec une sûreté et une sobriété dont je ne le soupçonnais pas capable. Ce système d'observation précise et terre-à-terre, de conversations notées au vol, dans leur nullité et leur ennui, me séduit absolument, et pourtant quelque chose me semble manquer à ce livre que j'aime, et mon plaisir n'est pas aussi grand que je le voudrais. Pourquoi? Je crois avoir trouvé la raison. C'est qu'il n'y a, au fond, point de philosophie là-dessous. *Un accident de Monsieur Hébert*, par je ne sais quelle tare originelle, n'impressionne guère plus qu'un fait divers. Et pourtant, c'est d'une jolie patte.[18]

In this letter Céard seems to be fighting for the approval of the *maître de Médan* at the expense of his rival, Hennique. Indeed, rather than seeing the clutch of novels of adultery written in the wake of Flaubert's death as a coherent project, perhaps it is more realistic to analyze them in terms of such rivalry. In spite of Rousseau's thesis that this novel has much more to do with Flaubert's model than Zola's, the letter to Hennique from Médan dated 25 November 1883 does not voice Céard's concerns about a novel which is, after all, dedicated to 'mon ami Emile Zola'. He praises 'un comique excellent' in all the encounters of Gabrielle and Ventujol, particularly the 'seduction' scene counterpointed with the sounds of the parade ground, and he notes that 'il y a là-dedans une originalité qui s'affirme, un sens très curieux de la bêtise humaine. Votre adultère est d'une imbécillité vraie à donner des frissons. Les conversations amoureuses sont surtout stupéfiantes comme cruautés photographiques'.[19] As much as Naturalism is a literature of tragic sympathy, it also clearly constitutes (to borrow from Artaud) a literature of cruelty.

Amongst the scenes Zola most enjoys are the *fausse-couche* and what he terms the 'dîner sur l'herbe'. Clearly the former has Naturalist credentials. Rousseau compares the gory realism of this most conspicuous moment in the novel with the *fausse-couche* of Adèle in *Pot-Bouille*.[20] The latter, though, relates to a whole range of cultural models which makes of the *déjeuner sur l'herbe* scene an intertextual focus of particular significance. Once more, then, *Un accident de Monsieur Hébert* plays upon artistic forms as well as social norms, as a dozen bourgeois from Versailles (including the triangle of the Héberts and Ventujol) set out for what seems to be an idyllic lunch in the country. Rather than remove Gabrielle to a fictitious Paris, chapter 6 promises to take her away from the modern city to the apparently timeless bois Martin, near Jouy-en-Josas, not far from Versailles, which has been inherited unexpectedly by the Perrin de Jancourt family. This bourgeois fiction of rural tranquillity is rudely disturbed by the arrival of local *paysans* who have right of way through Jancourt's property and ridicule their middle-class niceties, thereby bringing the lunch to a rather abrupt end. It is in this *déjeuner sur l'herbe* scene that Hennique foregrounds most effectively the clichés of adultery. For it is in this scene that the romantic and erotic codes of the novel of adultery are rudely interrupted by the social codes of class antagonism.

The biblical tale of fruit offered in the Garden is one of our most resonant narratives of sexual transgression, but the *déjeuner sur l'herbe* clearly has far more recent antecedents too, most conspicuously Manet's famous painting which was shown at the Salon des Refusés in 1863.[21] This contests as much as it echoes the genre painting of the eighteenth century, in particular the *fête champêtre* of the Rococo masters. Clearly this has its literary equivalents in the Romantic evocation of humanity regressing toward nature. In *Le Peintre de la vie moderne* Baudelaire mentions late eighteenth-century engravers and water-colourists such as Debucourt, Gabriel and Augustin de Saint-Aubin, who depict in an easily accessible medium the manners of the elegant world of Paris. According to Isaacson, Manet's painting 'stands as a nineteenth-century middle-class version of the aristocratic idyll of a bygone day', and Monet's unfinished version of his own *Déjeuner sur l'herbe* originally intended for the 1866 Salon 'expresses the simple pleasures of the hitherto disenfranchised'.[22] What Hennique juxtaposes in chapter 6 of *Un accident de Monsieur Hébert* are these self-consciously simple pleasures of the bourgeoisie and the derisory interventions of those still bereft of political power. Further models are the group photograph of pleasure seekers out of doors which attained great popularity in the 1860s and other paintings of small picnic scenes intended for a middle-class audience. Examples are Bazille's *Repos sur l'herbe* (1865) and James Tissot's *Déjeuner sur l'herbe* of the middle to late 1860s. Tissot's *Partie carrée* of 1870 is a costume piece on a larger scale which emphasizes the anecdotal or flirtatious side of the pleasurable gathering, and this is clearly echoed in Hennique's version of this set scene.

Once more satire and parody fuse, for it is not merely the cultural model which threatens to saturate in artifice this scene of nature. The bourgeois manufacture of this rural idyll is foregrounded explicitly in the opening pages of chapter 6 which describe how the servants arrive at the bois Martin in the morning to set the scene for this *déjeuner*. Loiseau, Miroix and Bertoux are little more than stagehands: 'il s'agissait de trouver une clairière capable de contenir une douzaine de personnes, sans gêne pour le service' (p. 120). The class-specificity of this fantasy of rural peace is made clear in the words of Eugène Miroix: 'moi, si j'étais patron . . . je mangerais dans ma salle à manger, et pas dans les bois; comme ça, les oiseaux ne flanqueraient pas sur mes bifteks' (p. 115). As he and Bertoux applaud the humming of Loiseau 'comme s'ils venaient d'assister à une audition, dans un café-concert', it is clear that their fantasy is to enjoy a world of municipal leisure which is already all too available to their masters. Loiseau goes on to explain how he would love to have been an artist and Bertoux tells his peers of an 'artisse' that he knew:

Tout p'tit qu'il était, fallait l'voir travailler! Son fort, c'était la bimbloterie. Un jour, il a fait une cathédrale . . . rien qu'avec son couteau . . . Oui, monsieur Loiseau, une cathédrale . . . comme un pâtissier. Il l'avait fourrée sur sa cheminée, et quand il venait des camarades, le soir, il mettait dedans un bout de bougie. (p. 118)

One does not have to be a Proustian to notice in this reference to a miniature cathedral the emblem of a coherent artistic structure. This transcription of elliptical popular speech by Hennique (which readers of *Alexis* will recognize) also suggests that these servants have more in common with the *paysans* than their own masters.

By the time the guests arrive the scene has been set by the servants. Their arrival is heralded by a parodic narratorial vision of rural bliss:

Là, aussi loin que s'étendait la vue, des pièces de blés et d'avoines hérissaient le sol, inégalement séparées les unes des autres par des éteules couverts de moyettes, par des nappes moelleuses de luzernes, par d'interminables champs de betteraves d'un vert luisant. Quelques charettes y stationnaient où des hommes et des femmes, en bras de chemises, coiffés de chapeaux de paille ou de mouchoirs, empilaient des bottes de seigle. (p. 119)

And so on. However, this fantasy has already been nuanced by the evocation of an industrial horizon reminiscent of Seurat: 'au loin, dans le ciel d'un bleu argent, une haute cheminée d'usine dominait un monticule, vomissait des tourbillons de fumée noire' (p. 117). Just as marriage is supposed to impose order on the disorder of desire, so the *déjeuner* is regulated according to a bourgeois timetable quite at odds with the aristocratic ease it is intended to mimic; and Mme Bissinger is served according to plan 'à midi précis' (p. 124). The curtain rises to reveal the theatre of bourgeois leisure, but disorder constantly threatens. The stage is surrounded by props which should properly remain concealed: 'plusieurs chapeaux pendus à des branches, un éparpillement d'ombrelles, de pardessus, de mantelets enceignaient les convives d'un inévitable désordre d'antichambre' (p. 127). Things go from bad to worse when a beggar whom the servants met in the morning comes to pester the party. The women in particular are furious and are forced to state the obvious: '«mais c'est très désagréable! . . . On n'est plus chez soi . . .»' (p. 136). The bourgeois fantasy of taming nature whilst retaining the flavour of otherness which makes it so enticing for the town-dweller is exposed here in all its self-delusion.

The conflict between the municipal bourgeois and the *paysans* reinforce class prejudices, and within class boundaries other forms of exclusive affiliation are fostered, most notably the homosocial bond between classmates Ventujol and Hébert, discussed above. They sit side by side at the *déjeuner*, and it is from this perspective that the male bond is made most explicit, for in this novel where the variability of point of view is paramount the two men look with the same admiration at the woman they share:

Le magistrat et [Ventujol] jetèrent un coup d'œil vers Mme Hébert. Elle était radieuse, entourait son mari et son amant d'un même nimbe, les couvait presque sous la chaleur de ses pensées: «C'était donc vrai! . . . Elle les voyait là . . . tranquilles . . . rajeunissant le passé, causant comme si tous deux ne la possédaient pas!» Leur entente la dilatait, l'enlevait de terre, la plongeait en une langueur si étrange et si douce qu'elle en avait mal à l'âme. (p. 129)

This unease on Gabrielle's part reflects the sense that her husband and her lover are so close as to be almost interchangeable, and this analogy between men echoes the many moments in the novel where Ventujol is posited as a figure of paternity. The irony is that the officer fathers neither Jules nor the daughter Gabrielle loses, but when Jules says that he too would like to be a soldier the symbolic equivalence between men seems complete. *Tel amant, tel fils.*

It is interesting to compare this triangular pattern of relationships with Manet's *Le Déjeuner sur l'herbe* where there are also three figures in the foreground. In this painting the legs and the feet of the female nude gazing at the viewer and of the reclining man on the right form a series of emblematic triangles. Their left feet are nearly touching, as are their right feet, but she sits beside the other man. The fourth figure, the woman standing in the pool, is the absent partner who would complete the quartet of characters (but this, of course, merely sets up another set of transgressive permutations as in Goethe's *Die Wahlverwandtschaften*).

Indeed, she also completes a larger triangle on the canvas connecting all the figures in the painting. However, Hennique's version may ultimately have more in common with the larger group depicted in the various versions of Monet's unfinished *Le Déjeuner sur l'herbe*. In what has come to be known as the Moscow sketch, the surprised couple sitting on the cloth by the crockery and food almost seem to have been interrupted by their fellow guests, on the left the trio of a man and two women, and on the right the quartet of three men surrounding the seated woman. The latter seems to be seated next to her partner, and yet she is returning the gaze of the man lying in front of the tree, his jacket removed and legs stretched out in an almost languid pose. As Ventujol reminds us, of course, 'tout dépend du point de vue auquel on se place'. Unlike the couple sitting on the cloth by the crockery and food in the final fragment, the gaze of the couple in the Moscow sketch is symbolically divided by this scene, the man looking up at the trio to the left, and the woman looking at the man lying in front of the tree, like the other woman on the cloth. Of course, these women looking at the man in front of the tree form another triangular pattern in the painting's foreground. Standing alone is the mysterious figure to the right of the tree who is, in all senses, shady. Sporting a top hat, he resembles the incongruous Hébert, also 'coiffé de son chapeau à haute forme' (p. 124).

Hennique's version shares an investment in the romantic and erotic codes of flirtation with these pictorial representations of this scene. Most instructive in the context of the subsequent plot are the reciprocal glances of Cécile and Ventujol (pp. 131, 139). Before this, though, the reader has already been shown a scene of working-class flirtation when the waitress in the *auberge* where the servants stop off for a morning drink observes, 'Il va faire chaud aujourd'hui', and Loiseau replies, 'Pas si chaud que dans votre lit, pour sûr' (p. 113). The most confident flirts are the satirically minded Morizot and the English-style dandy Flavinet Saint-Ange who is described thus: 'son cou semblait cerclé par un col de fer-blanc. Il avait une mince cravate de jaconas gris à pois bleus, une culotte marron à raies vertes, les pieds dans des guêtres jaunes' (p. 123).[23] In their discussion of *Sylvia*, the latest ballet at the Opéra, Flavinet argues, 'comme si le public avait besoin des jambes de ces dames, ne pouvait en trouver ailleurs d'équivalentes' (p. 133). Morizot retorts, 'Je suis d'avis que les jambes sont bonnes à examiner partout où on les rencontre, chez soi, dans la rue, à l'Opéra'.

The irony is that the face of the adulterous Gabrielle remains 'glacial': 'depuis sa faute, elle ne tolérait plus les expressions risquées,

haïssait les moindres sous-entendus grivois'. The paranoia of guilt instils
in her a fear of connotation, and a distinction seems to operate between
middle-class innuendo and genuine transgression. The impotence of
such *badinage* is exposed most clearly when a raucous group of local girls
arrive on the scene. In one of those suggestive moments of pseudo-
paternity Ventujol relieves Gabrielle by taking Jules in his arms (p. 142).
Morizot quips, 'donnez-lui à téter', but does not realize the extent of the
connotation in this remark. What he believes to be mild banter which
plays on a simple gender inversion (as if Ventujol were playing the role
of the mother) is interpreted in a far funnier (and more sexually-
charged) fashion by his unwelcome audience: 'les paysannes, dans le
chemin, éclatèrent d'un tel rire que le conseiller en devint cramoisi, eut
pleine conscience du mauvais goût de sa facétie'. Sexual connotation
runs riot as the speaker–audience relationship crosses class boundaries.
The fragile structure of bourgeois circumlocutions is exploded by the
troubling juxtaposition of the municipal bourgeoisie with the rural poor
whose crude sexuality is associated with untamed nature. When Flavinet
confronts the *paysannes*, they simply laugh at his 'chic anglais' and one
retorts in 'une voix presque mâle'. Gender inversion bespeaks the inversion of social power, and for all the *Besitzstolz* of Jancourt who tells
Gabrielle how he acquired the bois Martin 'le nez en l'air', it becomes
evident that the bourgeoisie is on foreign soil (p. 122). What the bourgeoisie cannot bear is dialogue between the classes, but the extent of
social antagonism is manifested in the violent fury of Mme Bissinger
and the quarrel between Jules and the *galopin* who spectates (pp. 122,
132).

The comedy of bourgeois propriety has already been indexed earlier
in the chapter by the suspense in the punctuation when 'M. de Jancourt,
la face empreinte d'une noble condescendance, proposa d'admettre aux
honneurs de la nappe . . . un des domestiques. On finit par accepter' (p.
125). Loiseau is equally embarrassed to be placed alongside his masters.
The irony is that this very episode is triggered by Jancourt's observation
that 'nous sommes treize', and is thus based on a superstition which
might be more readily identified with the poor whom the bourgeoisie
despise. There is a clear echo here of Gervaise's birthday party in
chapter 7 of Zola's *L'Assommoir* where père Bru is dragged in from the
street after her exclamation, 'nous sommes treize!'.[24] The introduction
of père Bru simply means that one bad omen replaces another.

Chapter 6 of *Un accident de Monsieur Hébert* discerns the naivety of the
bourgeois fantasy of classless pleasure. The spectacle of nature which

greets them on arrival is displaced by the spectacle of society, as the rural audience come to view these middle-class visitors when word spreads of this open-air comedy (first the *galopin*, then the beggar, and finally a larger crowd appear). At first it is Cécile de Jancourt who laughs at the onlookers from behind her fan, but soon the tables are turned as the oblique bourgeois world of suggestion, symbolized by the fan and articulated via innuendo and connotation, is subjected to another level of irony from the locals. This comic thematisation of the spectacle of class difference is itself ironically anticipated by the gentlemen's discussion of the forthcoming *exposition* in Paris. Walking straight out of Flaubert's *Dictionnaire des idées reçues*, Hébert notes with the 'œil atone' of his characteristic *hébétement*, 'une grand chose que les expositions . . . la manifestation pacifique du travail, des arts et de l'industrie' (p. 127).

In this case, of course, the *exposition* of the bourgeoisie is far from 'pacifique', and when the group beat a hasty retreat, the connotations of military defeat (particularly ironic in the presence of Ventujol) are all too clear. This time the middle-classes are forced back to Versailles, and Jancourt's tragi-comic refrain, 'partie manquée! . . . partie manquée!' echoes 'à chaque instant, comme des épaves sur l'eau, pendant une débâcle' (p. 141). The disorder of the 'débâcle' is also quite evident as the locals wave 'en signe d'adieu ironique': 'on s'installa comme précédemment, mais pêle-mêle, le plus vite possible cette fois' (pp. 143–4). As with the curious appearance of colonel Thuilier at the end of the previous chapter, the *déjeuner sur l'herbe* episode closes in a similarly enigmatic fashion. The radical newspaper in Versailles somehow manages to get hold of the story the next day. What is reported is a particular version of events which contradicts the narrator's account:

Le journal radical de Versailles contait, en deux colonnes, qu'une *orgie* avait eu lieu au bois Martin, *protégée par l'armée, sous l'aile de la magistrature;* que les femmes *avaient sali les buissons de leurs vomissements* . . . mais que les paysans des environs, les travailleurs, *ceux à qui la nation devait son pain de chaque jour!* avaient fait justice des coupables . . . *en les chassant.* (p. 144, Hennique's italics)

And so the chapter ends, with the narrative returning at the start of chapter 7 to the safe space of Versailles, without commenting on this contradictory report.

The novel ends, as has been seen above, with Gabrielle returning to her husband. This is anticipated in the onomastic echo at the end of chapter 8 when Gabrielle manages to get rid of Jancourt's old cousin. Rejected by Ventujol, having lost her baby, 'débarrassée de la vieille fille, Gabrielle regagna son canapé, s'y laissa tomber avec *hébétation*' (p. 228,

our italics). What Gabrielle falls back into is the dazed stupor of conjugal habit. This ending has lead at least one critic to contrast the conservative nature of Hennique's novel with *Madame Bovary*:

> Le monde de Hennique est un monde dont la structure est figée. Chacun y joue
> son rôle, peut s'en écarter momentanément, mais revient à la place qui lui est
> attribuée. Emma, elle, est libre, et sa quête du bonheur la conduira à choisir la
> mort, preuve de sa liberté . . . C'est alors la société qui apportera la solution au
> problème de Hébert. Sa mère lui conseille de garder sa femme . . . L'aspect
> fondamental du malaise d'Emma Bovary ne se retrouve pas chez Gabrielle
> Hébert. Il s'agit pour celle-ci d'un épisode dans une vie bien réglée, où elle ne
> risque rien. La remise en cause de la société n'existe pas dans le roman de
> Hennique.[25]

Rousseau's end-determined reading of the novel fails to take into
account the interpretative lacunæ which the narrator opens up and yet
refuses to probe with any analytical rigour. As Catherine Belsey argues
in her analysis of popular novelistic romances:

> The ending is not, after all, the whole story. Too often, in my view, commenta-
> tors on romance isolate the content of the story and look for explanations at the
> level of the signified, supposing that a satisfying resolution of the plot is the
> element that ensures a satisfied reader. What they neglect in the process is the
> pleasure of reading itself, the pleasure, that is, of reading classic realist fiction.[26]

Primary amongst the pleasure-giving lacunæ in *Un accident de Monsieur
Hébert* is the end of chapter 6 which clearly does involve 'la remise en
cause de la société'. Indeed, the sociological stakes are high anyway in a
novel of adultery set in a society based on the order of married life,
where the *union libre*, much debated in the *fin de siècle*, places people
outside of polite middle-class society, for instance: 'le *regretté* Majorelle
avait brusquement disparu de la circulation pour vivre en concubinage'
(p. 271, Hennique's italics).

   What the *déjeuner sur l'herbe* scene confirms is the social contextualization of desire. The bourgeois fantasy of the rural idyll in which the play
of flirtation can be safely couched is suddenly undermined by the
manifestation of class antagonism; social codes (town versus country;
bourgeois versus *paysans*; private role-play versus public spectacle)
demystify the codes of romantic and erotic exchange. This problematic
juxtaposition of codes is, moreover, reaffirmed at the end of the novel in
another meal scene. Hébert has learned of Gabrielle's infidelity, and this
leaves his wife with a dilemma: 'L'heure du dîner approchant, elle devint
très perplexe: lui fallait-il s'avouer malade, garder la chambre comme
une adultère de roman, ou affronter la présence d'Hébert, afin de

donner le moins de prise possible à la curiosité des domestiques?' (p. 302). Which code should she obey? The romantic code or the social code? Life as a novel or the novel of real life? Once again, the code of social difference is the determinant factor, and Gabrielle decides to come down and face the music. What follows is rather less of an ordeal than the adulterous wife might expect, but to return to the stage of bourgeois married life is in any case to return to the spectacle of role-play in which, as has been seen, nothing is more perturbing than interpretation by the *peuple*. As such, the old adage of 'Not in front of the servants' is observed . . . but the memory of the bois Martin remains, as does the alternative, radical reinterpretation of the *déjeuner sur l'herbe*, which the omniscient, omnivorous Naturalist narrator (who is still present in Zola's *Paris*) must swallow and yet cannot quite digest.

ANARCHISM UNDER THE CITY

Quelle étrangeté de métaphores![27]

Il lui semblait entendre un craquement formidable, la famille bourgeoise qui s'effondrait: le père chez une fille, la mère aux bras d'un amant, le frère et la sœur sachant tout, l'un glissant aux perversités imbéciles, l'autre enragée, rêvant de voler cet amant à sa mère pour en faire un mari.[28]

Before the century ends, the author of *Les Rougon-Macquart* does manage to conclude one more set of novels, the trilogy *Les Trois Villes*, which pursues the spiritual itinerary of Pierre Froment from *Lourdes* via *Rome*.[29] At the start of the opening novel in the trilogy, Pierre is on a pilgrim train heading for Lourdes. The first person to speak in *Lourdes* is the invalid, Marie, who is travelling with Pierre's party: 'Ah! les fortifications! . . . Nous voici hors de Paris, nous sommes partis enfin!' (p. 23). The trilogy, however, shares the circular structure of *Les Rougon-Macquart*, and like *Le Docteur Pascal*, *Paris* manages to 'boucler la boucle', this time by bringing Pierre back to the capital. Published in book form in 1898 after being serialised in *Le Journal* between September 1897 and February 1898, *Paris* provides Zola's readers with an image of the metropolis in all its complexity as the century draws to a close.

Rather than simply rehearsing the well-documented relations between *Paris* and the trilogy which it closes, we shall see how this novel registers a crisis in the Naturalist enterprise. Looking back over the nineteenth century and looking down over the city, *Paris* places a tremendous strain on its plot's powers of assimilation, with the incest motif manipulated as an extreme case in the cognitive endeavours of Naturalism.

This time the sexual scenario involves a pseudo-incestuous relationship, or, we might say, a fiction of incest.

For Zola to write a novel about the capital was to test in the public domain the resources of the Naturalist rhetoric of 'tout dire' which, as we have seen throughout this study, finds its ultimate test in the representation of a supposedly unthinkable incest (which is only too amenable to representation). As Christopher Prendergast notes, 'in theory, the Naturalist project aimed at an exhaustive cataloguing and mapping of the city, mastering the material by means of its complete transcription'. However, 'matter in Zola's world, and above all in Zola's city, is always at risk of exceeding the effort of the writing to subjugate it'. This engenders 'a certain vaporization of the sign, a loss of focus, a blur akin to the "brume" which so often hangs over Zola's Paris'.[30] The city, after all, is the place where, 'at every instant, there is more than the eye can see'.[31] It is clear from an interview which Zola gives to journalists from *Le Matin* and *L'Echo de Paris* in 1892 that his use of the capital city in the title is not simply a convenient label in keeping with *Lourdes* and *Rome*. It anticipates the novel's concerns logically as well as typographically. 'Je ne possède en ce moment', he says, 'que mon titre et rien de plus' (p. 1573). As Clive Thomson writes, 'attribuer à un roman un nom de ville m'a toujours paru un geste à la fois banal et audacieux. Audacieux, parce qu'ambitieux. (Comment peut-on écrire, par exemple, un roman qui s'intitule *Paris*? . . .)'.[32] Written in the wake of the 'Paris des précurseurs de Zola (Balzac, Hugo, Flaubert, Baudelaire, etc.) qui avait presque épuisé le sujet avant lui',[33] *Paris* clearly harbours a considerable 'anxiety of influence'.

As well as dealing with the problem of how to find appropriate metaphors for the city given its status as a saturated cultural icon, the novel also confronts the dilemma of how to make sense of the complexities of multiple urban plots in a readable format. At one level, it appears that everything has been said; at another, it seems impossible for Zola to say everything. The narrative weaves between the different milieux of Paris life, from the subculture of anarchism and radical politics, via images of cosy domesticity and religiosity, to the Decadent world of an effete aristocracy which degenerates into incest. Thomson notes in *Les Trois Villes* 'une grande multiplicité de personnages secondaires (une soixantaine dans *Paris*, par exemple)'.[34] This is a symptom of the plot's complexity. Whereas *A Rebours* is full of references to books and paintings but short of people, *Paris* is crowded with characters. The latter is, of course, the world that des Esseintes leaves. Indeed, *Paris* is in a sense the converse of

A Rebours. Whereas the latter begins by leaving the 'unwritable' city and ends by returning to it, *Paris* confronts that very 'unwritability'.

The rhetoric of Naturalism evident in *Le Docteur Pascal* is turned inward by the self-conscious doubting to which *Paris* is prey. Naturalism's surgical metaphor of dissection is subject to a masochistic rewriting. Guillaume, the politically radical scientist, insists that Marie, his betrothed, marries his brother, Pierre, the fallen priest, as it is they who are truly in love: 'il eut la cruauté d'insister, en chirurgien héroïque qui taille dans sa chair plus encore que dans celle des autres' (p. 1477). The quest for knowledge (symbolized by the scientist) no longer coincides with the quest of desire. In *Le Docteur Pascal*, of course, it is the object of desire, Clotilde, who is left to complete the project of uncle Pascal, who is both scientist and lover. In *Paris*, however, the scientist loses the woman.

The multiple strands of the plot are centred around the Sacré-Cœur which is under construction as the novel progresses. The denouement returns the reader to the basilica where the novel began, so the æsthetic principle of 'boucler la boucle' operates within the novel itself as well as in the trilogy as a whole. In this climax Pierre finds Guillaume in the cellars below and persuades him not to blow up the Sacré-Cœur and its faithful. Of course, Guillaume's anarchist politics reflect the historical *terreur noire* of the 1890s. Christopher Prendergast also relates this attempt to plant a bomb below the basilica to a historical and literary tradition:

The historical association of Paris underground with sedition and insurrection runs at least from Babeuf's meetings in the cellars of the Pantheon to the group of insurgents in 1848 who hid themselves in the Montmartre quarry (massacred and left there by Cavaignac's troops) and the anarchist plotters in the cellars of Sacré-Cœur described by Zola in *Paris* (Elie Berthelet's popular novel of the 1850s, *Les Catacombes de Paris*, which went through twenty editions in ten years, based its plot on a secret society descended from the Knights Templar and intent on blowing up the whole city).[35]

Both anarchism and incest can be linked in their relation to the symbolic representation of architecture. Whereas anarchism threatens to explode the constructs of public space, incest threatens to implode the necessary separations of domestic space. The anarchist explosion could be analyzed as a radical symbol of the Naturalists' *Entropic Vision* which provides the title for David Baguley's exemplary study of Naturalist fiction. The bomb produces an extremely violent dispersal of matter and release of energy, and as such a particularly conspicuous form of entropy. It is also worth noting that Elaine Showalter's account of the crises in the *fin de siècle* representation of sexuality is aptly entitled *Sexual Anarchy*. Zola, it will be noted, suggests a bond between sexuality and violence in his description of the cabaret singer, Legras, with his 'coup de mâchoire du mâle, qui se fait adorer des femmes en les terrorisant' (p. 1358). What may be termed 'the terrorism of seduction' is even more evocative in the context of Philippe Bonnefis's Freudian analysis of Zola's representation of the Sacré-Cœur, for he views the basilica as a symbol of maternal rotundity.[36]

This novel explores the paranoia of literary plots in the context of a radical politics whose very strategy involves the arousal and manipulation of public paranoia.[37] At one level, *Paris* almost acts as a parody of this hunt for plots. Within the terms of this story, however, that search seems justified as plots are indeed to be found everywhere in this city-as-novel. The narrative is focalized by Pierre's passage through the labyrinthine city in which he continually encounters the anarchist Salvat. In the context of the famed anonymity of the city the chance encounter as literary *topos* is repeated à la Marx to farcical proportions. In fact, Pierre, unaware of Salvat's anarchist links with Guillaume, is guilty of a grave misrecognition. Each time he sees Salvat – walking down the Champs Elysées, for instance, or when the anarchist is refused entry to the Chamber of Deputies – Pierre believes foolishly that the bulge in his pocket is 'sans doute quelque morceau de pain caché là' (p. 1222). What Pierre takes to be some bread is actually a political response to the lack of bread . . . an anarchist bomb. The irony is that Pierre is travelling around the city on a charity mission designed to bring succour to precisely the same underprivileged people whom the anarchists hope to liberate. Such misrecognitions dominate the plot.

Pierre's suspicions are aroused too late, when he comes across Salvat again, this time on the rue Scribe, and sees Guillaume greet him. Pierre follows them both back in circular motion to the rue Godot-de-Mauroy where, doing charity work on behalf of abbé Rose, he has seen Salvat earlier that morning outside the hôtel Duvillard, site of the Decadent intrigue of incest. It is in this scene that Pierre starts to sense the multiple connections which dynamise the plot in its varied contexts – anarchist, ecclesiastical, parliamentary, journalistic, Decadent, poverty-stricken, aristocratic, and amongst the *haute bourgeoisie*. This recognition of the network of intrigues, and hence of the redundancy of chance within the determined structures of the plot, is triggered by a recognition of what Salvat is doing. The violent *jouissance* of the anarchist bomb thrown by Salvat at the hôtel Duvillard runs counter to the textual *plaisir* of narrative coherence proffered at this point. The plot comes together as bodies and buildings fall apart. The reader will expect the *texte de plaisir*, whose coherence has just been asserted, to culminate in a satisfying narrative closure, but in that very act of assertion the analogical relationship between textual closure and spatial enclosures literally explodes.

The two brothers are also united by the explosion. The injured Guillaume asks Pierre to take him back to the home in Neuilly where they grew up. This in turn brings together the disparate factions of radical thought, as Guillaume is visited by the Communard Bade, who reads Saint-Simon and Fourier, by Morin, the evolutionist representing Proudhon and Comte, by the old-style Republican Nicolas Barthès, and by the anarchist Janzen. Pierre studies 'ces hommes venus là des quatre points des idées du siècle', who embody the compass-points on the map of the century's radical thought. He realises the need to synthesise 'le bilan du siècle' by reading Saint-Simon, Fourier, Cabet, Comte, Proudhon and Marx, with a knowledge of Rousseau amongst others, 'afin de se rendre au moins compte du chemin parcouru, du carrefour auquel on était arrivé' (p. 1266). So the dimensions of space in the novel chart the city's limits – both geographical and intellectual – and its time frame attempts to map out the nineteenth century. The novel is offered as a 'bilan' of nineteenth-century Paris.

The *carrefour* in *Paris*, however, is not viewed simply as a focal point. According to the city–body analogy which Zola borrows from Maxime du Camp, the heart of the metropolis is also a void.[38] Even though 'le cœur de la grande ville semblait battre là [la place de l'Opéra]', the traffic makes this 'le gouffre le plus dangereux du monde' (p. 1248). The urban centre is construed as a global *abîme*. Much later, at another meeting of radicals (this time at Guillaume's house), Pierre listens 'assis contre le vitrage, ouvert sur l'immensité braisillante de Paris' (p. 1438). The city frames radical debate, yet Paris's status as a political avant-garde hailing forth the brave new century is confused. Paris by night remains 'la grande énigme, le chaos noir', a riddle not resolved by the novel's attempts at mapping, be they literal or figurative.

Much of the novel's action involves the authorities' efforts to police these radicals. It is, however, the industrialist, Grandidier, who symbol-ises the crisis of power that undermines capitalist surveillance of labour. He lives beside his factory where Guillaume's son, Thomas, works, not just to supervise the workforce but really to tend to his deranged wife 'dans le pavillon morne, aux persiennes toujours closes' (p. 1526). Drained and shaken by another domestic drama, Grandidier responds to Pierre's appeal for charity with the *interrogatio*: 'Le pire malheur, le connaît-on? Qui peut parler du pire malheur, s'il n'a pas souffert le malheur des autres? . . .' (p. 1527). In a paradoxical mixture of industrial power and domestic impotence not dissimilar to Hennebeau in *Germinal*, Grandidier experiences a pain he cannot share. The omniscience implicit in a system of absolute ethical judgements based on religious values is seen to fail given the impossibility of effective empathy in what Marie-Claire Bancquart terms Zola's 'ville de la ségrégation'.[39] This is why the novel proposes a humanitarianism based on justice rather than charity.

The 'ségrégation' which works against such omniscience also under-mines the practice of Naturalist writing. Although the aim of 'tout dire' suggests the acceptance of all subject matter by virtue of a sort of epis-temophilic anti-taboo, the institution of an omniscient distance from subject matter by the Naturalist art of designation suggests a metaphor of pointing but not touching, that is, a taboo on touch. Hence *Paris* may know of and yet never quite know a Paris seen but not felt. The novel with its vast display of subcultures is, as it were, a text-museum where, in accordance with the referential illusion, the reader may look but not touch. It is the incest taboo, of course, which places constraints on inti-mate touching within the family, but, in the Decadent realm of the hôtel Duvillard concealed behind the aristocratic patronage of Pierre's charity work, it is not incest as such but what may be termed a fiction of incest which prevails. This fiction is yet one more form of the artifice characteristic of the Decadence.[40] By stealing her mother's lover, Gérard de Quinsac, Camille Duvillard triggers this fiction which thus asserts its dominance over the narrative of adultery played out between Camille's mother, Eve, and Gérard.

In an attempt to dissuade Gérard from marrying Camille, the reader will recall, Eve arranges a meeting at the restaurant in the Bois de Boulogne where she first met him (pp. 1386–90). This is inspired by 'l'idée poétique de retrouver là les premiers baisers pour qu'ils fussent les derniers peut-être'. In fact, this 'poetic' circularity, which, as we have seen, is an æsthetic structure favoured by Zola, is upset by another mis-recognition. The scene has changed, 'lorsqu'elle entra dans le cabinet, elle ne le reconnut point, si terne, si froid, avec son divan fané, sa table et ses quatre chaises'. Eve warns Gérard that his marriage to Camille would be 'presque un inceste'. As she says this, she takes his hands, 'telle qu'une mère qui cherche de bonnes raisons pour empêcher son grand fils de commettre quelque exécrable faute'. By acting towards Gérard as if he were her son, Eve's behaviour suggests a sibling incest between Camille and Gérard. Yet the logic of Eve's analogy falters, as it also implies that her relationship with Gérard bears the characteristics of mother–son incest. The adultery itself appears incestuous, and, by stealing her mother's lover, it is as if Camille is doing her father's bidding. Thus by a sort of contagion the incest paradigm infiltrates all manner of relationships. In this decadent milieu at the heart of this 'ville de la ségrégation', the necessary segregations which define family relations within the domestic unit collapse.

Eve arranges this rendez-vous with Gérard after a confrontation with her daughter at the Duvillard charity sale (pp. 1333–8). This is yet another scene of misrecognitions. At first Eve pities 'cette créature laide et contrefaite, qu'elle n'avait jamais pu s'habituer à reconnaître pour sa fille . . . Etait-ce possible qu'une telle disgrâce fût sortie de sa beauté souveraine . . . ?'. As their quarrel intensifies, 'il n'y avait plus là une mère et une fille, c'étaient deux rivales qui souffraient et combattaient'. Similarly, '[Eve] ne sut plus qu'elle était mère, qu'elle parlait à sa fille. La femme amoureuse seule demeurait, outragée, exaspérée par une rivale'. The love-hate tension latent in this mother–daughter bond is precipitated by their rivalry over Gérard. Camille, indeed, is introduced as an example of the same genetic *innéité* that docteur Pascal exhibits: 'Elle n'avait rien de son père, ni de sa mère: un des accidents imprévus, dans l'hérédité d'une famille, qui fait qu'on se demande d'où ils peuvent venir' (p. 1197). Within the mimetic order of heredity, she, like Pascal, is radically *invraisemblable*. Camille's escape from this visible order of family allegiances symbolises her subversive function within the family and her capacity to invert its hierarchy. At the charity sale, for instance, she tells her mother, 'Es-tu assez enfant! Oui, en vérité, c'est toi qui es l'enfant . . .'.

The highlighting of this tension between mother and daughter in terms of this fiction of incest also foregrounds the relationship between sexuality and violence in the novel. Images of the subversive power of the daughter are to be found at a number of points in the text. When the Duvillards first appear, Camille's eyes fix upon her mother, 'de son regard aigu, meurtrier comme un couteau' (p. 1198). Later she is infuriated by Pierre's 'questions naïves, qui lui retournaient le couteau dans le cœur!', questions about her mother's whereabouts when Eve is secretly meeting Gérard (p. 1237). In Camille's verbal attack launched against her mother at the charity sale, 'chaque phrase était entrée dans le cœur de sa mère, comme un couteau'.

Eve's maternal force is, however, reasserted by physical aggression as she attacks Camille with a handful of yellow roses and pricks blood from her daughter's left temple. Camille's ultimate success in marrying Gérard is testament nevertheless to the external power of symbolic verbal violence. The verbal 'knife' that castrates the phallic mother – as Freudians might put it – exerts a force within the family narrative akin to that of the anarchist bomb within the political order, concealed by Salvat in his 'sac à outils' (the reader may note the phallic connotation of 'outil').

The Naturalist fantasy of a childlike mastery over one's material is symbolised in the novel by a displacement between two scenes at either end of the novel which involve a child at play. The psychoanalytical resonances of 'outil' are only too clear when the anarchist Salvat tells his daughter Céline not to play with his 'sac' in front of Pierre, in case the priest sees what the anarchist's bag really contains. 'Je t'ai défendu de toucher aux outils', the father tells his daughter (p. 1185). This initial concealment triggers those misrecognition scenes analysed above in which Pierre mistakes Salvat's bomb for bread. In one of the final images of the novel Pierre and Marie's son, Jean, plays with the *moteur à explosion* invented by Guillaume and Thomas (p. 1566). The *moteur* represents a constructive use of potentially destructive science. As Phillipe Bonnefis comments on this image: 'La machine est l'isolant idéal. Proche de l'abîme qui actionne, elle offre en son sein une douce sécurité où tous les bruits extérieurs sont magiquement amortis. Qu'il fait bon vivre dans une machine!'[41] In this passage from the assertion of the taboo to a revelation of the child's mastery over the machine-as-toy, Zola inscribes the distance between the textual constructs of his own humanist ideology and the destructiveness of the anarchist. The circle which connects the beginning of the novel and its ending turns out to be an upward spiral.

Zola's attempt to write about the radicalism of both anarchism and the Decadence whilst maintaining a healthy distance from both is, however, fraught with difficulties. The courtesan Silviane, for instance, provides yet another focal point in the novel. She poses such a threat to the political and social order of Paris because she refuses to recognise the segregation of plots which the structuring of any traditional classic novel seems to demand. She dominates baron Duvillard's life by tying his political role to questions of desire. She is 'la tare, chez cet homme si solide et si puissant encore, dans le déclin de sa race' (pp. 1229–30). When he exclaims that he cannot bring down a government just to get her the role of Pauline in *Polyeucte* at the Comédie-Française, she asks, 'Pourquoi pas?' Hence the realm of high politics is usurped by low-life intrigue. One of Silviane's pleasures involves telephoning the baron in the middle of an important meeting. Here is the *jouissance* – doubled thematically and narratalogically – of one plot disrupting the continuity of another.

After dragging her entourage (and the plot) back to Montmartre, from the Café des Anglais to the Cabinet des Horreurs, in order to hear her former lover Legras sing, the bisexual Silviane becomes the object of princesse de Rosemonde's lesbian desires. In terms of Zola's hetero-sexual ideology of *Fécondité*, homosexuality is seen as no less barren than the cerebral love between Camille's brother, the effete Hyacinthe, and his Decadent companion, the princesse. Ironically, of course, the Cornelian intertext *Polyeucte* dramatises the renunciation of desires deemed harmful to the social order. The 'pose alanguie du renoncement universel' characteristic of Hyacinthe and the non-consummation of Morigny's love for Gérard's mother symbolise the failure on the part of this dying world to reproduce itself both sexually and socially.

Hyacinthe, moreover, wisely predicts to Rosemonde that she will one day yield to her lesbian desires, and in so doing he invokes the rhetoric of Zola's Naturalism in a context quite alien to Zola's values: 'vous irez bien un jour, il faut tout connaître' (p. 1357).[42] Fatalism drives characters towards perversion just as determinism drives the plot towards its close. As Zola's epistemophilic anti-taboo espouses the value of 'tout con-naître', it regresses into the idle perversity of the very Decadence it abhors. The order of Naturalist writing is thus continually haunted by the sexual disorders it diagnoses, of which incest enjoys the heaviest cul-tural charge. At the same time, the Naturalist novel (as both individual text and literary movement) is haunted by the fear that it has ended pre-maturely, and that a 'will-to-closure' has ultimately denied the opportu-nity of 'tout dire'. But the scopic drive which propels Naturalism's desire to point, look and tell remains largely blind to its own ideological predis-positions and passions. Indeed, the very attempt (on the part of Zola and Hennique *inter alia*) to master both romance and politics (or, we might say, private and public plots) should be contrasted with the popular romance fiction of women writers at the turn of the century such as Marcelle Tinayre and Daniel Lesueur for whose heroines a public life would usually signal a scandal.[43]

Coda: Bourget's 'Un divorce' and the 'honnête femme'

Prétendre définir l'Amour, c'est-à-dire tous les Amours, constitue, pour quiconque a vécu, une insoutenable prétention et presque un enfantillage.[1]

Le divorce est le sacrement de l'adultère.[2]

The most conspicuous sign of the crisis in family life towards the end of the century was, as we have already seen, the debate on divorce which culminated in the *Loi Naquet* of 1884. Though this legislation did not offer the provisions of modern divorce law and hardly triggered a rush to the courts by dissatisfied spouses, its symbolic significance was unmistakable. In France this was a trigger in the modern process which, to borrow Anthony Giddens's terms, translated marriage 'into a signifier of commitment, rather than a determinant of it'.[3] For though different to the divorce law suppressed in 1816, the avowal on the part of the republican state that marriage was a conditional contract, rather than the incontrovertible sacrament hallowed by the Catholic Church, reflected the Revolution's discourse on the family in a manner which sought to bracket out the imperial regressions of the intervening century. In the politics of the *fin de siècle* the certainty of Balzac's 'deux vérités éternelles' seemed long gone, as the republican state drove towards self-definition, in contradistinction to the Church rather than in league with it.

Paul Bourget's novel, *Un divorce* (1904), provides a reactionary retrospection on the social effects of this new order of family life by pursuing the deleterious effects of Gabrielle's second marriage on the next generation embodied in her son, Lucien, conceived with her first husband, Chambault. Though 'tout chez Gabrielle Darras dénonçait une personne de la haute bourgeoisie française', this appearance conceals the mid-life crisis of this remarried forty year old divorcee.[4] Though now unfashionable amongst æsthetically orientated literary criticism (in Singer's terms 'in a sort of limbo, no longer popular, not yet classic'),[5] Bourget has much to teach cultural historians about the official values of turn-of-the-century bourgeois society. Often difficult to stomach no doubt because his narrators wear their ideology on their sleeve, Bourget nevertheless shared with Zola the domination of that vital terrain where the academic and the popular meet. Whereas Zola's most quintessential Naturalist plots blossomed outwards from an essentially liberal position in order to paint in the externals of various social domains, Bourget remained within the order of mimesis which guaranteed readability in the mainstream but worked inwards from the traditional perspective of the psychological novel. The extent of his ideologically charged faith in the social necessity of secure family life is revealed by the fact that in the same year as the publication of *Un divorce* Bourget also co-edited with Michel Salomon a collection of Bonald's writings.

Zola invokes divorce as both a glib rhetorical sleight of hand and a grave moral calamity. In the first instance divorce is invoked as a comic sanction in the battle of the sexes. In his scathing review of Olympe Audouard's *Guerre aux hommes!* printed in *L'Evénement* on 27 February 1866, Zola pretends to agree with the pro-divorce lobby: 'Le divorce serait une excellente chose: il permettrait aux maris de se débarrasser des femmes embarrassantes'.[6] Six weeks after the review of Audouard, *L'Evénement* printed Zola's review of Mme Champleix's *Un divorce* (written under the pseudonym of André Léo) which had appeared in *Le Siècle* before being published in book format. As in the case of Audouard, once again Zola shows himself to be at one remove from truly radical thought: 'La conclusion me paraît être celle-ci: on doit s'étudier mutuellement avant de se marier, car, une fois mariés, on ne peut briser le lien qui vous unit, sans emporter la chair et le cœur.' In his article on 'Le divorce et la littérature', as we have seen in chapter 1, Zola is similarly glib, bemoaning the effects on novelists that the legalization of divorce would have as adultery and crimes of passion would no longer be acceptable either as forms of social behaviour or therefore as narrative possibilities for Naturalist authors. Zola's facetiousness lies in his apparent concern about negative narrative effects to the exclusion of any pleasure in the potentially positive social effects of legalizing divorce. What this facetiousness brings out, though, is the relationship between what might be termed the order of family life and the order of narrative. E. M. Forster's famous observation that classic novels have to end with either a marriage or a death reflects a view of family plots as defined by the two key transactional moments in which legal texts (marriage

contracts and wills) restructure the economic and affective order of
family life. The advent of divorce adds another transactional moment to
this list and allows for narrative situations in which widowers and widows
are not the only figures who may find life after wedlock.

Bourget's position is a little like that of the man in his short story,
Complicité, who sees his best friend's wife kissing another man. Should he
be honest or should he protect his friend's blind happiness? In other
words, should he (like Bourget) tell for the umpteenth time the story of
adultery? It has been standard practice to read the banality of adultery
in Paul Bourget's writing as testament to his own cultural centrality and
banality. In the words of Thibaudet (which reflect those of many contemporary critics of his early work), 'L'adultère n'est plus chez lui exception scandaleuse comme chez Flaubert, mais vraiment l'arbre de couche
du roman'.[7] The motif of adultery is certainly one of the aspects which
allows Bourget to share with Zola that key cultural location between
intellectualization and accessibility where the novel functions so ably as
a popular genre. In this particular novel, however, Bourget exploits that
very reputation as the author of tales of seduction in order to show the
displacement of the fiction of adultery by the fiction of divorce. When
Gabrielle starts to confess to Euvrard, the priest (like the typical reader)
assumes that he is about to hear a tale of illegitimacy, 'Cette femme était
mariée. Elle l'avait dit elle-même. Elle avait commis une faute. Son
enfant n'était pas du mari' (p. 13). It is only her pride which forces him
to reassess the narrative context in which he finds himself, 'Non, elle
n'était pas l'héroïne repentante d'une banale histoire d'adultère'. As
Gabrielle herself claims, in terms to which we shall return in the final
pages of this book, 'Je n'ai pas à me reprocher ce que vous croyez. Je suis
une honnête femme'. Precisely because of his own investment in the
motif, Bourget can effectively undo the presuppositions of his readers.
For, in the metaphorical terms lent by computerspeak, we might say that
adultery has become the default narrative within the common culture,
in other words the lowest common denominator which provides the
standard format and layout of bourgeois narratives.

The name of 'adultery' is retained as a reactionary way of denoting
triangular relationships. Gabrielle recalls Euvrard's condemnation of
her second marriage: 'Vous vivez . . . avec un homme qui n'est pas votre
mari, et que vous appelez votre mari, alors que vous êtes réellement
mariée à un autre. C'est un adultère pire, puisqu'il constitue en même
temps un outrage public à Dieu' (p. 200). By a further irony Darras cas-
tigates the priest as the third party who has upset their marriage when

Gabrielle explains that her return to faith has led to her belief that they are not married in the eyes of God. He feels 'une âpreté plus haineuse encore, celle du mari pour qui le confesseur n'est pas le représentant anonyme et impersonnel du Juge invisible, mais un homme apparu entre l'épouse et l'époux' (p. 234). She simply cites the Gospel: 'Tout homme qui renvoie sa femme et en épouse une autre, commet l'adultère. Toute femme qui quitte son mari et en épouse un autre, commet un adultère' (p. 242). In his anger at Euvrard he, however, cannot help but feel 'un élancement de jalousie, aussi aigu, aussi perçant que celui dont il eût tressailli devant la preuve d'une perfidie d'un autre ordre' (p. 255).

Whereas the marriage plot of *Bel-Ami* is doubled by the divorce plot in which the novel culminates, *Un divorce* refashions family narrative by looking at the effects of a divorce which precedes narrative time in the novel but remains as an inescapable hamartia from which Gabrielle and Lucien cannot escape. Traditional endings are intercalated in the course of the narrative with the effect that by the end of the tale, the major protagonists are left in limbo, neither happy nor dead. By getting married and yielding her maiden name, Nouet, Gabrielle's life should in a sense have been *dénoué*, but the Ariadne's thread rewound by divorce and remarriage threatens to strangle her. The engagement of Lucien and Berthe provides one such *fausse fin* at the end of chapter 5, as does the death of Chambault at the end of chapter 8 and Lucien's adieu at the end of the penultimate chapter 9. In fact Chambault's death is the source of fresh suspense as it raises the possibility of a religious marriage between Darras and Gabrielle if only she can persuade him that she is a widow 'sortie de cette équivoque du divorce' and not a divorcee liberated long before Chambault's death.

When the row over Berthe between Lucien, Gabrielle and Darras reaches fever pitch in chapter 6, the 'plaie découverte' at the heart of this second marriage is exposed by Lucien's observation that only his 'vrai père' has the right to forbid his marriage to Berthe. The essential scandal of Darras's involvement, as far as Lucien is concerned, lies in the chronological impropriety whereby the son precedes the new husband in the history of the family. As Lucien tells his stepfather, 'elle était ma mère avant d'être ta femme', so due to this transgression of narrative order the roles of wife and mother are seen to collide rather than cohere: 'Je verrai si elle est ta femme plus qu'elle n'est ma mère' (p. 225). When Gabrielle recovers from her swoon, she feels compelled to tell Darras that Lucien is right and that God is punishing her. In the indictment of their 'adulterous' love, she confirms, 'nous ne sommes pas mariés' (p. 228).

It is this philosophical difference between Gabrielle and Darras which is underscored by the pedestrian irony in the title of the final chapter: 'Prison'. Turning the republican discourse of liberation on its head, Bourget suggests that 'la terrible tentation de cette loi impie du divorce' (p. 353) has incarcerated Gabrielle in an impossible situation from which there is no benign denouement. By an ironic circularity Darras visits Euvrard in his desperation, just as Gabrielle has done at the very start of the novel. This chapter plays with the classic forms of novelistic closure by toying with Gabrielle's desire for a religious ceremony to confirm her marriage to Darras. She views herself as a widow, but he contends, 'Non, tu n'es pas ma maîtresse. Tu es ma femme. Non, je ne suis pas ton amant. Je suis ton mari' (p. 357). So by simply denying the fact of her divorce and remarriage, Gabrielle returns to the permutations of the adulterous scenario which Berthe's choice of *union libre* is designed to erase. By the end, though, the reader (like Gabrielle) is left unsure as to whether her desires will be granted by Darras to whom she has returned: 'Y avait-il une issue à la situation où les avait acculés leur mariage dans le divorce?' (p. 397). Though ideologically unambivalent, the plot ends by consigning its heroine to the uncertainty of 'une mélancolie infinie où luisait cependant un peu d'espoir'.

The urgency of Bourget's social anxieties undoes any subtlety which he may possess as a storyteller, and his narrator cannot resist the postulation of theses intended to halt interpretative indeterminacy. Whereas *A Rebours* diverts the plotting of narrative events by an indulgence in descriptive inventory, *Un divorce* allows the paternalist authority of its narrator to interrupt the fashioning of an autonomous fictional universe. In order to puncture the suspension of disbelief and reassert the primacy of the social referent (such that the imperative of socially useful instruction dominates the goal of textual pleasure), the narrator of this *roman à idée* can barely resist bringing the reader back from fiction to *actualité*, for instance by footnoting a reference to Enrico Morselli's *Per la polemica sul divorzio* (p. 28). By the end of the novel the strain of such philosophizing is starting to show as the narrator finally finds a metaphorical shorthand for his critique of Darras's thinking in the latter's fear that Gabrielle and Jeanne have fled to join Lucien: 'Ce détail montrera mieux qu'une longue analyse le désarroi où l'inquiétude avait jeté cette intelligence, très précise d'ordinaire et très méthodique' (p. 369). But even the metaphorical code itself is robbed of its charm by this interventionist foregrounding by the narrator of the persuasive authority of figurative language.

The narrator finds his model reader in the figure of père Euvrard, the confessor whom Gabrielle visits at the start of the novel. Once he overcomes the shock of finding that he is not the allocutor in a default narrative of adultery, his role as moral adviser provides the alibi for a didactic commentary on the story. Humbled by 'les abominables mesures de 1903' (p. 6) which help to divide Church and State, Euvrard has had to move home, and when Gabrielle visits him in the opening scene of the novel to confess her fears, she enters a lugubrious building which bears three busts: Antinous (the beautiful melancholy youth who commits suicide) and those sources of light, Diana and Apollo. The latter in particular represents the purifying power of a figure sent (like Euvrard, so the narrative implies) to preserve the state from the decadent malady of worldweariness embodied by Antinous. Like Zola, Bourget's fantasy of intellectual mastery results in an attempt to absorb the antithetical positions of science and religion (as in the union of Pascal and Clotilde, and the resolution of sibling strife in *Paris*). The problem in this novel is that the wife of the secular Darras returns to religion. Euvrard embodies this union of philosophically opposed stances as he is also a teacher of mathematics. The ensuing metaphors of equation and equilibrium, however, inform a Catholic standpoint from which divorce is seen to upset in quasi-metaphysical fashion the asymmetrical conjunction of genders in married life, in other words its 'mathématique secrète' (p. 42).

As model reader, Euvrard's interest is rekindled by the realization that Gabrielle's real dilemma comes from the rebirth of her religious faith as she prepares her daughter for her first communion. The problem is that as a remarried woman she has no right to absolution from the Catholic Church. Euvrard explains that the Church cannot sanction her second marriage by annulling her first, even if she divorced Chambault because of his terrible drinking. He explains, 'Quand [l'Eglise] marie deux êtres, elle enregistre bien un contrat, mais irrévocable, puisqu'il se double d'un sacrement' (p. 25). He challenges Gabrielle to bring her secular second husband back to the faith. This is the challenge upon which her plot turns. This initial confession allows Euvrard to spout the Catholic line on the legal reforms of 1884. Brimming with subsequent tales of tragic divorces, he impugns the 'criminel article qu'ont introduit dans notre Code les pires ennemies de l'ordre social, les destructeurs de la famille' (p. 29). He argues that Gabrielle's sin is to have sacrificed the social good for the benefit of her individual happiness, producing 'un type de foyer anarchique'. It is important to stress that it is neither the reprobate qualities of a second husband nor a tale of adulterous betrayal on her part which makes her bid for happiness so untenable in the eyes of Euvrard. It is simply that the 'polygamie successive' of divorce (which might nowadays be termed serial monogamy) creates an 'anarchie et fièvre éternelle' (p. 28). Once more the political language of anarchism is used to amplify the moral decadence of the 'foyer posé à faux' which triggers or 'motivates' the interruption of the narrative quietude of the married couple by dividing the family unit. (Berthe's first lover, Méjan, apparently visits that veritable historical icon of anarchism, Elisée Reclus.) The ironic sadness is that the remarried woman has fewer theological privileges than the adulterous wife who can at least confess and take communion (p. 48). This same language of anarchical individualism is used in the final pages of the novel to condemn Darras's 'idées sur la société, singulièrement contradictoires', for he is categorized along with those *moralistes* 'chez lesquels le souci du bien général s'associe à des principes d'un individualisme foncièrement anarchique' (p. 374). The most socially destructive force of this kind is, in Bourget's view, the 'loi d'anarchie et de désordre', the *Loi Naquet*.

Whereas the Don Juan narratives, *Pot-Bouille* and *Bel-Ami*, articulate the serial desires of the arch seducer, Bourget's novel reasserts the traditional values of exclusive reciprocity which marries an intensely romantic view of love with a conservative version of family values at odds with the burgeoning goal of erotic self-fulfilment. This cult of uniqueness depends upon the cherishing of female virginity and a mystification of its loss. Just as Nana bears the traces of the genetic imprint left on Gervaise by that first lover, Lantier, so in a not wholly dissimilar fashion Gabrielle can never quite escape the influence of that first marriage to Chambault. Darras (like Coupeau) is doomed to failure in his bid to erase the determinant force of that originary moment. In the highly charged atmosphere in the wake of Chambault's death, the connotative force of the name of the father (which includes the upheaval and disorder of *chamboulement*) is suggested when Gabrielle tries to find Darras in the library in order to bring about a reconciliation between him and Lucien. Unable to turn the door knob and find her new husband, she leans in despair against the doorframe, the *chambranle*. Even in death this first husband represents the uncrossable threshold between her and Darras. The secularism of Darras is lent heathen (because non-Christian) overtones by virtue of his hybrid origins: 'Il y avait de l'Arabe dans la coupe de cette figure busquée, et dans ce corps souple aux extrémités très fines', hence 'le Bédouin apparaisse dans le civilisé'

(p. 57). So his 'religion à rebours' is presented as 'fanatisme' in a strategic manœuver designed to disassociate scientific secularism and rationality.

The second man (be it Coupeau or Darras) cannot undo the primary moment of seduction (be it outside or inside marriage), and this effect of doubling is itself duplicated in the sorry fate of the family. For Lucien, like his stepfather Darras, is the second man, the quintessential *fin de siècle* figure who arrives too late. When the two argue about the viability of adopting Berthe's child, Lucien uses this very analogy between their lives to defend his decision. Even when Lucien and Berthe kiss after he has heard Berthe's version of her past, declared his love for her and adopted her son, the ghostly half-presence of that third party, Méjan, lingers in their minds, 'sachant si bien, l'un et l'autre, quel fantôme venait de les séparer' (p. 161). In the wake of Chambault's death, Lucien gives up the idea of formally marrying Berthe and resolves to leave for Germany where he will give her son his name and legalize their status in two years' time. In this 'suprême et logique épisode' of the family tragedy, 'le second mariage manifestait sa radicale incompatibilité avec les débris du premier' (p. 340). In another triangular pattern Darras himself intervenes as a disturbing presence in Gabrielle's relationship with her son: 'Lucien n'avait jamais vécu avec Mme Darras dans cette pleine et entière intimité qui rend deux êtres si présents l'un à l'autre qu'ils se sentent sentir. Il avait toujours rencontré Darras entre eux' (p. 197). A prefiguration of this plot is discernible in the early novel *André Cornélis* (1887) where a man takes revenge when he discovers that his father was murdered by his mother's second husband.

The Naturalist fiction of genealogy is reconstructed in *Un divorce* by the interlinking of family plots; the imperfection of Gabrielle's life is visited upon her son, as he ends up agreeing to cohabit with the thoroughly modern Berthe. If the twice-married Gabrielle is excessive, the unmarried Lucien is insufficient. His relationship with Berthe seems doomed as 'une fatalité acharnée' (p. 209) is inscribed in this reduplication of plots. Because he does not enjoy the 'autorité du sang' (p. 85), Darras is in no position to force Lucien to see sense. For the stepfather remains 'le nouveau venu au foyer, l'étranger', the interloper, the stranger in the house, as long as the first husband is still alive (p. 95).

A different theory of paternal rights is propounded in Max du Veuzit's one-act play, *Paternité*, premiered at the Grand Théâtre du Havre on 31 March 1908. When a biological father, Maurice Villiers, returns to collect his daughter Julia from her wealthy stepfather, Paul Romagny, she refuses to leave with Maurice and throws herself into the arms of the man who has raised her. Divorced from Julia's mother who has just died, Maurice discovers that blood is not sufficient to assert paternal rights. As he admits to Paul in the sixth and final scene:

Aujourd'hui, l'enfant vous préfère à moi, c'est tout naturel . . . . . . Un homme ne doit jamais oublier qu'il est père ni momentanément abdiquer ses droits au profit d'un autre . . . Le divorce n'est pas en cause. Le divorce sépare l'homme et la femme, le père et la mère, mais il ne diminue pas les devoirs de ceux-ci vis-à-vis de leurs enfants.[8]

This play on the paradoxically 'natural' quality of the step relationship echoes an ironic refrain through the piece. Paul explains to Maurice in Scene 4 that Lucienne is of course distraught at the thought that she might have to leave this second home which has become her primary home, and he does so with the observation that 'c'est un peu naturel'. The final scene stages the triangular encounter where Lucienne must choose between progenitor and *éducateur*. When she chooses the latter and thus privileges the experience of nurture over the fact of nature, Maurice resigns himself with the emphasis 'c'est si naturel'. The biological is no longer seen by Veuzit as natural.

Things do not work out so smoothly for the stepfather in Bourget's novel. In preparation for his encounter with Chambault at the start of chapter 8 (which turns out to be a meeting with Berthe), Darras feels an inferiority as he thinks of this man who knew his wife as a virgin and who enjoys 'des droits du sang qu'il conservait malgré tout sur Lucien' (p. 285). Contrary to all of those well-known nineteenth-century narratives of adultery fuelled by the fear of paternal uncertainty, the rights of biological paternity are asserted precisely when the 'social father', the stepfather, appears to have usurped the former's position within the nuclear family structure. For, as we are told when Lucien subsequently arrives to visit Chambault on his deathbed, 'le père le plus criminel reste un père' (p. 303). What Berthe offers Lucien is the deluded promise that they might escape their past (and thereby prove themselves properly modern) by asserting the autonomy of their romantic bond, free of familial and legal constraints. In this meeting with Darras she argues, 'Quand on a deux familles, on n'en a pas; et [Lucien] n'en a pas . . . Sa famille, ce sera moi et lui, il sera la mienne. Nous nous suffirons' (pp. 299–300). According to Bourget's narrative this 'doctrinaire de sincérités intransigenates' is precisely the type of *femme nouvelle* against which the patriarchal family must defend itself (p. 177). In Berthe's eyes *fin de siècle* Paris represents the possibility of the end of traditional wedlock if not the end of the family: 'Paris, c'était la clôture définitive de scènes domestiques extrêmement pénibles' (p. 155). She has already had a son by her previous partner, that 'cabotin du féminisme' Etienne Méjan, who abandoned her once she fell pregnant. She argues:

J'ai pensé et je pense encore qu'un vrai mariage consiste dans la libre union de deux êtres qui associent leurs destinées par leur choix personnel, sans d'autres témoins de cette promesse que leurs consciences. J'ai pensé et je pense encore qu'une femme ne perd plus l'honneur pour avoir contracté un tel lien, et s'être trompée, que si elle avait épousé à l'église et à la mairie un misérable qui l'eût trahie et abandonnée enceinte. (p. 151)

In a world without marriage, adultery is as such no longer possible. She is viewed as particularly dangerous because, 'elle n'avait ni dans son regard, ni dans sa voix, cet air de défi, si déplaisant chez la plupart des adeptes du féminisme' (p. 124). Her intellectual heroes are Claude Bernard, Flaubert and Dostoevsky who inspire in her 'un nihilisme systématique' (p. 129). Lucien only comes round to accepting the validity of cohabitation when, in the wake of his biological father's death, he gives up the idea of actually marrying Berthe. As he explains to his mother at the end of chapter 9:

Nous pensons que la valeur morale du mariage réside uniquement dans l'engagement des consciences . . . Le vrai mariage, le seul qui soit absolument exempt de convention mensongère, c'est l'union libre. Si j'ai voulu d'abord épouser Mlle Planat légalement, c'est que le mariage légal est une preuve publique de l'estime. (p. 344)

The irony is that the secular republican, Darras, is in a far better position than the pious Gabrielle to understand what this young couple plan to do: 'Il y a tout de même une doctrine dans l'union libre. Elle est folle, mais ce n'est pas le libertinage' (p. 350).

Bourget's strategy is to constrain Berthe within a 'doxic' vision of women as creatures of instinct and nature in spite of her radical upbringing. His narrator sees a natural instinct where the cultural influence of this doxic vision makes Berthe secretive about her past when she falls in love with Lucien. The narrator extrapolates:

Une jeune fille peut avoir reçu l'éducation la plus infectée d'idées révolutionnaires, – c'était le cas de Berthe Planat, – s'être intoxiquée des pires paradoxes, avoir cru à l'égalité absolue des sexes, professé le mépris des conventions sociales et en particulier du mariage, proclamé et pratiqué, hélas! dans des conditions qui l'excusaient presque, le droit à l'union libre: il suffit qu'un amour sincère s'éveille en elle. De s'être donnée sans sacrement et sans contrat lui fait une honte irraisonnée et invincible, comme un instinct. (p. 141)

The narrator fails to entertain the opinion that this is merely the residual effect of a nurturing ambience of normativity at odds with 'contagious' radicalism, and not the instinctual effect of natural *pudeur*. The notion of saving oneself for that first and last sexual partnership (in other words the teleology of virginity) simply corroborates the cult of uniqueness in bourgeois romantic love.

The blinding passion she feels in chapter 5, 'Fiançailles', as she goes to meet Lucien at the Arènes is presented as 'la revanche en elle de la femme sur la féministe, . . . de la créature impulsive et tendre, incomplète et incertaine, dont la faiblesse réclame l'appui viril, sur l'orgueilleuse et la raisonneuse qui avait enfantinement rêvé de se tenir debout contre la société, par l'unique force de l'acte individuel' (p. 180). Not unlike Gabrielle, she is perceived as guilty of an anti-social individualism. However, this supposed egotism crumbles as Berthe fulfils the age-old archetype of the emotional woman, 'une amoureuse suspendue aux gestes, au désir, à la volonté de celui qu'elle aime', in explicit contrast with the rational male, 'l'intellectuel dressé à tout systématiser dans ses sentiments et ses actes' (p. 182). As Lucien tries to persuade Berthe of the validity of a civil marriage, ironically these 'enfants du vingtième siècle' fail to note the significance of this location, 'ces décombres restés visibles d'une ville ensevelie' (p. 191). In spite of the revolutionary modernity of their opinions, this son of a divorcee and this anarchist student cannot resist the 'archaeology' of 'les coutumes ancestrales'. It is therefore especially ironic that the narrator should be so sensitive to Darras's sexism when he ascribes Gabrielle's theological crisis to 'une crise purement sentimentale, et sans doute d'origine nerveuse' (p. 243). As the narrator notes, 'cet adversaire de tous les préjugés avait ce préjugé-là: il était très près de confondre les émotions religieuses et l'hystérie'.

However, an altogether different account of *union libre* is to be found in Armand Charpentier's novel, *Une honnête femme* (1892), which underlines the primacy of sex for pleasure rather than sex for reproduction. Not to be confused with other Charpentiers of greater repute, Armand spent much of his now mostly forgotten career at the heart of Parisian cultural life. His absence from most twentieth-century literary histories is conspicuous, even though he was a regular of Edmond de Goncourt's *Grenier* (perhaps because Edmond de Goncourt recounts how guests such as the Rosny brothers, Rodenbach and Frantz Jourdain would mock Charpentier mercilessly once he had left the room).[9] However, he is mentioned as a promising young novelist by his contemporary E. M.

Rienzi in the *Panthéon des lettres, des sciences et des arts* of 1893. Charpentier sided with Zola during the Dreyfus Affair, and on 27 January 1898 he wrote to him proposing a banquet in his honour on the eve of his trial. The idea was that the presence of personalities such as Anatole France and Emile Duclaux would impress the jury, but Zola politely declined the offer.[10] Nevertheless, Charpentier decided, along with others such as Mirbeau, to compose an 'Adresse à Emile Zola' for *L'Aurore* on 2 February. Indeed, if Charpentier is remembered at all, it is for his *Historique de l'affaire Dreyfus* (1933) and *Les Côtés mystérieux de l'affaire Dreyfus* (1937). In this vein the entry for Charpentier by M. Prévost in the *Dictionnaire de biographie française* describes him as a 'disciple . . . de Zola'.[11] Rienzi, however, writes of the Charpentier of the early 1890s, 'c'est un des rares «jeunes» qui ne cherchent pas à suivre les sentiers battus par les maîtres du naturalisme'. Indeed, Armand Charpentier is one of those overlooked authors who informs the wider debate on the *femme nouvelle* and her role within shifting family structures. In his interrogation of the traditional family, his writing underpins the growing support of *union libre* (as opposed to marriage) which we can see in radical quarters during the *fin de siècle*. The problem of status in such unions is exemplified by the actual case of Challemel-Lacour who retained his long-term relationship with a married woman when he attained high public office during the Third Republic. As Jean Estèbe suggests, for the forces of order the crisis triggered by the respectability of such sexual radicalism is in truth a crisis of naming: 'Situation étrange qui embarrasse les policiers chargés de veiller sur lui: comment nommer une personne qui n'est pas une épouse légitime mais qui n'est plus vraiment une maîtresse?'[12]

Charpentier's heroine, Hélène Bernard, retains her status as 'une honnête femme' because although she is unfaithful to her husband, Edouard Morisset, she remains true to what Tanner calls 'that interior organ of authentic preference and revulsion',[13] her heart, and to her reasonable desire for pleasure (and as such the novel makes an implicit retort to earlier fictions such as Victor Cherbuliez's *Le Roman d'une honnête femme* and Octave Feuillet's *Le Journal d'une femme*). According to the received ethical ideal that a woman should have sex neither prior to nor outside marriage, only the widow might hope for a second sexual partner. In theory only the death of a husband might free a woman from the unique conjugal bond. Her motto might have been: once fallen, forever fallen. Once Mme Cécile d'Eblis, the friend of Feuillet's diarist Charlotte, has yielded to the prince de Viviane, the only way for her to escape the stain of adultery is to commit suicide, and her motives are not to be confused with Emma Bovary's. As Cécile laments, 'Ah! j'avais été honnête femme jusque-là, je t'assure! . . . et penser que je ne puis plus l'être jamais . . . jamais . . . que j'ai cette tache au front, cette honte au cœur pour le reste de ma vie! . . .'[14] By the time Charpentier writes, another narrative of female decency is plausible in which the primary value of devotion is put into question. The new amorous ideal of such turn-of-the-century fiction is aptly defined by Giddens's term 'confluent love'. For this 'active, contingent love . . . jars with the "for-ever", "one-and-only" qualities of the romantic love complex'.[15] As he argues: 'Confluent love for the first time introduces the *ars erotica* into the core of the conjugal relationship and makes the achievement of reciprocal sexual pleasure a key element in whether the relationship is sustained or dissolved.'

Charpentier contrasts the authenticity of such sexual *disponibilité* favourably with the hypocrisy of a wife who will make a fool of a wealthy admirer by accepting his generosity only to return, as it were, unscathed to her husband and family. The effects of the cloistering of women, which Zola has already addressed, return in comical vein in *Une honnête femme*. Hélène is so naive on her wedding night that she does nothing when she finds her husband rummaging through her underwear drawer. She asks herself, 'Pourquoi donc Edmond fouille-t-il dans ma commode? Il a beau être mon mari, il pourrait bien attendre un peu . . . Enfin! maman m'a dit de ne rien lui dire et de le laisser faire . . .' What is taken for fetishism is in fact ineptitude. What Balzac calls 'la danse dans la chambre nuptiale'[16] takes place in her parents' house, and Hélène's mother has told Edouard that she has left his nightshirt in one of the drawers, but in the comical confusion of the dark conjugal bedroom Edouard gets the wrong drawer. Both daughter and son-in-law are acting upon the wisdom of Mme Bernard, and both are woefully misled. Typically marriage does not mean an immediate escape from the society of relatives into the private realm of the couple. One paradoxical effect of such prudishness, though, was actually to intensify the solitude of couples which we take to be so modern. During the Second Empire it was standard bourgeois practice to display a bride's trousseau, but this became ever less the norm as the couple's right to privacy was asserted. In the words of one contemporary commentator, 'Cette exhibition froissait les sentiments délicats; les objets de lingerie intime d'une femme ne doivent pas ainsi s'étaler aux yeux et à la vue de tous.'[17]

What drives Hélène to adultery is not just an affective void in her life, but also what might be termed a pleasure deficit, 'Du râle, elle ignore les douceurs, ne les soupçonne même point.' ('Le râle' is akin to the 'petite mort'.) Edouard, her husband, just cannot understand why she does not react to his masculine prowess in the way that other women have reacted – or seem to have reacted. It is only through conversation with other women that she discovers what she is missing out on:

La curiosité . . . l'incite à l'adultère. Avec cette franchise, quelquefois même cette crudité de paroles qu'ont les femmes entre elles quand nul homme ne les écoute, sa mère, sa sœur, ses amies lui ont décrit les joies passionnelles. Par ces confessions, elle a compris, qu'elle n'était pas femme, bien que mère et que sa chair conservait encore une virginité: l'ignorance du spasme.

Only after sleeping with Paul Vincent can she – and the narrator – conclude, 'Le mystère . . . n'existe plus: elle est femme.' One could of course argue that for all of his enlightenment, Charpentier's implicitly male narrator plays through the fantasy of disrupting the privacy of the female homosocial bond, and that it is only by a renegotiation of the heterosexual contract that Hélène is brought closer to a sense of gendered identity, but Charpentier's text does at least make clear the high stakes involved in the cultural concern for wifely adultery as a regime of pleasure which the will-to-knowledge of the male gaze cannot master.

The passage from the received view of hysterical female desire to a reconstructed perception of female desires within marriage can be anticipated in Dartigues's otherwise unreconstructed *De l'amour expérimental ou des causes d'adultère chez la femme au XIXe siècle* (1887), classified by subtitle as an 'Etude d'hygiène et d'économie sociale'. Initially he cites the stereotypical rhetoric of unfathomable femininity, described as 'cet inextricable labyrinthe de caprices, de dissimulation, de volontés inconstantes, où se joue une sensibilité vive, exaltée, plus mobile que l'air', and the classic fear of female desire as 'un feu concentré qui couve sous la cendre, et qui n'en porte que des atteintes plus profondes à la sensibilité nerveuse'.[18] But this emphasis on female desires merely serves to underline the need for men to attend to the sexual needs of a wife: 'Rien ne dégoûte plus une femme de son mari, rien n'est plus capable de la pousser à l'adultère, que la malencontreuse disposition d'un homme qui se satisfait promptement, sans aucun préambule de caresses, sans s'inquiéter de ce qui éprouve une femme.' Thus a century after the founding revolutionary moment of political rights in France, the sexual right to mutual pleasure is boldly asserted in an argument which, like Léon Blum's advocation in *Du mariage* (1907) of premarital sexual experience for both partners, aims at social cohesion based on the heterosexual satisfaction of educated senses. As Dartigues warns: 'Le mari ne doit jamais oublier que sa femme a autant de droit que lui aux sensations voluptueuses de l'amour, et que c'est par là qu'il sauvegarde la chasteté du foyer.' A further century later, it would be naive, if pleasurable, to imagine that the revolution which conjoins the political and the sexual is complete.

Notes

INTRODUCTION: FIN DE SIÈCLE, FIN DE FAMILLE?

1 Paul Bourget, *Physiologie de l'amour moderne* (Paris, Lemerre, 1891), p. 140.
2 Edmond and Jules de Goncourt, *Journal*, 3 vols., ed. Robert Ricatte (Paris, Robert Laffont, 1989), vol. 3, pp. 664–5 (February 1892).
3 Roger Shattuck, *The Banquet Years* (New York, Vintage, 1955), p. 5.
4 Tony Tanner, *Adultery in the Novel* (Baltimore, Johns Hopkins University Press, 1979).
5 Denis de Rougemont, *Love in the Western World* (New York, Anchor Books, 1957); first published as *L'Amour er l'Occident* (Paris, Plon, 1939).
6 Catherine Belsey, *Desire: Love Stories in Western Culture* (Oxford, Blackwell, 1994), p. ix.
7 Léon Jaybert, *De l'adultère dans les différents âges et chez les différentes nations* (Paris, Poulet-Malassis, 1862), p. 7.
8 Theodore Zeldin, *France 1848–1945: Ambition and Love* (Oxford University Press, 1979).
9 For a recent account of such cultural mutations, see *Scarlet Letters: Fictions of Adultery from Antiquity to the 1990s*, ed. Nicholas White and Naomi Segal (Basingstoke, Macmillan, 1997).
10 Tanner, *Adultery*, pp. 15, 86.
11 Adam Phillips, *Monogamy* (London, Faber and Faber, 1996), p. 91.
12 Guy de Maupassant, 'L'Adultère' in *Chroniques,* 3 vols. (Paris, Union générale d'éditions (10/18), 1980), vol. 1, pp. 397–402 (p. 398). Maupassant's italics.
13 See Tony Williams, 'Champfleury, Flaubert and the Novel of Adultery', *Nineteenth-Century French Studies*, 20 (1991–2), pp. 145–57, which argues persuasively that if Champfleury's *Les Bourgeois de Molinchart* 'taught Flaubert anything, it was a lesson in how *not* to write a novel of adultery' (p. 145).
14 Lynn Hunt, *The Family Romance of the French Revolution* (London, Routledge, 1992), p. xiii.
15 Chantal Gleyses, *La Femme coupable: Petite histoire de l'épouse adultère au XIXe siècle* (Paris, Imago, 1994), p. 7.
16 Jules Cauvière, *De la répression de l'adultère* (Paris, Imprimerie Chaix, 1905), p. 5.

17 Richard von Krafft-Ebing, *Psychopathia Sexualis* (London, Mayflower-Dell, 1967), p. 9.
18 Gustave Flaubert, *Œuvres complètes*, 16 vols. (Paris, Club de l'Honnête Homme, 1971–75), vol. 13, p. 472.
19 Guy de Maupassant, 'Le Roman', *Romans*, ed. Louis Forestier (Paris, Gallimard/Pléiade, 1987), pp. 711–12.
20 André Maurois, *Cinq visages de l'amour* (New York, Didier, 1942), pp. 130–1.
21 Roddey Reid, *Families in Jeopardy: Regulating the Social Body in France, 1750–1910* (Stanford University Press, 1993), pp. 8–9.
22 Tanner, *Adultery*, p. 368.
23 André Theuriet, 'Paternité', *Revue des deux mondes*, 124 (1894), pp. 756–96 (796, 785), and 125 (1894), pp. 38–72 (51–3, 62).
24 Champfleury, *Histoire de l'imagerie populaire* (Paris, Dentu, 1886), pp. 223–30.
25 Bourget, *Physiologie de l'amour moderne*, p. 111.
26 Jaybert, *De l'adultere*, pp. 90, 92, 102–3.
27 *La Grande Encyclopédie: inventaire raisonné des sciences, des lettres et des arts*, ed. P. E. M. Berthelot, H. Derenboury, F.-C. Dreyfus *et al.*, 31 vols. (Paris, Lamirault, 1886–1902), vol. 16, pp. 1161–2. Our italics.
28 Rachel G. Fuchs, *Poor and Pregnant in Paris: Strategies for Survival in the Nineteenth-Century* (New Brunswick, NJ, Rutgers University Press, 1992), p. 4.
29 See Naomi Segal, *The Adulteress's Child: Authorship and Desire in the Nineteenth-Century Novel* (Cambridge, Polity Press, 1992) and Alison Sinclair, *The Deceived Husband: A Kleinian Approach to the Literature of Infidelity* (Oxford University Press, 1993).
30 See Michael Black, *The Literature of Fidelity* (London, Chatto and Windus, 1975) and Judith Armstrong, *The Novel of Adultery* (Basingstoke, Macmillan, 1976).
31 See in particular *A History of Private Life*, ed. Phillipe Ariès and Georges Duby, tr. Arthur Goldhammer, 5 vols. (Cambridge, MA, London, Bellknap Press, 1987–91), vol. 4, *From the Fires of Revolution to the Great War*, ed. Michelle Perrot (1990).
32 See Christopher Prendergast, *The Order of Mimesis* (Cambridge University Press, 1986).
33 Reid, *Families in Jeopardy*, p. 70.
34 J.-P. Dartigues, *De l'amour expérimental ou des causes d'adultère chez la femme au XIXe siècle* (Versailles, Litzelmann, 1887), p. 39.
35 Peter Gay, *The Bourgeois Experience: Victoria to Freud*, 2 vols. (Oxford University Press, 1984–6), vol. 1, p. 430.
36 Alain Corbin, 'The Secret of the Individual', in *A History of Private Life*, vol. 4, pp. 457–547 (p. 491).
37 Cited in Anne Martin-Fugier, *La Bourgeoise* (Paris, Grasset, 1983), p. 337.
38 This area is synthesised by David Cheal in his *Family and the State of Theory* (New York, Harvester Wheatsheaf, 1991), chapter 4, 'Private and public: dialectics of modernity, division 11', pp. 81–118.
39 Lynda M. Glennon, *Women and Dualism* (New York, Longman, 1979), p. 23. Glennon's italics.

40 Jürgen Habermas, *The Structural Transformation of the Public Sphere*, trans. Thomas Burger (Cambridge, Polity Press, 1989).

41 Kristin Ross, *The Emergence of Social Space: Rimbaud and the Paris Commune* (Basingstoke, Macmillan, 1988), p. x. See also Christopher Prendergast, *Paris and the Nineteenth Century* (Oxford, Blackwell, 1995).

42 Gaston Bachelard, *La Poétique de l'espace* (Paris, Presses Universitaires de France, 1964), p. 200.

43 Roland Barthes, *Le Plaisir du texte* (Paris, Seuil, 1973), p. 19. Barthes's italics.

44 Perrot, 'Roles and Characters', in *A History of Private Life*, vol. 4, p. 231.

45 *ibid.*, p. 235.

46 Perrot, 'The Family Triumphant', in *A History of Private Life*, vol. 4, p. 124.

47 Bernard Gallina, *Eurydices fin de siècle: Emma Bovary et le roman naturaliste* (Udine, Aura Editrice, 1992).

48 Henry Céard, *Une belle journée* (Geneva, Slatkine, 1970), p. 260.

49 Céard, *Lettres inédites à Emile Zola*, ed. C. A. Burns (Paris, Nizet, 1958), p. 116.

50 Cited in Colin Burns, 'Henry Céard and his Relations with Flaubert and Zola', *French Studies* (1952), pp. 308–24 (316).

51 *ibid.*, p. 308.

52 Terence Cave, *The Cornucopian Text: Problems of Writing in the French Renaissance* (Oxford, Clarendon, 1979), pp. 3–4.

53 Emile Zola, *Les Rougon-Macquart*, 5 vols., ed. Henri Mitterand (Paris, Gallimard (Pléiade), 1960–7), vol. 3, pp. 795, 798.

54 Michael Wood, 'No Second Chance: Fiction and Adultery in *Vertigo*' in *Scarlet Letters*, pp. 189–98 (p. 198).

55 Alain Corbin, *Women for Hire: Prostitution and Sexuality in France after 1850*, trans. Alan Sheridan (Cambridge, MA, Harvard University Press, 1990), pp. 174–85.

56 See in particular René Girard, *Deceit, Desire, and the Novel*, trans. Yvonne Freccero (Baltimore, Johns Hopkins University Press, 1972). Originally appeared as *Mensonge romantique, vérité romanesque* (1961).

57 Eve Kosofsky Sedgwick, *Epistemology of the Closet* (New York, Harvester Wheatsheaf, 1991), p. 73.

58 Bourget, *Physiologie de l'amour moderne*, p. 329.

59 'Chronique', *Gazette des tribunaux*, 3 September 1890.

60 Anne-Marie Sohn, 'The Golden Age of Male Adultery: The Third Republic', *Journal of Social History*, 28 (1995), pp. 469–90 (470).

61 Michel Foucault, *Histoire de la sexualité, I: La Volonté de savoir* (Paris, Gallimard, 1976), p. 49.

62 Marc Angenot, *Le Cru et le faisandé: Sexe, discours et littérature à la Belle Époque* (Brussels, Labor, 1986), p. 178.

63 Jeffrey Weeks, *Sex, Politics and Society: The Regulation of Sexuality since 1800*, (2nd edn; London, Longman, 1989), p. x.

64 Friedrich Engels, *L'Origine de la Famille, de la Propriété privée et de l'Etat*, trans. Henri Ravé (1884; Paris, Georges Carré, 1893), pp. ix, 88, 79, 82, 96.

65 Eve Kosofsky Sedgwick, *Between Men* (New York, Columbia University Press, 1985), p. 1.

66 See Jean Borie, *Le Célibataire français* (Paris, Sagittaire, 1976).
67 Emile Verhæren, 'Métempsychose de romancier', *L'Art moderne*, 19 October 1890.
68 Cited in J.-K. Huysmans, *Lettres inédites à Jules Destrée*, ed. G. Vanwelkenhuyzen (Geneva, Droz, 1967), p. 78, n. 4.
69 See Jennifer Waelti-Walters and Steven C. Hause, eds., *Feminisms of the Belle Epoque: A Historical and Literary Anthology* (Lincoln, University of Nebraska Press, 1994).
70 For an indispensable account of the female-authored corpus of the period, see Jennifer Waelti-Walters, *Feminist Novelists of the Belle Epoque: Love as a Lifestyle* (Bloomington, Indiana University Press, 1990).
71 E. M. Forster, *Aspects of the Novel* (London, Edward Arnold, 1927), p. 128.
72 G. W. F. Hegel, *Aesthetics: Lectures on Fine Art*, trans. T. M. Knox, 2 vols. (Oxford, Clarendon, 1975), vol. 2, p. 1216.

I DEMON LOVER OR EROTIC ATHEIST?

1 Friedrich Nietzsche, *Genealogy of Morals*, essay 2, section 17, in *Complete Works*, ed. Oscar Levy, 18 vols. (Edinburgh: T. N. Foulis, 1909–13), vol. 13, p. 103.
2 Phillips, *Monogamy*, p. 91.
3 Linda Hutcheon, *A Theory of Parody: The Teachings of Twentieth-Century Art Forms* (New York, Methuen, 1985), p. 26.
4 Émile Zola, 'Le féminisme et le désarmement', *Gil Blas*, 2 August 1896.
5 Zola, 'Le divorce et la littérature', *Œuvres complètes*, 15 vols., ed. Henri Mitterand (Paris, Cercle du livre précieux, 1966–9), vol. 14, pp. 543–7 (544).
6 Zola, 'L'Adultère dans la bourgeoisie', *ibid.*, pp. 531–7.
7 Honoré de Balzac, *Petites misères de la vie conjugale* in *La Comédie humaine*, 12 vols. (Paris, Gallimard (Pléiade), 1976–81), vol. 12, p. 27.
8 Emile Zola, *Pot-Bouille* in *Les Rougon-Macquart*, ed. Henri Mitterand, 5 vols. (Gallimard (Pléiade), 1960–7), vol. 3, p. 93, Subsequent interpolated references in this chapter are made to this edition.
9 Zola, 'L'Adultère dans la bourgeoisie'.
10 Zola, 'Femmes honnêtes', in *Œuvres complètes*, vol. 14, pp. 538–542.
11 Zola, *Correspondance*, 10 vols., ed. B. H. Bakker (Presses de l'Université de Montréal; Paris, C.N.R.S., 1978–95), vol. 1, p. 197.
12 See Jonathan Culler, *Flaubert and the Uses of Uncertainty* (Ithaca, Cornell University Press, 1985), pp. 195–8.
13 George Sand, *André* (Paris, Michel Lévy, 1869), p. 42.
14 *Ibid.*, p. 15. Our italics.
15 Katryn J. Crecchius, *Family Romances: George Sand's Early Novels* (Bloomington and Indianapolis, Indiana University Press, 1987), pp. 141–62.
16 Isabelle Hoog Najinski, *George Sand: Writing for her Life* (New Brunswick, Rutgers University Press, 1991). As we shall see in chapter 5, *A Rebours* also explores this relationship between nobility and the working classes, in the form of des Esseintes and the servant couple.
17 Sand, *André*, p. 3 Sand's italics.

18 Shoshana Felman, *The Literary Speech Act: Don Juan with J. L. Austin, or Seduction in Two Languages*, trans. Catherine Porter (Ithaca, Cornell University Press, 1983), pp. 28, 31. Felman's italics.
19 Molière, *Dom Juan* in *Œuvres complètes* (Paris, Seuil, 1962), p. 296.
20 Gustave Flaubert, *Madame Bovary* (1857; Paris, Livre de Poche, 1983), p. 381.
21 Choderlos de Laclos, *Les Liaisons dangereuses* (1782; Paris, Folio, 1972), pp. 403–6; letters 141–2.
22 Stephen Kern, *The Culture of Love: Victorians to Moderns* (Cambridge, MA, Harvard University Press, 1992), p. 315.
23 Flaubert, *Madame Bovary*, p. 176.
24 Belsey, *Desire*, p. 183.

2. THE RHYTHMS OF PERFORMANCE

1 Paul Bourget, *Physiologie de l'amour moderne*, (Paris, Lemerre, 1891), p. 108.
2 Emile Zola, *Pot-Bouille* in *Les Rougon-Macquart*, ed. Henri Mitterand, 5 vols. (Gallimard (Pléiade), 1960–7), vol. 3, p. 93, subsequent interpolated references in this chapter are made to this edition.
3 See Calvin S. Brown, 'Music in Zola's Fiction, Especially Wagner's Music', *PMLA*, 71 (1956), pp. 84–96, and Calvin S. Brown and Robert J. Niess, 'Wagner and Zola Again', *PMLA*, 73 (1958), pp. 48–52.
4 *The New Grove Dictionary of Music and Musicians*, ed. Stanley Sadie (London, Macmillan, 1980), vol. 12, pp. 246–56.
5 Émile Zola, *Œuvres complètes*, 15 vols., ed. Henri Mitterand (Paris, Cercle du livre précieux, 1966–9), vol. 4, pp. 694, 695.
6 Giacomo Meyerbeer, *Les Huguenots*, libretto by E. Scribe (Paris, Maurice Schlesinger, 1836).
7 Jacques Noiray compares this with the ridiculous duel between Frédéric Arnoux and Cisy (*'Pot-Bouille*, ou *«L'Éducation sentimentale»* d'Emile Zola', *Cahiers naturalistes*, 69 (1995) pp. 113–26 (115). The theme of the abortive duel also echoes Julien Sorel.
8 Grétry, *Zémire et Azor*, libretto by Jean-François Marmontel (Paris, Houbaut, 1771).
9 Reference is made to this source in Georges de Froidcourt (ed.), *La Correspondance générale de Grétry* (Bruxelles, Brepols, 1962), p. 61. Suzanne Clerex invokes the *Mille et une nuits* as a model for such exoticism in *Grétry* (Bruxelles, La Renaissance du Livre, 1944), p. 53.
10 David Charlton, *Grétry and the Growth of Opéra-comique* (Cambridge University Press, 1986), p. 99.
11 Richard A. Lanham, *A Handlist of Rhetorical Terms* (Berkeley, University of California Press, 1991), pp. 92, 100.
12 See Emily Apter, *Feminizing the Fetish: Psychoanalysis and Narrative Obsession in Turn-of-the-Century France* (Ithaca, Cornell University Press, 1991).
13 Linda Hutcheon, *A Theory of Parody: The Teachings of Twentieth-Century Art Forms* (New York, Methuen, 1985), p. 6.

14	Cf. James H. Reid (amongst others) observes that 'in Flaubert's novels, nine-teenth-century French fiction is beginning to parody the textual aspects with which the realist novel constructs the concept of reality' (*Narration and Description in the French Realist Novel* (Cambridge University Press, 1993), p. 64).

15	Zola, *Correspondance*, 10 vols, ed. B. H. Bakker (Presses de l'Université de Montréal; Paris, C.N.R.S., 1978–95), vol. 4, p. 295.

16	David Baguley, *Naturalist Fiction: The Entropic Vision* (Cambridge University Press, 1990), p. 153. Cf. Naomi Segal's discussion of the fairytale qualities of Julien Sorel (*The Adulteress's Child* (Cambridge, Polity Press, 1992), pp. 63–75 (66)).

17	This 'incisive satirical comedy' is analysed by Brian Nelson in his 'Black Comedy: Notes on Zola's *Pot-Bouille*', *Romance Notes*, 17 (1976), pp. 156–61. He compares the novel to a Feydeau farce with its 'burlesque theatricality' and 'comic-grotesque caricature'.

18	Henry Céard, *Une belle journée* (Geneva, Slatkine, 1970), p. 338.

19	It is worth noting, though, that the doctor categorizes the stupidity we find in Marie as the product of *éducation*, whereas there are moments where Zola suggests a separate category of innate stupidity, for example in the first detailed plan: 'Les 3 adultères, *sans passion sexuelle*: par éducation, par détraquement physiologique, et par bêtise' (p. 1619). In the article 'L'adultère dans la bourgeoisie' all three types of adulteress are explained in terms of *milieu*, and in particular *éducation* (as well as other genetic factors).

20	Pierre Bourdieu, *The Field of Cultural Production* (Cambridge, Polity Press, 1993), p. 72.

21	Nelson notes 'the cumulative sense of circular monotony' in the novel in 'Black Comedy', p. 158.

22	This fascination with the perpetually replenished desire of the Don Juan figure, with his 'lusting after a state of *perpetual* desire' (James Mandrell, *Don Juan and the Point of Honour: Seduction, Patriarchal Society and Literary Tradition* (University Park PA, Pennsylvania State University Press, 1992), p. 41) underpins the irony of Edmond Rostand's *The Last Night of Don Juan* (1921).

23	In his notes, Mitterand explains the importance of this Flaubertian inter-text, 'sous l'influence de *L'Education sentimentale*, relue avec admiration l'année précédante, il tentait de resserrer et d'assécher son style' (p. 1623). Indeed, he goes on to explain the very title of the novel in terms of a quota-tion from part 3, chapter 1, of *L'Education sentimentale*, 'Rosanette voyait leur chambre avec les métiers rangés en longueur contre les fenêtres, le pot-bouille sur le poêle, le lit peint en acajou, une armoire en face, et la soupente obscure où elle avait couché jusqu'à quinze ans' (p. 1638). Zola praises *L'Education sentimentale* in a review for *Le Voltaire* (9 December 1879) reprinted in *Mélanges critiques*, 'Le livre est un continuel avortement, avortement d'une génération, avortement d'une époque historique' such that 'l'«histoire» manque' (*Œuvres complètes*, vol. 12, pp. 606–9 (p. 607)). He also praises it in his presentation of Flaubert in *Les romanciers naturalistes* (*Œuvres complètes*, vol.

11, pp. 110–12). See also Noiray's observation that 'Dans *Pot-Bouille*, l'intrigue est à peu près absente. Il n'y a pas d'«histoire», mais une succession de sketches' (p. 122).

24 Reprinted in Zola, *Œuvres complètes*, vol. 4, p. 689.

25 Guy de Maupassant, 'Emile Zola', *Chroniques*, 3 vols. (Paris, Union générale d'éditions (10/18), 1980), vol. 1, p. 386.

26 Bill Overton, *The Novel of Female Adultery: Love and Gender in Continental European Fiction, 1830–1900* (Basingstoke, Macmillan, 1996), p. 5.

27 Bourget, *Physiologie de l'amour moderne*, p. 257.

28 Corbin, *Women for Hire*, pp. 174–5.

29 Emile Zola, *Nana* in *Les Rougon-Macquart*, ed. Henri Mitterand, 5 vols. (Paris, Gallimard (Pléiade), 1960–4), vol. 2, p. 1118.

30 *Ibid.*, p. 1485.

31 Michel Serres, *Feux et signaux de brume* (Paris, Grasset, 1975). Elsewhere Serres makes it explicit that the Don Juan figure embodies a principle of capitalist exchange drawn out to its logical extreme ('Apparition d'Hermès: *Dom Juan*' in *Hermès I: La communication* (Paris, Ed. de Minuit, 1969), pp. 233–45).

32 For an account of women's problematic investment in cultural capital, see for example Anne Martin-Fugier's account of the status of female lecturers in *La Bourgeoise*.

3. 'BEL AMI': FANTASIES OF SEDUCTION AND COLONIZATION

1 See Jean Borie, *Le Célibataire français* (Paris, Sagittaire, 1976).

2 Guy de Maupassant, *Romans*, ed. Louis Forestier (Paris, Gallimard (Pléiade), 1987), pp. 214–15. Subsequent interpolated references in this chapter are made to this edition.

3 See Claudine Giacchetti, *Maupassant: espaces du roman* (Geneva, Droz, 1993).

4 Catherine Belsey, *Desire: Love Stories in Western Culture* (Oxford, Blackwell, 1994), p. 191.

5 Christopher Lloyd, *Maupassant: Bel-Ami* (London, Grant & Cutler, 1988), pp. 19–20.

6 See Leo Bersani, *Homos* (Cambridge, MA, Harvard University Press, 1995).

7 Emile Zola, *Les Rougon-Macquart* ed. Henri Mitterand, 5 vols. (Paris, Gallimard (Pléiade), 1960–7), vol. 3, p. 13.

8 Clotilde has already set him up almost as her *grisette* in a room on the rue de Constantinople (p. 266), and it becomes clear that she already has in her pay that vital figure in the interaction of private and public space, the concierge, who seems as duplicitous as M. Gourd.

9 Paul Bourget, *Physiologie de l'amour moderne*, (Paris, Lemerre, 1891), p. 182.

10 At other points Maupassant suggests how the crowd can threaten the identification, and implicitly identity, of families. When the family goes to see Pierre sail away in the final pages of *Pierre et Jean*, M. Roland complains, 'On ne peut jamais reconnaître les siens dans le tas' (p. 827).

11 Gustave Flaubert, *Madame Bovary* (1857; Paris, Livre de Poche, 1983), p 224.

See Tanner, *Adultery in the Novel* (Baltimore, John Hopkins University Press, 1979), pp. 266–73.

12 Colonial references abound in Maupassant. In chapter 2 of *Pierre et Jean*, for instance, Pierre's dream of 'tous les pays qui sont nos contes de fées à nous qui ne croyons plus à la Chatte blanche ni à la Belle au bois dormant' articulates the power of fantasy which the colonial adventure exerts (*Romans*, p. 738).

13 Forestier cites as examples Zola's *La Curée*, which we shall examine in due course, and Maupassant's *La Serre* (pp. 1360, 1424).

14 Louis Forestier compares this scene to Louis Morin's *Flagrant délit* and Feydeau's *La Puce à l'oreille*.

15 Shoshana Felman, *The Literary Speech Act: Don Juan with J. L. Austin, or Seduction in Two Languages*, trans. Catherine Porter (Ithaca, Cornell University Press, 1983), pp. 11, 28.

16 *Ibid.*, pp. 37–9.

17 See Rachel G. Fuchs, *Poor and Pregnant in Paris: Strategies for Survival in the Nineteenth Century* (New Brunswick, NJ. Rutgers University Press, 1992), pp. 20, 37.

18 Lucie Delarue-Mardrus, *Marie, fille-mère* (Paris, Fasquelle, 1908).

19 'Republican Politics and the Bourgeois Interior in Mid-Nineteenth-Century France' in ed. Suzanne Nash, *Home and its Dislocations in Nineteenth-Century France* (Albany, SUNY Press, 1993), pp. 193–214 (p. 202). In his example, though, which is 'the republican text par excellence for children', Mme Alfred Fouillée's *La Tour de France par deux enfants* (1877), 'the *recherche de la paternité* is undertaken at the level of metaphor'.

20 Fuchs, *Poor and Pregnant*, pp. 69, 93.

21 Maupassant, 'L'Adultère' in *Chroniques*, 3 vols. (Union générales d'éditions (1018), 1980), vol 1, p. 401.

22 Marie Maclean, 'The Heirs of Amphitryon: Social Fathers and Natural Fathers' in eds. Nicholas White and Naomi Segal, *Scarlet Letters: Fictions of Adultery from Antiquity to the 1990s* (Basingstoke, Macmillan 1997), pp. 13–33.

4. INCEST IN 'LES ROUGON-MACQUART'

1 Alphonse de Calonne, 'L'Exposition de 1900 à Paris', *Revue des deux mondes*, 127 (15 January 1895), p. 366.

2 See Zola's letter to Jacques Van Santen Kolff dated 25 January 1893 in his *Correspondance*, ed. B. H. Bakker, 10 vols. (Presses de l'Université de Montréal; Paris, C.N.R.S., 1978–95), vol. 7, p. 358.

3 Émile Zola, *Les Rougon-Macquart*, 5 vols., ed. Henri Mitterand (Paris, Gallimard (Pléiade), 1960–7), vol. 5, p. 1218. Subsequent interpolated references in this chapter are made to the volumes in this edition.

4 See Ronnie Butler, 'La Révolution française, point de départ des *Rougon-Macquart*', *Cahiers naturalistes*, 60 (1986), pp. 89–104.

5 Reprinted in Zola, *Œuvres complètes*, ed. Henri Mitterand 15 vols. (Paris, Cercle du livre précieux, 1966–9), vol. 14 pp. 822–27.

6 Zola, 'Tolstoï et la question sexuelle', reprinted in *Cahiers naturalistes*, 20 (1962), pp. 171–3.

7 Gérard Genette, *Seuils* (Paris, Seuil, 1987), pp. 110, 121.

8 Alain Decaux, 'Jeanne Rozerot (1867–1914)', *Cahiers naturalistes*, 64 (1990), pp. 225–31 (p. 228).

9 Cited in Emile Zola, *Les Œuvres complètes* (Paris, Bernouard, 1927–8), vol. 12, p. 355. All other references to Zola's complete works are made to the Cercle du livre précieux edition (ed. by Henri Mitterand and cited above).

10 'De la description', in *Le Roman expérimental*, reprinted in *Œuvres complètes*, vol. 10, pp. 1299–1302.

11 Jean Borie, *Zola et les mythes, ou de la nausée au salut* (Paris, Seuil, 1971), p. 128.

12 Zola, *Œuvres complètes*, vol. 12, p. 677.

13 Sigmund Freud, *Totem and Taboo*, trans. J. Strachey (London, Routledge and Kegan Paul, 1950), p. 27.

14 See Jean Kæmpfer, *D'un naturalisme pervers* (Paris, Corti, 1989).

15 See David Baguley, 'Rite et tragédie dans *L'Assommoir*', *Cahiers naturalistes*, 52 (1978), pp. 80–96.

16 Reprinted in *Roland Barthes par Roland Barthes* (Paris, Seuil, 1975), p. 183.

17 Gilles Deleuze and Felix Guattari, *Mille plateaux* (Paris, Ed. de Minuit, 1980), p. 11.

18 Zola, *Œuvres complètes*, 14, pp. 785–90 (p. 788).

19 Emile Durkheim, 'La prohibition de l'inceste et ses origines', *L'Année sociologique*, 1 (1896–97), pp. 1–70 (35).

20 Gustave Flaubert, *Madame Bovary* (1854: Paris, Livre de Poche, 1983), p. 196.

21 Docteur Edouard Toulouse, *Enquête médico-physiologique sur la supériorité intellectuelle: Emile Zola* (Paris, Flammarion, 1896), p. 259.

22 Zola, *Œuvres complètes*, vol. 15, p. 440.

23 *Ibid.*, pp. 425, 417, 418, 421, 418, 419.

24 *Ibid.*, p. 423.

25 See Janice Best, *Expérimentation et adaptation: Essai sur la méthode naturaliste d'Emile Zola* (Paris, Corti, 1986), pp. 127–48.

26 Zola, *Œuvres complètes*, vol. 15, pp. 514, 425–6.

27 Zola, *Œuvres complètes*, vol. 15, p. 156.

28 See David Baguley, *Zola et les genres* (University of Glasgow French and German Publications, 1983).

29 See Robert Lethbridge, 'Zola: Decadence and Autobiography in the Genesis of a Fictional Character', *Nottingham French Studies*, 17, 1 (1978), pp. 39–51 (46).

30 See Evelyne Cosset, 'L'Avidité de possession foncière: problématique narrative de *La Terre*', *Cahiers naturalistes*, 61 (1987), pp. 26–33.

31 Prosper Lucas, *Traité philosophique et physiologique de l'hérédité naturelle dans les états de santé et de maladie du système nerveux*, 2 vols. (Paris, Baillière, 1847–50), 1, pp. 24 (Lucas's italics), 96 (Lucas's use of upper case), 102.

32 Adeline Daumard, *Les Bourgeois et la bourgeoisie en France depuis 1815* (Paris, Aubier, 1987), p. 161.

33 Henry Bordeaux, *Histoire d'une vie*, 13 vols. (Paris, Plon, 1951–73), vol. 8, p. 350.

34 Lucas, *Traité philosophique*, vol. 1, p. 195.
35 Carlo Ginzburg, 'Morelli, Freud and Sherlock Holmes: Clues and Scientific Method', *History Workshop Journal*, 9 (1980), pp. 5–36. See also Christopher Prendergast, *The Order of Mimesis* (Cambridge University Press, 1986), pp. 212–53.

5. THE CONQUEST OF PRIVACY IN 'A REBOURS'

1 James Huneker, 'The Pessimist's Progress: J.-K. Huysmans', in *Egoists: A Book of Supermen* (London, T. Werner Laurie, 1909), pp. 167–206 (p. 175).
2 Joris-Karl Huysmans, 'Paris retrouvé' (1901–2), appeared as 'Un article inédit' in *Bulletin Joris-Karl Huysmans*, 51 (1966), pp. 426–27.
3 Martine Martiarena, 'Réflexions sur la Notice d'*A Rebours*', *A Rebours*, 29 (1984), pp. 11–14 (p. 12).
4 Joris-Karl Huysmans, *A Rebours* (Paris, Gallimard (Folio), 1977), p. 79. Subsequent interpolated references in this chapter are made to this edition.
5 For a related discussion of narcissism in *A Rebours*, see Nicholas White, 'Narcissism, Reading and History: Freud, Huysmans and other Europeans', *Paragraph*, 16 (1993), pp. 261–73.
6 Julia Kristeva, *Pouvoirs de l'horreur: Essai sur l'abjection* (Paris, Seuil, 1980), p. 101.
7 Marie Maclean, 'The Heirs of Amphitryon: Social Fathers and Natural Fathers' in Nicholes White and Naomi Segal (eds.), *Scarlet Letters* (Basingstoke, Macmillan, 1997), p. 26.
8 Marius-Ary Leblond, *La Société française sous la Troisième République d'après les romanciers contemporains* (Paris, Félix Alcan, 1905), p. 140.
9 See Claude Lévi-Strauss, *Les Structures élémentaires de la parenté* (Paris, Presses Universitaires de France, 1949) and Jacques Derrida, *De la grammatologie* (Paris, Ed. de Minuit, 1967).
10 Joris-Karl Huysmans, *Œuvres complètes*, 23 vols., ed. Lucien Descaves (Paris, Crès, 1928–34), vol. 2, pp. 51–2.
11 Christopher Lloyd, *J.-K. Huysmans and the* Fin-de-siècle *Novel* (Edinburgh University Press, 1990), p. 19.
12 Joris-Karl Huysmans, 'Lucien Descaves', in Robert Brunel, and André Guyaux (eds.), *Les Cahiers de l'Herne: Huysmans* (Paris, Herne, 1985), p. 431. Our italics.
13 Huysmans, *Œuvres*, vol. 14, p. 28.
14 Joris-Karl Huysmans, *Lettres inédites à Jules Destrée*, ed. G. Vanwelkenhuyzen (Geneva, Droz, 1967), p. 178.
15 The review in question can be found in Jules Barbey d'Aurevilly, *Le XIXe siècle: des œuvres et des hommes*, ed. Jacques Petit, 2 vols. (Paris, Mercure de France, 1964–66), vol 2, pp. 338–43.
16 *Ibid.*, p. 339.
17 Huysmans, 'Cauchemar', *Croquis parisiens*, in *Œuvres complètes*, vol. 8, p. 163.
18 See René-Pierre Colin, *Schopenhauer en France: un mythe naturaliste* (Presses universitaires de Lyon, 1979), part III, chapter 4, 'Huysmans consolé, puis déçu',

pp. 181–92.

19 Elme-Marie Caro, *Le Pessimisme au XIXe siècle* (Paris, Hachette, 1878), pp. 1, 196–7, 208.

20 Cited in *Lettres à Destrée*, pp. 178–9, n. 5.

21 *Le Radical*, 11 July 1884.

22 François Livi, *J.-K. Huysmans: 'A Rebours' et l'esprit décadent*, (Paris, Nizet, 1972), p. 179.

23 Caro, *Le Pessimisme*, p. 9.

24 Huysmans, *Œuvres*, vol. 1, p. 38.

25 *Ibid.*, p. 48.

26 Lloyd, *J.-K. Huysmans*, p. 39.

27 Joseph Halpern, 'Decadent Narrative: *A Rebours*', *Stanford French Review*, 2 (1978), pp. 91–102 (p. 96).

28 A translation of Schubert's 'Des Mädchens Klage', dated 1814–16.

29 See Mallarmé, *Œuvres*, ed. Yves-Alain Favre (Paris, Garnier, 1992), pp. 30–1.

30 Pierre Cogny, 'Quinze lettres inédites de J.-K. Huysmans au Docteur Roger Dumas', *Bulletin J.-K. Huysmans*, 67 (1977), pp. 1–27 (p. 10).

31 Huysmans, *Œuvres*, vol. 9, pp. 17, 28–30, 39.

32 *Ibid.*, pp. 70–71.

33 *Ibid.*, vol. 1, p. 117.

34 Jennifer Birkett, *The Sins of the Fathers: Decadence in France 1870–1914* (New York, Quartet, 1986), p. 3.

35 Hence the aggressive rejection of Walter Bruno's 'Dekadenz und Utopie in J.-K. Huysmans's *A Rebours*', *Germanisch Romanische Monatschrift*, 56 (1975), pp. 214–29, by Gerhard Damblemont's '*A Rebours* et l'Allemagne', in *Bulletin J-K. Huysmans*, 76 (1984), pp. 3–7 (p. 7).

36 See the fragment 'Le Texte politique' in *Roland Barthes par Roland Barthes* (Paris, Seuil, 1975), p. 150, and the gloss offered by Andrew Brown, *Roland Barthes: The Figures of Writing* (Oxford, Clarendon Press, 1992), p. 51.

37 Fritz Schalk, 'Fin de siècle', in *Fin de siècle: zu Literatur und Kunst der Jahrhundertwende*, ed. Roger Bauer *et al.* (Frankfurt am Main, Vittorio Klostermann, 1977), p. 4.

6. PAINTING, POLITICS AND ARCHITECTURE

1 Adoré Floupette [pseudonym of Henri Beauclair and Gabriel Vicaire], *Les Délinquescences. Poèmes décadents* (Milan, Cisalpio-Goliardica, 1979).

2 Gustave Flaubert, *Le Dictionnaire des idées reçues* in *Bouvard et Pécuchet* (1881; Paris, Folio, 1979), pp. 486, 495.

3 O. R. Morgan, 'Léon Hennique (1851–1935). His Life and Works' (Master's thesis, University of Nottingham, 1961), p. 18.

4 Other major Naturalist novels of adultery completed in the immediate aftermath of Flaubert's death include, as we have seen, Henry Céard, *Une belle journée* (1881), J.-K. Huysmans, *En ménage* (1881), and Emile Zola, *Pot-Bouille* (1882).

5 Morgan, 'Léon Hennique (1851–1935)', pp. 98–9.

6 Jean-Joseph Rousseau, 'L'Œuvre romanesque de Léon Hennique'. (Doctoral thesis, Université de Nantes, 1984), pp. 138, 135.

7 O. R. Morgan, 'Léon Hennique and the Disintegration of Naturalism', *Nottingham French Studies*, 1.2 (1962), pp. 24–33 (p. 29).

8 Léon Hennique, *Un accident de Monsieur Hébert* (Paris, Charpentier, 1884), p. 40. All subsequent interpolated references in the first part of this chapter are taken from this edition.

9 Morgan, 'Léon Hennique (1851–1935)', p. 97.

10 As has been observed by Morgan, the ironic counterpointing of the 'seduction' with the orders from the parade ground below bears comparison with the Comices agricoles scene in *Madame Bovary*. See Morgan, 'Léon Hennique (1851–1935)', p. 96, and 'Hennique and the Disintegration of Naturalism', p. 28.

11 Gustave Flaubert, *Œuvres complètes*, 16 vols. (Paris, Club de l'Honnête Homme, 1971–5), vol. 16, p. 308.

12 René Dumesnil, *Histoire de la littérature française 9: Le Réalisme et le Naturalisme*, ed. Jean Calvert (Paris, del Duca de Gigord, 1955). Dumesnil does underline Hennique's sense of the comic: 'il eut, comme Huysmans, le sens de l'humour dont Zola et surtout Paul Alexis furent assez dépourvus' (p. 366).

13 For an analysis in the context of *Le Rouge et le Noir* of how the notion of the *imprévu* may represent a threat to the codes of realism, see Prendergast, *The Order of Mimesis* (Cambridge University Press, 1986), pp. 119–47.

14 Rousseau, 'L'Œuvre romanesque', pp. 149, 152.

15 René Dumesnil, *La Publication des* Soirées de Médan (Paris, Malfère, 1933), p. 66.

16 Cf. the way in which the decadence of Paris offers an ironic anticipation of the military collapse of 1870–1 in Emile Zola's novel of prostitution *Nana* (1880) as the crowds shout 'À Berlin! à Berlin! à Berlin!' in the final chapter (*Les Rougon-Macquart*, 5 vols., ed. Henri Mitterand (Paris, Gallimard (Pléiade), 1960–7), vol. 2, pp. 1471–85).

17 Cf. the end of Joris-Karl Huysmans, *A Rebours*, where this idea of Paris as cure is also highlighted when the doctor orders des Esseintes to return to the capital (p. 349).

18 Henry Céard, *Lettres inédites à Emile Zola*, ed. C. A. Burns (Paris, Nizet, 1958), p. 248.

19 Emile Zola, *Correspondance*, 10 vols., ed B. H. Bakker (Presses de l'Université de Montréal; Paris, C.N.R.S., 1978–95), vol. 4, pp. 436–37.

20 Rousseau, 'L'Œuvre romanesque', pp. 145–8.

21 For an instructive account of influences exerted on and by Manet, see Joel Isaacson, *Monet: Le Déjeuner sur l'herbe* (London, Allen Lane, 1972).

22 *Ibid.*, p. 41.

23 Isaacson argues that a stress on the flirtatious aspect of the *déjeuner* scene is characteristic of English genre painting contemporary with Manet (*ibid.*, p. 56).

24 Zola, *Les Rougon-Macquart*, vol. 2, pp. 571–2.

25 Rousseau, 'L'Œuvre romanesque', p. 159.

26 Catherine Belsey, *Desire: Love Stories in Western Culture* (Oxford, Blackwell, 1994), p. 35.

27 Ferdinand Brunetière, 'Le *Paris* de M. E. Zola', *Revue des Deux Mondes*, 146 (1898), pp. 922–34 (p. 932).

28 Emile Zola, *Œuvres complètes*, 15 vols., ed. by Henri Mitterand (Paris/ Lausanne, Cercle du livre précieux, 1966–9), vol. 7, p. 1239. All subsequent interpolated references to *Paris* in the second part of this chapter are taken from this edition.

29 The circumstances of composition are recounted by René Ternois, 'Discours à Médan (1956)', *Cahiers naturalistes*, 2 (1956), pp. 272–83. Ternois stresses the overlapping between the conclusion of *Les Rougon-Macquart* and the conceptualisation of *Les Trois Villes*.

30 Christopher Prendergast, *Paris and the Nineteenth Century* (Oxford, Blackwell, 1995), pp. 71–72.

31 Kevin Lynch, *The Image of the City* (Cambridge, MA, MIT Press, 1960), p. 1.

32 Clive Thomson, 'Une typologie du discours idéologique dans *Les Trois Villes*', *Cahiers naturalistes*, 54 (1980), pp. 96–105 (p. 97). In opposition to the critical commonplace which sees the trilogy as a stepping stone between *Les Rougon-Macquart* and the unfinished cycle *Les Quatre Evangiles*, Thomson argues persuasively that these novels are *romans à thèse*.

33 Stefan Max, *Les Métamorphoses de la grande ville dans* Les Rougon-Macquart (Paris, Nizet, 1966), p. 8. In spite of its title, Max's study concludes by relating Zola's earlier representations of cities to *Les Trois Villes*. See also Claude Duchet, 'Pathologie de la ville zolienne', in *Du visible à l'invisible: pour Max Milner*, ed. Stéphane Michaud, 2 vols. (Paris, Corti, 1988), vol. 1, pp. 83–96.

34 Thomson, 'Une typologie', p. 99.

35 Prendergast, *Paris and the Nineteenth Century*, p. 83.

36 See Philippe Bonnefis, 'Le cri de l'étain', *Revue des sciences humaines*, 160 (1975), pp. 514–38.

37 Christopher Prendergast uses Carlo Ginzburg's 'conjectural paradigm' to analyse the patriarchal paranoia of the nineteenth-century Family Romance as a crisis of legitimacy. See the section 'Plots and Paranoia' in his *The Order of Mimesis*, pp. 216–32.

38 See Maxime du Camp, *Paris, ses organes, ses fonctions et sa vie dans la seconde moitié du XIXe siècle*, 6 vols. (Paris, Hachette, 1869–75).

39 Marie-Claire Bancquart, *Images littéraires du Paris 'fin-de-siècle': 1880–1900* (Paris, Ed. de la Différence, 1979), p. 244.

40 Cf. Zola's simulacrum of incest in the drama, *Renée*, where he uses 'l'expédient, la tricherie, pour dire le mot, qui esquive l'inceste réel, en établissant que Saccard n'est que de nom le mari de Renée' (*Œuvres complètes*, vol. 15, p. 417).

41 'Le cri de l'étain', p. 517. Michel Serres suggests how the *moteur* functions as a metaphor for Naturalist writing in his *Feux et signaux de brume*.

42 Cf. *La Curée* where Renée, in her 'insatiable besoin de savoir et de sentir',

considers lesbian pleasures as she searches for 'une jouissance unique, exquise, où elle mordrait toute seule' (*Les Rougon-Macquart*, vol. 1, p. 422).

43 I am particularly grateful to Diana Holmes for her helpful comments on this issue.

CODA: BOURGET'S 'UN DIVORCE' AND THE 'HONNÊTE FEMME'

1 Paul Bourget, *Physiologie de l'amour moderne* (Paris, Lemerre, 1891), p. iv.
2 Jean-François Guichard, *Journal de Paris*, February 1797.
3 Anthony Giddens, *The Transformation of Intimacy: Sexuality, Love and Eroticism in Modern Societies* (Cambridge, Polity, 1992), p. 192.
4 Paul Bourget, *Un divorce* (Paris, Plon, 1904), p. 1. Subsequent interpolated references in this chapter are made to this edition.
5 Armand Edwards Singer, *Paul Bourget* (Boston, Twayne, 1976), p. 10.
6 Emile Zola, *Œuvres complètes*, ed. Henri Mitterand, 15 vols. (Paris, Cercle du livre précieux, 1966–9), vol. 10, pp. 381, 430.
7 Albert Thibaudet, *Histoire de la littérature française de 1789 à nos jours* (Paris, Stock, 1936), p. 430.
8 Max du Veuzit, *Paternité* (Montivilliers, Hervé Rillet, 1908), pp. 31–2, 26, 29.
9 Edmond and Jules de Goncourt, *Journal*, ed. Robert Ricatte, 3 vols. (Paris, Robert Laffont, 1989), vol. 3, pp. 665, 803, 917–18, 1123–4.
10 Emile Zola, *Correspondance*, ed. B. H. Bakker, 10 vols. (Presses de l'Université de Montréal; Paris, C.N.R.S., 1978–95), vol. 9, p. 157.
11 *Dictionnaire de biographie française*, ed. M. Prévost and Roman d'Amat (Paris, Letouzey et Ané, 1959), vol. 8, p. 630.
12 Jean Estèbe, *Les Ministres de la République, 1871–1914* (Paris, Presses de la fondation nationale des sciences politiques, 1982), p. 81.
13 Tony Tanner, *Adultery in the Novel* (Baltimore, Johns Hopkins University Press, 1979), p. 104.
14 Octave Feuillet, *Le Journal d'une femme*, 17th edn (Paris, Calmann Lévy, 1878), pp. 302–3.
15 Giddens, *The Transformation of Intimacy*, pp. 61–2.
16 Honoré de Balzac, *Petites misères de la vie conjugale* in *La Comédie humaine* (1847; Paris, Gallimard (Pléiade), 1981), vol. 12, p. 24.
17 La Baronne d'Orval, *Usages mondains, Guide du Savoir-Vivre universel* (Paris, 1881). Cited in Martin-Fugier, *La Bourgeoise*.
18 J.-P. Dartigues, *De l'amour expérimental ou des causes d'adultère chez la femme au XIXᵉ siècle* (Versailles, Litzelmann 1887), pp. vii, 92, 124–5.

Bibliography

Unless otherwise stated, books in French were published in Paris.

Angenot, Marc, *Le Cru et le faisandé: sexe, discours et littérature à la Belle epoque* (Brussels, Labor, 1986).

Apter, Emily, *Feminizing the Fetish: Psychoanalysis and Narrative Obsession in Turn-of-the-Century France* (Ithaca, Cornell University Press, 1991).

Armstrong, Judith, *The Novel of Adultery* (Basingstoke, Macmillan, 1976).

Bachelard, Gaston, *La Poétique de l'espace* (Presses Universitaires de France, 1964).

Baguley, David, *Naturalist Fiction: The Entropic Vision* (Cambridge University Press, 1990).

'Rite et tragédie dans *L'Assommoir*', *Cahiers naturalistes*, 52 (1978), pp. 80–96.

Zola et les genres (University of Glasgow French and German Publications, 1983).

Balzac, Honoré de, *Petites Misères de la vie conjugale* in *La Comédie humaine* (1847; Gallimard (Pléiade), 1981), vol. 12.

Bancquart, Marie-Claire, *Images littéraires du Paris 'fin-de-siècle': 1880–1900* (Ed. de la Différence, 1979).

Barbey d'Aurevilly, Jules, *Le XIXe siècle: des œuvres et des hommes*, ed. Jacques Petit, 2 vols. (Mercure de France, 1964–6).

Barthes, Roland, *Le Plaisir du texte* (Seuil, 1973).

Roland Barthes (Seuil, 1975).

Bauer, Roger, *et al.* (eds.), *Fin de siècle: zu Literatur und Kunst der Jahrhundertwende* (Frankfurt am Main, Vittorio Klostermann, 1977).

Belsey, Catherine, *Desire: Love Stories in Western Culture* (Oxford, Blackwell, 1994).

Bersani, Leo, *Homos* (Cambridge, MA, Harvard University Press, 1995).

Best, Janice, *Expérimentation et adaptation: essai sur la méthode naturaliste d'Emile Zola* (Corti, 1986).

Birkett, Jennifer, *The Sins of the Fathers: Decadence in France 1870–1914* (New York, Quartet, 1986).

Black, Michael, *The Literature of Fidelity* (London: Chatto and Windus, 1975).

Bonnefis, Philippe, 'Le cri de l'étain', *Revue des sciences humaines*, 160 (1975), pp. 514–38.

Bordeaux, Henry, *Histoire d'une vie*, 13 vols. (Plon, 1951–73).

Borie, Jean, *Le Célibataire français* (Sagittaire, 1976).

Zola et les mythes, ou de la nausée au salut (Seuil, 1971).

Bourdieu, Pierre, *The Field of Cultural Production* (Cambridge, Polity, 1993).

Bourget, Paul, *Un divorce* (Plon, 1904).

Physiologie de l'amour moderne (Lemerre, 1891).

Brown, Andrew, *Roland Barthes: The Figures of Writing* (Oxford, Clarendon, 1992).

Brown, Calvin S., 'Music in Zola's Fiction, Especially Wagner's Music', *PMLA*, 71 (1956), pp. 84–96.

Brown, Calvin S., and Robert J. Niess, 'Wagner and Zola Again', *PMLA*, 73 (1958), pp. 48–52.

Brunel, Robert, and André Guyaux (eds.), *Les Cahiers de l'Herne: Huysmans* (Herne, 1985).

Brunetière, Ferdinand, 'Le *Paris* de M. E. Zola', *Revue des Deux Mondes*, 146 (1898), pp. 922–34.

Bruno, Walter, 'Dekadenz und Utopie in J.-K. Huysmans's *A Rebours*', *Germanisch Romanische Monatschrift*, 56 (1975), pp. 214–29.

Burns, Colin, 'Henry Céard and his Relations with Flaubert and Zola', *French Studies* (1952), pp. 308–24.

Butler, Ronnie, 'La Révolution française, point de départ des *Rougon-Macquart*', *Cahiers naturalistes*, 60 (1986), pp. 89–104.

Calonne, Alphonse de, 'L'Exposition de 1900 à Paris', *Revue des deux mondes*, 127 (15 January 1895), p. 366.

Camp, Maxime du, *Paris, ses organes, ses fonctions et sa vie dans la seconde moitié du XIXᵉ siècle*, 6 vols. (Hachette, 1869–75).

Caro, Elme-Marie, *Le Pessimisme au XIXᵉ siècle* (Hachette, 1878).

Cauvière, Jules, *De la répression de l'adultère* (Imprimerie Chaix, 1905).

Cave, Terence, *The Cornucopian Text: Problems of Writing in the French Renaissance* (Oxford, Clarendon, 1979).

Céard, Henry, *Une Belle Journée* (Geneva: Slatkine, 1970).

Lettres inédites à Emile Zola, ed. C. A. Burns (Nizet, 1958).

Champfleury, *Histoire de l'imagerie populaire* (Dentu, 1886).

Charlton, David, *Grétry and the Growth of Opéra-comique* (Cambridge University Press, 1986).

Cheal, David, *Family and the State of Theory* (New York, Harvester/ Wheatsheaf, 1991).

'Chronique', *Gazette des tribunaux*, 3 September 1890.

Clerex, Suzanne, *Grétry* (Brussels: La Renaissance du Livre, 1944).

Cogny, Pierre, 'Quinze lettres inédites de J.-K. Huysmans au Docteur Roger Dumas', *Bulletin J.-K. Huysmans*, 67 (1977), pp. 1–27

Colin, René-Pierre, *Schopenhauer en France: un mythe naturaliste* (Presses universitaires de Lyon, 1979).

Corbin, Alain, *Women for Hire: Prostitution and Sexuality in France after 1850*, tr. Alan Sheridan (Cambridge, MA, Harvard University Press, 1990).

Cosset, Evelyne, 'L'avidité de possession foncière: problématique narrative de *La Terre*', *Cahiers naturalistes*, 61 (1987), pp. 26–33.

Crecchius, Katryn J., *Family Romances: George Sand's Early Novels* (Bloomington/ Indianapolis, Indiana University Press, 1987).

Culler, Jonathan, *Flaubert and the Uses of Uncertainty* (Ithaca, Cornell University Press, 1985).

Damblemont, Gerhard, '*A Rebours* et l'Allemagne', *Bulletin J-K. Huysmans*, 76 (1984), pp. 3–7.

Dartigues, J.-P., *De l'amour expérimental ou des causes d'adultère chez la femme au XIXe siècle* (Versailles, Litzelmann, 1887).

Daumard, Adeline, *Les Bourgeois et la bourgeoisie en France depuis 1815* (Aubier, 1987).

Decaux, Alain, 'Jeanne Rozerot (1867–1914)', *Cahiers naturalistes*, 64 (1990), pp. 225–231.

Delarue-Mardrus, Lucie, *Marie, fille-mère* (Fasquelle, 1908).

Deleuze, Gilles, and Felix Guattari, *Mille plateaux* (Ed. de Minuit, 1980).

Derrida, Jacques, *De la grammatologie*, (Ed. de Minuit, 1967).

Duchet, Claude, 'Pathologie de la ville zolienne' in *Du visible à l'invisible: pour Max Milner*, ed. Stéphane Michaud, 2 vols. (Corti, 1988), vol. 1, pp. 83–96.

Dumesnil, René, *La Publication des* Soirées de Médan (Malfère, 1933).
    Le Réalisme et le naturalisme, vol. 9, in *Histoire de la littérature française*, ed. Jean Calvet (Del Duca de Gigord, 1955).

Durkheim, Emile, 'La prohibition de l'inceste et ses origines', *L'Année sociologique*, 1 (1896–97), pp. 1–70.

Engels, Friedrich, *L'Origine de la famille, de la propriété privée et de l'état*, tr. Henri Ravé (Georges Carré, 1893 (1884)).

Estèbe, Jean, *Les ministres de la République, 1871–1914* (Presses de la fondation nationale des sciences politiques, 1982).

Felman, Shoshana, *The Literary Speech Act: Don Juan with J.L.Austin, or Seduction in Two Languages* tr. Catherine Porter (Ithaca, Cornell University Press, 1983).

Feuillet, Octave, *Le Journal d'une femme*, 17th edn (Calmann Lévy, 1878).

Flaubert, Gustave, *Le Dictionnaire des idées reçues* in *Bouvard et Pécuchet* (Folio, 1979).
    Madame Bovary (Livre de Poche, 1983).
    Œuvres complètes, 16 vols. (Club de l'Honnête Homme, 1971–5).

Floupette, Adoré, [pseud. of Henri Beauclair and Gabriel Vicaire], *Les Délinquescences. Poèmes décadents* (Milan, Cisalpio-Goliardica, 1979).

Forster, E. M., *Aspects of the Novel* (London, Edward Arnold, 1927).

Foucault, Michel, *Histoire de la sexualité, I: La Volonté de savoir* (Gallimard, 1976).

Freud, Sigmund, *Totem and Taboo*, tr. J. Strachey (London, Routledge and Kegan Paul, 1950).

Froidcourt, Georges de (ed.), *La Correspondance générale de Grétry* (Bruxelles, Brepols, 1962).

Fuchs, Rachel G., *Poor and Pregnant in Paris: Strategies for Survival in the Nineteenth Century* (New Brunswick, NJ, Rutgers University Press, 1992).

Gallina, Bernard, *Eurydices fin de siècle: Emma Bovary et le roman naturaliste* (Udine, Aura Editrice, 1992).

Gay, Peter, *The Bourgeois Experience: Victoria to Freud*, 2 vols. (Oxford University Press, 1984–6).

Genette, Gérard, *Seuils* (Seuil, 1987).

Giacchetti, Claudine, *Maupassant: espaces du roman* (Geneva: Droz, 1993).

Giddens, Anthony, *The Transformation of Intimacy: Sexuality, Love and Eroticism in Modern Societies* (Cambridge, Polity, 1992).

Ginzburg, Carlo, 'Morelli, Freud and Sherlock Holmes: Clues and Scientific Method', *History Workshop Journal*, 9 (1980), pp. 5–36.

Girard, René, *Deceit, Desire, and the Novel*, tr. Yvonne Freccero (Baltimore, The Johns Hopkins University Press, 1972). Originally appeared as *Mensonge romantique, vérité romanesque* (1961).

Glennon, Lynda M., *Women and Dualism* (New York, Longman, 1979).

Gleyses, Chantal, *La Femme coupable: Petite histoire de l'épouse adultère au XIXᵉ siècle* (Imago, 1994).

Goncourt, Edmond and Jules de, *Journal*, 3 vols., ed. by Robert Ricatte (Robert Laffont, 1989).

La Grande Encyclopédie: inventaire raisonné des sciences, des lettres et des arts, 31 vols. (Lamirault, 1886–1902).

Grétry, *Zémire et Azor*, text by Jean-François Marmontel (Houbaut, 1771).

Guichard, Jean-François, *Journal de Paris*, February 1797.

Habermas, Jürgen, *The Structural Transformation of the Public Sphere*, tr. Thomas Burger (Cambridge, Polity, 1989).

Halpern, Joseph, 'Decadent Narrative: *A Rebours*', *Stanford French Review*, 2 (1978), pp. 91–102.

Hegel, G. W. F., *Æsthetics: Lectures on Fine Art*, tr. T. M. Knox, 2 vols. (Oxford, Clarendon, 1975).

Hennique, Léon, *Un accident de Monsieur Hébert* (Charpentier, 1884).

Huneker, James, 'The Pessimist's Progress: J.-K. Huysmans', in *Egoists: A Book of Supermen* (London, T. Werner Laurie, 1909), pp. 167–206.

Hunt, Lynn, *The Family Romance of the French Revolution* (London, Routledge, 1992).

Hutcheon, Linda, *A Theory of Parody: The Teachings of Twentieth-Century Art Forms* (New York, Methuen, 1985).

Huysmans, Joris-Karl, *A Rebours* (Gallimard (Folio), 1977).

  Lettres inédites à Jules Destrée, ed. G. Vanwelkenhuyzen (Geneva, Droz, 1967).

  Œuvres complètes, 23 vols., ed. Lucien Descaves (Crès, 1928–34).

  'Paris retrouvé', (1901–2), appeared as 'Un article inédit' in *Bulletin Joris-Karl Huysmans*, 51 (1966), pp. 426–7.

Isaacson, Joel, *Monet: Le Déjeuner sur l'herbe* (London, Allen Lane, 1972).

Jaybert, Léon, *De l'adultère dans les différents âges et chez les différentes nations* (Poulet-Malassis, 1862).

Kæmpfer, Jean, *D'un naturalisme pervers* (Corti, 1989).

Kern, Stephen, *The Culture of Love: Victorians to Moderns* (Cambridge, MA, Harvard University Press, 1992).

Krafft-Ebing, Richard von, *Psychopathia Sexualis* (London, Mayflower-Dell, 1967).

Kristeva, Julia, *Pouvoirs de l'horreur: Essai sur l'abjection* (Seuil, 1980).

Laclos, Choderlos de, *Les Liaisons dangereuses* (Folio, 1972).

Lanham, Richard A., *A Handlist of Rhetorical Terms* (Berkeley, University of California Press, 1991).

Leblond, Marius-Ary, *La Société française sous la Troisième République d'après les romanciers contemporains* (Félix Alcan, 1905).

Lethbridge, Robert, 'Zola: Decadence and Autobiography in the Genesis of a Fictional Character', *Nottingham French Studies*, 17.1 (1978), pp. 39–51.

Lévi-Strauss, Claude, *Les Structures élémentaires de la parenté* (Presses Universitaires de France, 1949).

Livi, François, *J.-K. Huysmans: A Rebours et l'esprit décadent* (Nizet, 1972).

Lloyd, Christopher, *J.-K. Huysmans and the Fin-de-siècle Novel* (Edinburgh University Press, 1990).

Maupassant: Bel-Ami (London, Grant & Cutler, 1988).

Lucas, Prosper, *Traité philosophique et physiologique de l'hérédité naturelle dans les états de santé et de maladie du système nerveux*, 2 vols. (Baillière, 1847–50).

Lynch, Kevin, *The Image of the City* (Cambridge, MA, MIT Press, 1960).

Mallarmé, Stéphane, *Œuvres*, ed. Yves-Alain Favre (Garnier, 1992).

Mandrell, James, *Don Juan and the Point of Honour: Seduction, Patriarchal Society and Literary Tradition* (University Park PA, Pennsylvania State University Press, 1992).

Martiarena, Martine, 'Réflexions sur la Notice d'*A Rebours*', *A Rebours*, 29 (1984), pp. 11–14.

Martin-Fugier, Anne, *La Bourgeoise* (Grasset, 1983).

Maupassant, Guy de, *Chroniques*, 3 vols. (Union générale d'éditions (10/18), 1980).

Romans, ed. Louis Forestier (Gallimard (Pléiade), 1987).

Maurois, André, *Cinq visages de l'amour* (New York, Didier, 1942).

Max, Stefan, *Les Métamorphoses de la grande ville dans Les Rougon-Macquart* (Nizet, 1966).

Meyerbeer, Giacomo, *Les Huguenots*, text by E. Scribe (Maurice Schlesinger, 1836).

Molière, *Œuvres complètes* (Seuil, 1962).

Morgan, O. R., 'Léon Hennique (1851–1935). His Life and Works', Master's thesis, University of Nottingham (1961).

'Léon Hennique and the Disintegration of Naturalism', *Nottingham French Studies*, 1.2 (1962), pp. 24–33.

Najinski, Isabelle Hoog, *George Sand: Writing for her Life* (New Brunswick, Rutgers University Press, 1991).

Nelson, Brian, 'Black Comedy: Notes on Zola's *Pot-Bouille*', *Romance Notes*, 17 (1976), pp. 156–61.

Nietzsche, Friedrich, *Complete Works*, ed. Oscar Levy, 18 vols. (London, Allen and Unwin; Edinburgh, T. N. Foulis, 1909–13).

Noiray, Jacques, '*Pot-Bouille*, ou «*L'Education sentimentale*» d'Emile Zola', *Cahiers naturalistes*, 69 (1995), pp. 113–26.

Nord, Philip, 'Republican Politics and the Bourgeois Interior in Mid-Nineteenth-Century France' in ed. Suzanne Nash, *Home and its*

Dislocations in Nineteenth-Century France (Albany, SUNY Press, 1993), pp. 193–214.

Overton, Bill, *The Novel of Female Adultery: Love and Gender in Continental European Fiction, 1830–1900* (Basingstoke, Macmillan, 1996).

Perrot, Michelle (ed.), *From the Fires of Revolution to the Great War* (1990), vol. 4, *A History of Private Life*, ed. Phillipe Ariès and Georges Duby, tr. Arthur Goldhammer, 5 vols. (Cambridge, MA, Belknap Press of Harvard University Press, 1987–1991).

Phillips, Adam, *Monogamy* (London, Faber and Faber, 1996).

Prendergast, Christopher, *The Order of Mimesis* (Cambridge University Press, 1986).

Paris and the Nineteenth Century (Oxford, Blackwell, 1995).

Prévost, M., and Roman d'Amat (eds.), *Dictionnaire de biographie française* (Letouzey et Ané, 1959).

Le Radical, 11 July 1884.

Reid, James H., *Narration and Description in the French Realist Novel* (Cambridge University Press, 1993).

Reid, Roddey, *Families in Jeopardy: Regulating the Social Body in France, 1750–1910* (Stanford University Press, 1993).

Rougemont, Denis de, *Love in the Western World* (New York, Anchor Books, 1957); first published as *L'Amour er l'Occident* (Plon, 1939).

Rousseau, Jean-Joseph, 'L'Œuvre romanesque de Léon Hennique', doctoral thesis, Université de Nantes (1984).

Sadie, Stanley (ed.), *The New Grove Dictionary of Music and Musicians* (London, Macmillan, 1980).

Sand, George, *André* (Michel Lévy, 1869).

Sedgwick, Eve Kosofsky, *Between Men* (New York, Columbia University Press, 1985).

Epistemology of the Closet (New York, Harvester Wheatsheaf, 1991).

Segal, Naomi, *The Adulteress's Child: Authorship and Desire in the Nineteenth-Century Novel* (Cambridge, Polity Press, 1992).

Serres, Michel, *Feux et signaux de brume* (Grasset, 1975).

Hermès I: La communication (Ed. de Minuit, 1969).

Shattuck, Roger, *The Banquet Years* (New York, Vintage, 1955).

Sinclair, Alison, *The Deceived Husband: A Kleinian Approach to the Literature of Infidelity* (Oxford University Press, 1993).

Singer, Armand Edwards, *Paul Bourget* (Boston, Twayne, 1976).

Sohn, Anne-Marie, 'The Golden Age of Male Adultery: the Third Republic', *Journal of Social History*, 28 (1995), pp. 469–90.

Tanner, Tony, *Adultery in the Novel* (Baltimore, The Johns Hopkins University Press, 1979).

Ternois, René, 'Discours à Médan (1956)', *Cahiers naturalistes*, 2 (1956), pp. 272–83.

Theuriet, André, 'Paternité', *Revue des deux mondes*, 124 (1894), pp. 756–96, and 125 (1894), pp. 38–72.

Thibaudet, Albert, *Histoire de la littérature française de 1789 à nos jours* (Stock, 1936).

Thomson, Clive, 'Une typologie du discours idéologique dans *Les Trois Villes*', *Cahiers naturalistes*, 54 (1980), pp. 96–105.

Toulouse, Docteur Edouard, *Enquête médico-physiologique sur la supériorité intellectuelle: Emile Zola* (Flammarion, 1896).

Verhæren, Emile, 'Métempsychose de romancier', *L'Art moderne*, 19 October 1890.

Veuzit, Max du, *Paternité* (Montivilliers: Hervé Rillet, 1908).

Waelti-Walters, Jennifer, *Feminist Novelists of the Belle Epoque: Love as a Lifestyle* (Bloomington, Indiana University Press, 1990).

Waelti-Walters, Jennifer, and Steven C. Hause (eds.), *Feminisms of the Belle Epoque: A Historical and Literary Anthology* (Lincoln, University of Nebraska Press, 1994).

Weeks, Jeffrey, *Sex, Politics and Society: The Regulation of Sexuality since 1800*, 2nd edn (London, Longman, 1989).

White, Nicholas, 'Narcissism, Reading and History: Freud, Huysmans and Other Europeans', *Paragraph*, 16 (1993), pp. 261–73.

White, Nicholas, and Naomi Segal (eds.), *Scarlet Letters: Fictions of Adultery from Antiquity to the 1990s*, (Basingstoke, Macmillan, 1997).

Williams, Tony, 'Champfleury, Flaubert and the Novel of Adultery', *Nineteenth-Century French Studies*, 20 (1991–2), pp. 145–57.

Zeldin, Theodore, *France 1848–1945: Ambition and Love* (Oxford University Press, 1979).

Zola, Emile, *Correspondance*, 10 vols., ed. B.H. Bakker (Presses de l'Université de Montréal; Paris, C.N.R.S., 1978–95).

'Le féminisme et le désarmement', *Gil Blas*, 2 August 1896.

Les Œuvres complètes (Bernouard, 1927–28).

Œuvres complètes, 15 vols., ed. Henri Mitterand (Cercle du livre précieux, 1966–9).

Les Rougon-Macquart, 5 vols., ed. Henri Mitterand (Gallimard (Pléiade), 1960–7).

'Tolstoï et la question sexuelle', repr. in *Cahiers naturalistes*, 20 (1962), pp. 171–3.

Index

CAMBRIDGE STUDIES IN FRENCH

General editor MICHAEL SHERINGHAM (*Royal Holloway, London*)

Editorial board: R. HOWARD BLOCH (*Columbia University*), MALCOLM BOWIE
(*All Souls College, Oxford*), TERENCE CAVE (*St John's College, Oxford*),
ROSS CHAMBERS (*University of Michigan*), ANTOINE COMPAGNON
(*Columbia University*), PETER FRANCE (*University of Edinburgh*),
CHRISTIE MCDONALD (*Harvard University*), TORIL MOI (*Duke University*),
NAOMI SCHOR (*Harvard University*)